T0247361

YEAR OF THE
ROCKET

YEAR OF THE
ROCKET

John Candy, Wayne Gretzky,
a Crooked Tycoon, and the Craziest
Season in Football History

PAUL WOODS

sh.
SUTHERLAND
HOUSE
TORONTO, 2021

Sutherland House
416 Moore Ave., Suite 205
Toronto, ON M4G 1C9

Copyright © 2021 by Paul Woods

All rights reserved, including the right to reproduce this book or portions thereof in any form whatsoever. For information on rights and permissions or to request a special discount for bulk purchases, please contact Sutherland House at info@sutherlandhousebooks.com

Sutherland House and logo are registered trademarks of The Sutherland House Inc.

First edition, September 2021

If you are interested in inviting one of our authors to a live event or media appearance, please contact publicity@sutherlandhousebooks.com and visit our website at sutherlandhousebooks.com for more information about our authors and their schedules.

Manufactured in the United States
Cover designed by Jason Logan
Book composed by Karl Hunt

Library and Archives Canada Cataloguing in Publication
Title: Year of the Rocket : John Candy, Wayne Gretzky,
a crooked tycoon, and the craziest season
in football history / Paul Woods.
Names: Woods, Paul (Paul Stuart), 1957- author.
Identifiers: Canadiana 20210239808 |
Subjects: LCSH: Toronto Argonauts (Football team)—
History—20th century.
Classification: LCC GV948.3 T67 W663 2021 |
DDC 796.335/6409713541—dc23

ISBN 978-1-989555-44-6

To Simon and Caleb

Contents

The Summer of
Argonaut Love

OR ONE NIGHT—for the first time ever, really—the most important, talked-about, watched, and hyped event in Canada's largest city was, of all things, a football game.

On July 18, 1991, if you wanted to be where the action was, you had to be at SkyDome, the self-described "world's greatest entertainment centre," to witness the unveiling of the new Toronto Argonauts.

Many of the 41,178 spectators who trooped into the colossal facility on a typically muggy summer evening were Argo fans who had been to SkyDome, and its predecessor, Exhibition Stadium, before. But there were also a lot of folks there for the first time, and for reasons other than football.

"We came to see the show," a young woman excitedly told a TV crew. Oh, and "the game, too."

But mostly the show. For this was meant to be a show unlike anything Toronto had seen. Just a week after the Toronto Blue Jays had played host to baseball's best players in the major league all-star game at SkyDome, the Argonauts were about to stage their own showcase event, complete with Hollywood celebs, legendary musicians, and the debut of the most-talked-about player ever to step on a Canadian football field.

This moment had been anticipated for five months, ever since the lightning bolt in February 1991. Hockey star Wayne Gretzky and comedian John Candy were teaming with Los Angeles Kings owner Bruce McNall to purchase the Toronto Argonauts. Tinseltown pizzazz was coming to a Canadian Football League that had appeared to be on the brink of extinction.

McNall, who made his fortune collecting and trading ancient coins, was the most important power broker in hockey. By acquiring Gretzky from the Edmonton Oilers, he had transformed the sport from something popular in Canada and pockets of the U.S. northeast into a commodity marketed across most of America. Attendance at Kings games skyrocketed as Californians and their stars—John Candy, Kirk Russell, Michael J. Fox, Ronald Reagan—lined up to watch the Great One rack up goals and assists.

McNall's empire had expanded beyond coins and hockey players to encompass other "collectibles," from prize-winning racehorses to rare baseball cards. Now he was bringing his apparent Midas touch to Canada, accompanied by two of its most beloved citizens. Gretzky, the skinny kid from Brantford, Ontario, who set mind-boggling, never-to-be-beaten scoring records. And Candy, the round-faced Torontonian behind such uproarious and memorable TV and movie characters as Johnny LaRue, Uncle Buck, and Del Griffith.

The funniest man Canada had ever produced, the greatest hockey player ever to lace up skates, and a slick coin-dealer-turned-sports magnate. As Brian Cooper, whom they hired as executive vice-president of the Argos, described it nearly three decades later: "The king of comedy, the king of hockey, and the guy who owns the Kings—it's a powerful group."

It was powerful enough to do something that from today's perspective seems outlandish, preposterous, unthinkable. They signed the most highly-touted prospect in professional football, a young man so fast and exciting he was worthy of the same nickname as an iconic Canadian athlete of an earlier generation. Move over, Rocket Richard, here comes Raghib "Rocket" Ismail, stolen away from the mighty National Football League on the very day he was expected to be anointed as its next star.

McNall, Gretzky, and Candy made Rocket Ismail the highest-paid player in football history. Not Canadian football history. *Football* history. He was to be paid at least 18 million dollars over four years. In return for these riches, Ismail was expected not only to be a superstar on the field, but to reignite interest among Torontonians and, indeed, people all across Canada, in the teetering CFL.

And it all started tonight.

* * *

The day before the game, a private jet bearing the silver-and-black colour scheme of hockey's Los Angeles Kings had landed on the runway at Pearson International Airport. Stepping off the tricked-out Boeing 727 and into a fleet of stretch limousines were the comedian Martin Short, actor Jim Belushi, Oscar-nominated actress Mariel Hemingway, *The Breakfast Club* icon Ally Sheedy, and *Slap Shot* star Michael Ontkean, to name a few. Wayne Gretzky's wife, Janet Jones, was there as well, along with daughter Paulina. Even "Super Dave" Osborne, the perpetually optimistic comedic daredevil whose stunts always, in the end, went horribly wrong, joined the entourage. That might have been an omen.

Another plane had also landed the previous day after a transatlantic flight. Donald "Duck" Dunn, Steve Cropper, Matt "Guitar" Murphy and several other legendary musicians were the house band behind Elwood (Dan Aykroyd) and "Joliet" Jake Blues (John Belushi) in the 1980 movie *The Blues Brothers*. Now touring without the late Belushi, and restyled as the Elwood Blues Revue, they interrupted a string of dates in Europe to perform at halftime for a rumoured fee of a half-million dollars. "Some people wisely invest in real estate," says Matt Cauz, a Toronto broadcaster who was a 16-year-old Argo fan in 1991. "Others fly the horn section in from Italy."

The band was the feature attraction at a pre-game party the night before the game. That little shindig at the Horseshoe Tavern had been Candy's idea. "We need to set the world on fire," he told Bret Gallagher, his assistant. "We need hysteria, we need craziness."

Soon after agreeing to buy a twenty-per-cent share of the Argos, Candy had solicited help from his former Second City Comedy mate Aykroyd, who grew up in Kingston, Ontario. Aykroyd was tight with the owners of the Horseshoe, a natural venue for the party, which drew an overflow crowd of celebs and gawkers wanting a peek at the glitzy new Argonauts organization.

Drinks flowed. Aykroyd blew a mean blues harp at the front of his red-hot band. Candy sang and mugged from the stage.

"It was the single greatest sports party I've ever been at," says Doug Smith, who has covered Canadian sports for four decades. "That includes Olympic welcome parties and Blue Jays parties and Raptors parties."

Less than 24 hours later, the party shifted to the massive domed stadium, its roof open under the stars. While players on the Argos and the Hamilton Tiger-Cats warmed up on the artificial turf, the new owners of the Argonauts strolled around the field to thunderous applause. The grinning, Fred Flintstone-esque McNall performed a ceremonial kickoff alongside Gretzky and Candy. The three-piece Jeff Healey Band sang the Canadian national anthem *a cappella*. Candy, nearby, mouthed the words along with them.

At halftime, Aykroyd took to a makeshift stage in the north end zone, dancing and jiving as his band launched into the blues standard *Sweet Home Chicago*, with the words changed to "sweet home Toronto."

"One and one is two," sang Aykroyd. "Two and two is four. I see Belushi and Candy coming up in that back door." And sure enough, Candy, in jaunty fedora and shades, and Jim Belushi, replacing brother John, were up on stage, adding their voices and white-man dance steps to the jam.

When the players left the field after the fourth quarter, Aykroyd, Candy, Belushi, and the Elwood Blues Revue returned for a post-game set, joined by Hemingway, Sheedy, and Ontkean, among others.

"We've never played a better house in our lives," says Aykroyd. "That night was probably the greatest gig we've ever played. Boy, was Toronto ready for this. It was just ripe when we walked into that stadium that night."

"I've seen the NBA final, watched the NFL Super Bowl, I've watched my horse run the Kentucky Derby," Gretzky said, "but tonight I really watched something spectacular."

Suzan Waks, McNall's senior financial executive, had a joyous exchange with Cooper, as the stadium shook. "The Blues Brothers are playing!" Cooper exulted. "We did this! Can you believe we did this?"

"How many regular-season Argo games in history could you say were an event?" asks Steve Simmons, Canada's most widely read sports columnist. "The game was a 'where were you?' moment. There haven't been many of those."

It was almost impossible not to come away believing it was the dawn of a new era in Canadian football. Even Marty York, a longtime CFL nemesis in the *Globe and Mail*, was effusive in his assessment. "This simply had to be construed, even by the cynics—even by the legions of detractors—as a remarkably stirring night for the long-beleaguered Toronto Argonauts," he wrote. "It was as if, on this night, the CFL emerged from the dead and kissed its archaic mentality goodbye."

The new Argo ownership group was naturally thrilled with the whole show, from 8,000 walk-up ticket sales to an entertainment spectacle that seemed sure to win over new fans.

After closing down the SkyDome, the entire Hollywood and Blues Revue contingent, plus Argo staffers and plenty of scene-makers, repaired to the trendy Ultrasound Lounge on Queen Street West for the post-game party to end all post-game parties.

Aykroyd has a vivid memory of his friend Candy sitting on the roof of Ultrasound, his long hair framed against the illuminated skyline of Toronto. "How youthful he looked. Just full of life and laughter, at the peak of his existence. It was an awe-striking light, just effulgent. The light of the city was touching him there. . . . He was king of the city.

"The love . . . was so evident that night, and the weeks running up to it and afterwards, too. That whole summer was a summer of Argonaut love."

Just six months earlier, a summer of Argonaut love would have been inconceivable. The Argos were a different team, with a different owner, a different vibe, and no prospect of becoming the biggest thing in Toronto.

Just Wild About Harry

HARRY ORNEST WAS AT RISK of becoming bored. Having just turned 65, he had earned the right to settle into a comfortable retirement in southern California. But Ornest had spent much of his adult life chasing adventures in the world of professional sports, and he wasn't inclined to stop just because he was getting old.

A casual remark by Ornest's wife clarified the situation for him. "Please tell me what type of work you do," Ruth Ornest said to her husband one day, "so I can tell people what type of work you are out of."

"When she said that to me, I realized I had to get a job," Ornest said a couple of years later, shortly after he had purchased the Toronto Argonauts. "At this stage of my life it would be pretty hard for anyone to hire me, so I went out and bought a job. But listen, I dig it. I like the idea of owning a team."

If anything, that was an understatement. Ornest *loved* owning a professional sports team. Over the years, he had taken runs at buying about a half-dozen franchises in North America's four big leagues. "If there was a sports team and he didn't own it, he loved trying to figure out how he might," Bill Dwyre wrote in the *Los Angeles Times*.

Ornest first achieved his dream by acquiring hockey's St. Louis Blues at a fire-sale price in 1983. Like pretty well every other deal he ever made, it produced a healthy return on the investment, with Ornest reportedly pocketing between $11 million and $18 million when he sold the club three years later. There was a catch, however. It was reported that the Blues sale created a pressing tax issue for Ornest: he had two years after selling to find a new sporting investment or face a hefty tax bill. So Ornest did what he likely would have done anyway: he searched for another team to buy.

One month before the apparent tax deadline, Ornest found what he was looking for. As 1988 turned to 1989, Harry Ornest became the fifth majority owner in the 116-year history of the Canadian Football League's Toronto Argonauts.

The Carling O'Keefe brewery had been trying to sell the Argonauts for nearly two years. Carling insisted it was in no hurry to sell, but it was clear the brewery wanted out after a decade of owning the club. Its executives were as happy to find Ornest as he was to find them.

Born in 1923 in Edmonton, Harry Ornest got his first job at the age of seven, delivering newspapers door to door. He tried and failed to make it as a baseball player, and worked as a linesman in eight NHL games. But with just six teams and three regular refs in the league, he wasn't destined to move up to a senior on-ice officiating role.

Looking for ways to make money, Ornest discovered vending machines, the kind that dispensed candy bars and cigarettes. He installed them in movie theatres across western Canada. Coins started rolling in—so many that Ornest, who had also branched out into real estate, eventually moved his family to Beverly Hills, where Harry pursued his dream of snaring a big-league sports team.

In 1983, Ralston Purina, the pet-food company that owned the St. Louis Blues, was trying to sell the club to a group that would move it to Saskatoon, Saskatchewan. When NHL governors refused to approve the sale, Ralston essentially handed back the keys to the franchise. A group led by Ornest bought the team and its arena, with Ornest taking out a second mortgage on the family home to finance the purchase.

He proceeded to apply his tight-fisted management style to the Blues' operation. Some of his methods were charming, such as trying to keep the arena clean by helping to pick up trash. But pinching pennies could go to extremes. An indoor soccer team sued Ornest, claiming the Blues had charged a fee for depreciation of the arena's pipe organ.

His profitable sale of the Blues after three years of ownership opened the door for Ornest's next sporting venture.

* * *

The Toronto Argonauts are one of the oldest sports franchises in North America, dating back almost a century and a half. The team began in 1873 as an offshoot of the Argonaut Rowing Club, which saw rugby-style football as an invigorating pastime for its members when they weren't out sculling on the Humber River.

The rowing club sold the football operation in 1956 to a consortium of businessmen led by John Bassett, publisher of the *Toronto Telegram* and head of the company that created Toronto's first private TV station, CFTO.

Bassett, who bought out his partners during the 1960s, sold the club in 1974 to hotelier Bill Hodgson. Hodgson brought Carling O'Keefe in as a minority partner in 1976, then sold the balance of his holding to the brewery two years later.

Carling O'Keefe, the country's third-place beermaker behind Labatt and Molson, operated the team for a decade before selling a 95-per-cent stake to Ornest in 1988. From Ornest's viewpoint, the timing couldn't have been better, with the team about to move into a massive new stadium that was considered state of the art.

"I believe the Canadian Football League is on the upswing," the new owner said. "When you combine the city of Toronto with the SkyDome and the Argos, it ain't bad at all. The Argos are older than Union Station. They're hallowed."

The new SkyDome, with its wondrous retractable roof, was key to Ornest's interest in the team. It was "not only the eighth wonder of the world," he said, "but also the ninth. Who wouldn't want to watch the Argos in the SkyDome? [It's] the most significant thing that's happened to the Canadian Football League in its history."

Ornest was excited enough to predict the Argos would average 40,000 fans a game in 1989, up from 23,158 in 1988. He reckoned that curiosity about the new stadium would boost ticket sales, and he wouldn't have to spend a nickel on promotion.

The Argos fell well short of Ornest's rosy prediction, drawing an average crowd of 35,069 (based on announced attendance). Journalists believed that figure was padded, and the team drew just 22,000 for its home playoff game after the 1989 season.

As he had done in St. Louis, Ornest ran a decidedly lean operation in Toronto. There were just 11 employees in the Argo business office in 1989, and their marketing and communications miscues contributed to the low attendance. When the season ended and Ornest was preparing to return to Beverly Hills (where Ruth stayed year-round), he had equipment manager Danny Webb help pack up his possessions. On the way to Ornest's suite in the Sutton Place hotel, they cut through the lobby bar. "He stopped to grab peanuts [off tables] and pour them into his blazer jacket," says Webb. Argo offices were full of ballpoint pens emblazoned with the Sutton Place logo, presumably snatched off housekeeping carts.

One day Ornest found assistant coach Mike Levenseller printing a game plan. Levenseller's mistake was using only one side of the paper. "This machine copies on both sides," the owner admonished the assistant coach. "When you don't do that, it costs me a nickel for every paper you use."

One of Ornest's first, and least popular, moves as owner was to redesign the Argos' logo. Since 1977, Argo helmets had borne the image of a football that doubled as a boat, with oars protruding through waves under a billowing sail adorned with a large A. Ornest hated the logo. "All you see is that big A on top of a boat. It's hard to identify with that."

He ordered up a new logo: all-caps ARGOS with a sharp point flowing out of the A and underlining the rest of the word. Its virtue, he said, was that the new logo contained the name of the team (whose full name, he had decreed, was no longer the Argonauts).

The new owner also futzed around with the team's time-honoured primary colours, Oxford Blue (dark) and Cambridge Blue (light), in homage to the sculling traditions at two English universities. He offended purists by adding a red accent, just as he had added red to the Blues' gold-and-blue colour scheme.[1]

Ornest instituted a rule that each media member covering a game could have only one complimentary hot dog or slice of pizza in the press

---

1   Ornest's wordmark was annoyingly similar to the all-caps GIANTS script worn at the time by one of New York's NFL teams. The Ornest logo was scrapped in 1991 after he sold the team. The full name Argonauts was restored, and red never again appeared on its uniforms. After years of demands from a vocal segment of the Argo fanbase, a slightly modified version of the boat logo was brought back by the organization in 2019.

box at SkyDome. "It looked like U.S. marshals hovering around the food line to make sure you didn't take a second hot dog," said the *Edmonton Journal's* Cam Cole. When a veteran journalist, a rather large individual, complained about the policy, Ornest reportedly shot back, "We're saving your life."

He wouldn't feed them much, but Ornest, unlike most team owners, had plenty of time for members of the Fourth Estate, regularly and cheerfully sparring with high-profile commentators. Some columnists telegraphed their own affection for him by routinely referring to him by his first name, or sometimes Harry O.

A down-to-earth individual with a common touch, sleepy eyes and a sly grin, Ornest was easy to like, whatever his quirks. When he met anyone who seemed younger than him, he would typically ask the person's age and say, "I've got ties older than you." (The general feeling was that the statement was probably true.)

Brian Snelgrove, a team employee who drove his boss home to Sutton Place most nights, remembers a man who was remarkably approachable, with no airs. "Harry's office was just inside the doors at Exhibition Stadium. Anybody who came in, whether it was the delivery guy, a student, or even somebody looking for directions, he'd have them in his office."

Ornest was willing, even eager, to engage with his teams' fan bases. Phone calls to the Argo front office were sometimes answered by the owner himself. At Blues games, Harry "would hang in the standing area with the common folk, and watch the game with them," his son Mike says.

And despite his legendary frugality, Ornest was generous in his own way. He always paid for lunch. And he loved to hand out team baubles. "When anybody would come over to the house, they never left empty-handed," says daughter Laura. "They would leave with a baseball cap, a T-shirt or something for their kids."

There were limits to his generosity, though. Initially thrilled to have his team play in SkyDome, Ornest became livid when he learned the outlandish price he had to pay its exclusive food-service supplier for the hot dogs served to journalists covering games, and that the team did not get a cut of revenue taken in by the restaurant overlooking the playing field.

There were also protracted battles over rent. Scheduling was another sore point. Somehow the Argos and Jays, sharing the stadium, had both been granted a contractual right to first choice of dates. Something had to give, and the Argonauts were forced to play second fiddle.

As CEO of SkyDome, Richard Peddie fought some bitter battles with Ornest. In his 2013 book *Dream Job*, Peddie described a meeting in Ornest's office. Each man got angry, each swore, each stood up, menacingly. Peddie was 43 years old at the time, Ornest 67.

"I was thinking," Peddie wrote, "if we did come to blows and he felled me, I would have been beaten up by an elderly man. If I downed him, I would be accused of abusing a senior. I couldn't win this battle." Things eventually calmed down.

* * *

On the field, the team Ornest had purchased was not nearly as gaudy as the temple to which it had moved. None of the three quarterbacks who played regularly in 1989 managed to complete even half of their passes, and the group as a whole threw for just 15 touchdowns against 34 interceptions. A year after winning 14 times, Toronto lost 11 of 18 games.

A couple of guys who would loom large later were part of the dismal season, however. Darrell K. Smith and Mike Clemons were destined to be major pieces of the Argonauts over the next few years, although that wasn't apparent in 1989.

Smith had joined the team in 1986, flashing considerable promise as a rookie and then exploding in 1987 for one of the greatest years any Toronto receiver ever had. He caught 79 passes for 1,392 yards and ten touchdowns, earning a CFL all-star selection and helping the Argos to the Grey Cup game (in which he dropped a deep pass that might have given Toronto a better fate than its 38-36 loss to Edmonton).

His impressive output continued in 1988, with 73 receptions for 1,306 yards and seven TDs. On track for even better statistics halfway through 1989, Smith inexplicably stopped being targeted by Toronto's mediocre quarterbacks, and finished the year with 69 catches, 959 yards and two touchdowns.

When the Argos lined up for the East Division semifinal that November, he was not in uniform. He had been benched by head coach Bob O'Billovich, and replaced by a guy named Brian Bedford, who managed just 14 receptions in his entire CFL career.

That benching might have had something to do with O'Billovich's displeasure over an off-field incident in which Smith severely cut his hand. The receiver claimed it was caused when he broke a drinking glass, but there were loud whispers about his lifestyle. Smith made no secret of his taste for the nightlife of Toronto. "He played hard and partied hard," says teammate Bob Skemp. "I partied hard, too, and I drank—that and pain medication. But D.K. was just a level higher." Hard partying never seemed to affect Smith's performance, though. He lifted weights obsessively, and proudly displayed a ripped six-pack.

Smith's new teammate, Clemons, was in the lineup for that playoff game in 1989, but he also wasn't someone O'Billovich was inclined to trust.

Clemons had burst onto the Argo scene partway through training camp. After playing half of the 1987 season for the Kansas City Chiefs, he tried out a year later with the Tampa Bay Buccaneers, only to be told the team was going with someone younger. "I'm only 23 years old!" Clemons fumed.

Offered a contract by the Calgary Stampeders, he was about to fly to training camp when the team ran into a roster squeeze and released him. Argo president Ralph Sazio, an alumnus of the same school Clemons attended, William and Mary University, immediately sent him a contract.

On the practice field, Clemons drew instant attention. Professional football is generally not contested by men as short and slight as the five-foot-five, 170-pound Clemons. Prospective teammates Chris Schultz and Kelvin Pruenster each stood more than a foot taller and outweighed the young man by a hundred or more pounds.

The *Toronto Star* suggested the new recruit might be mistaken "for the equipment manager. Or perhaps the water boy. Maybe even the person who climbs inside the team's mascot costume. But a professional football player? Naw."

But Clemons wasn't just the smallest player on the field; he was also the guy no one could seem to tackle. "Who and what is that?" wondered receiver Paul Masotti as he watched the little guy bounce off defenders all over the field.

In perhaps the last significant act of his eight-year tenure as head coach, O'Billovich bestowed upon Clemons the wonderfully descriptive nickname he still answers to three decades later. Impressed with the rookie's elusiveness, Obie described Clemons to reporters as "bouncing around out there like a pinball." The moniker instantly stuck to the respectful young man with an engaging smile.

Pinball's size worried Toronto's coaches, though. "That guy's just too little," O'Billovich told his assistants.

Clemons had one final crack at making the team by suiting up as a kick returner for the season opener. Defensive backs Carl Brazley and

Doran Major, who had quickly grown fond of the Pinball, took it upon themselves to make sure he got the best possible chance to make a lasting impression on Toronto's kickoff and punt-return units. "The plan was to clear out some guys and give some blocks and at least give him a shot," says Brazley. "And Mike put on a show."

Indeed. In that opening game against Edmonton, Clemons amassed 184 yards on kickoff and punt returns, not including 69 yards on a runback negated by a penalty. The first time he touched the ball in Canadian football, on the opening play of the game, he dodged and danced around tacklers for more than 40 yards.[2]

Despite coining the endearing nickname, O'Billovich didn't do much to get Clemons the ball in 1989. Pinball dressed for 11 games, returned 50 punts and touched the ball 49 other times as a runner, receiver, kick returner, and option passer (completing his only pass for a touchdown). He also scored one of the shortest punt-return touchdowns of all time, racing 25 yards to the end zone after he snagged a ball as it bounced back towards the punter in a wind-swept game in Winnipeg. In the playoff game for which Smith had been benched, all Clemons did was return eight kicks for a mere 63 yards.

By the end of that game, the man who paid the bills had seen enough. Harry Ornest knew it was time to blow up the Argos' football operation. Obie's time as Argo coach was over.

---

2   Clemons fumbled on that first play, something that thankfully did not become a habit. In his 12-year CFL career, he fumbled 53 times out of 2,740 touches, for an average of less than two fumbles per 100 opportunities.

Gods of Football

FTER A DISMAL, dispiriting first year in SkyDome, Harry Ornest and president Ralph Sazio fired head coach Bob O'Billovich a few days after the Argos bowed out meekly at home in the 1989 playoffs. The team had won just seven games, and had failed to fill its new stadium.

Sazio had only one name on the list of potential new head coaches for the Toronto Argonauts. The coach who refused to believe his team would ever lose. Who let his players horse around, as long as they were ready on game day. Who practically invented the concept of swagger. Don "The Don" Matthews was a former linebacker from Idaho who had made his name as an assistant coach with the Edmonton Eskimos and as head coach of the B.C. Lions.

Matthews had six Grey Cup rings and a reputation as a master defensive strategist whose teams always played aggressively. Rather than drop his linebackers and defensive backs into zones, forcing the opposing offence to complete passes in narrow windows, he'd send six, seven, even eight men to attack the passer while leaving a handful of defensive backs in man-to-man coverage downfield. The high-risk strategy played right into his motto: "If you're not living on the edge, you're taking up too much space."

Matthews himself lived blissfully on the edge. He bombed around town in a Corvette or astride a Harley-Davidson. He worked his way through four wives over the years. "I can't help myself," he once told Argo linebacker Don Moen. "I love beautiful women."

Matthews had just spent the 1989 season as Edmonton's defensive co-ordinator after having been fired, inexplicably, by the Lions. With him calling the shots on defence, the Eskimos had won a record 16 games. So his agent, Gil Scott, wasn't surprised when Sazio said he wanted Matthews as his next coach. Scott, and anyone who paid attention to the CFL, knew Matthews was the best head coach available.

Sazio and Scott agreed on a salary, and Matthews' hiring was announced on November 22, 1989, four days before the first Grey Cup ever played in SkyDome, and three days after the 16-win Eskimos had been upset at home by nine-win Saskatchewan in the Western Final.

News reports about Matthews' arrival made much of the fact that the new head coach had been hired before a general manager was in place. (Sazio had been handling the GM job himself, but was looking to retire.) Usually, a general manager hires and oversees the head coach. The chain of command is clear, and if the team fails, the coach is far more likely than the GM to walk the plank.

Sazio coyly told reporters the next general manager would be the boss, as usual, "but Harry and I are not going to hire any general manager who does not feel he's lucky as hell to have Don Matthews for a head coach."

Behind the scenes, Ornest and Sazio had already identified their next GM: Michael P. McCarthy.

The 37-year-old had spent the past five seasons as assistant general manager and director of football operations for the Hamilton Tiger-Cats. He had worked previously for two teams in the United States Football League, as a scout for the NFL's New England Patriots, and as an assistant coach at the University of Oklahoma.

Thickly muscled, McCarthy had an impish grin and an impressive thatch of carefully coiffed brown hair. He looked like a chia pet on top of a fire hydrant. He had been an outstanding linebacker at Southwestern College in Kansas, despite standing just five-foot-seven in a big man's sport. As a senior in 1974, he made 180 tackles, more than any other player in U.S. college football, yet playing pro football was out of the question. "I had the heart and the stats," he once said, "but not the size."

While they were wooing him, Sazio and Ornest asked McCarthy for his opinion of Matthews. "Well, he's a cocky kind of guy," he told them. "If you want to hire him, I have no problem. Go ahead and hire Don."

McCarthy's hiring as Argo general manager was announced a week after Matthews came on board. Now the two men and their healthy egos, a potentially combustible combination, had to find a way to work together. Both assured reporters there would be no problem.

Although Matthews' hiring had been made public first, McCarthy insists the customary chain of command was always in place, as Sazio had promised. Matthews "found out right away from Harry Ornest who his boss [was]. Me."

If Matthews was "the Don," McCarthy, too, had an exalted title. Sports columnist Stephen Brunt dubbed him "God of football," a mixture of sarcasm and appreciation for both how well-connected and effective McCarthy was in the sport, and how much being well-connected and effective meant to him.

Some Argo players had a more derisive nickname for the general manager. They called him Tattoo, after the diminutive sidekick of the mysterious Mr. Roarke on *Fantasy Island*. (The actor who played Tattoo, Hervé Villechaize, was born with dwarfism.) "He would be walking through the lines at camp," says defensive end Mike Campbell, "and we'd be like, 'The plane, Boss! The plane!'"

Like many football men, McCarthy could be rough around the edges. He relentlessly needled Jo-Anne Polak of the Ottawa Rough Riders, the first female general manager in pro football. At one point, newspapers reported that he planned to hire her for the low-level role of administrative assistant. Polak, who was never actually approached about an Argo job, laughs it off as Mike being Mike. "He was always really nice to me. That's just a minor annoyance."

Some reporters who covered the Argos came to think that McCarthy was full of himself. Sit down for a chat with him and he'd immediately regale you with tales of working alongside American football legends such as Chuck Fairbanks, Barry Switzer, and George Allen, or close encounters with Richard Nixon, Ronald Reagan, and Madonna.

But McCarthy always answered his phone, returned calls, and freely fed both gossip and scoops to journalists. "Mike is charming-abrasive," says reporter Paul Hunter. "I never got the feeling he wasn't telling you the truth. With Don [Matthews], you never knew if he was playing you or trying to manipulate or massage something to make himself look better. I don't think Mike was duplicitous at all."

* * *

20

Matthews and McCarthy were determined to terrorize CFL defences and get Toronto back to the Grey Cup game. And there was one subject on which they absolutely agreed: there was no way the Argos could do either with the mediocre quarterbacking the team had received in 1989.

McCarthy knew how to fix that problem. Get Matt Dunigan.

The new general manager had heard about a rift that was developing in Vancouver between Dunigan and the B.C. Lions. While musing publicly about signing a highly touted college quarterback named Major Harris, McCarthy secretly arranged a meeting in Chicago with Lary Kuharich, B.C.'s new head coach. The two talked for ten hours about the possibility of a trade that would send Dunigan to the Argonauts.

There was a catch, though. In 1988, the Lions had obtained Dunigan in a trade that wasn't fully consummated for nearly a year. When all of the pieces were finally dispersed, the Lions had given up no fewer than six players to the Edmonton Eskimos for Dunigan.[3]

That deal had decimated B.C.'s defence and sent the Lions to the cellar in 1989, while helping the Eskimos win a record 16 games. So any trade sending Dunigan out of Vancouver would have to be just as lopsided to win support from Lions fans. B.C. needed to get a pile of players back for him.

Feigning great reluctance to strip apart his roster, McCarthy let Kuharich talk him into sending a half-dozen Argos to Vancouver. "I would have gone as high as ten," he later told a reporter. His reasoning was straightforward: "We're the flagship franchise of the CFL and we needed to have the league's big-name marquee player playing in the world's best stadium."

---

3   As evidence of Dunigan's value, Edmonton general manager Hugh Campbell said at the time that he would happily send all six players back to the Lions if he could reacquire the quarterback. "When you trade someone like that, you can't get enough stuff back, whether it's money or players."

Two of the traded Argos were genuine stars: Jearld Baylis, a dominating force at nose tackle, and linebacker Willie Pless, who ended up in the Canadian Football Hall of Fame. But to call the four other guys nondescript would be kind. Slotback Emanuel Tolbert was a former star nearing the end of his career. Linebacker Tony Visco and defensive back Todd Wiseman were journeymen backups. Quarterback Rick "Hollywood" Johnson was more interested in pursuing an acting career than playing football.

Around the league, there was astonishment at how little Toronto had given up. Calgary head coach Wally Buono said he liked Pless, but "I'd rather line up against Willie Pless than Matt Dunigan. You can always find linebackers and defensive linemen, but by the time you find a quarterback like Dunigan, you're usually fired."

"No wonder there isn't a straight face in the Argos' front office," wrote Allan Maki in the *Calgary Herald*. "Dunigan for Jearld Baylis and Willie Pless and the biggest collection of stiffs since Madame Tussaud got into the wax business? Stop it. You're killing us."

Reaction to the deal in Toronto was ecstatic. Since moving into SkyDome, the Argos had generated no buzz around town. Now they had a guy who was not only the best quarterback in the league, but also its most marketable commodity, by far.

A guy cut from the same cloth as Joe Namath: strong-armed, ruggedly handsome, bit of a southern drawl, great head of hair whether worn as a mop of curls, a dyed-blonde wavy mullet, or an old-fashioned brush cut. And oodles of swagger: the guy had an earring and blew gigantic pink bubbles while throwing warmup tosses in a sleeveless, midriff-baring sweatshirt. He would stare daggers at a teammate who didn't run the right pass pattern or throw the necessary block, then flash that teammate a sly wink and a grin that can only be described as shit-eating.

He won football games, too. Plenty of them. Dunigan was a guy who could return the Argos to the Grey Cup and put fans in their mammoth new stadium. "A living and breathing football saviour," the Sun's Steve Simmons called him.

* * *

Matt Dunigan grew up in Texas, where the four Fs rule: family, faith, friends, and football, not necessarily in that order. He was recruited to play quarterback at Louisiana Tech University, where one of his predecessors was Terry Bradshaw, who led the Pittsburgh Steelers to four Super Bowl championships during the 1970s. Dunigan, who became the starting quarterback as a sophomore, passed for 7,100 yards over three seasons, shattering Bradshaw's school record of 4,459.

Despite a strong arm and a fearless, aggressive nature, Dunigan was not what the National Football League favoured in the early 1980s. It prized pivots who could stand tall in the pocket. Big men like John Elway, Dan Marino, and Jim Kelly, all of whom came out of college in the same year Dunigan finished up at Louisiana Tech, and all of whom wound up in the Pro Football Hall of Fame.

At five-foot-ten, Dunigan wasn't tall, and he wasn't inclined to stand around if receivers didn't get open right away. He'd just as soon take off and run with the ball.

Knowing he would not be drafted into the NFL and had only a faint hope of winning a job there as an undrafted free agent, Dunigan chose to sign with Edmonton in 1983. His arrival coincided with two momentous events in Eskimo history: the end of an unprecedented run of five Grey Cup championships in a row, and the last year in Canada for star quarterback Warren Moon. Dunigan served as Moon's understudy for a year, then ascended to the starting role. He immediately won over fans in Edmonton, and all across the league, with his swashbuckling, never-play-it-safe mindset.

Like most Texas kids in the 1970s, Dunigan had grown up admiring Dallas Cowboys quarterback Roger Staubach. But he secretly preferred Billy Kilmer, who played the pivot position for Dallas' arch-rivals in Washington. "[Kilmer] wasn't that gifted, talent-wise, but he had tenacity and leadership abilities," Dunigan once said.

Dunigan himself had many of the qualities he saw in Kilmer. A fiery leader, he knew his playbook inside out, and he expected members of his offence to do the same. If a player failed at his assignment, Dunigan would get in his face. "Get your shit together!" he'd yell.

The supremely confident receiver Darrell K. Smith was never shy about demanding the ball, but Dunigan allowed no yapping in the huddle. "It was my huddle," Dunigan asserts. "I was doing the talking, not them." Players who didn't shut up got an earful. "If you want to keep talking, we'll just [take a delay-of-game penalty] and cut to the chase," Dunigan would tell them. That generally silenced the yappers.

* * *

In 1986, Dunigan led the Eskimos to the Grey Cup game. They were run over by a ferocious Hamilton Tiger-Cats defence that sacked Dunigan and his backup, Damon Allen, ten times on the way to a 39-15 demolition.

A year later, the Eskimos were back in the Grey Cup, heavily favoured against an upstart Argonauts team. Things did not go well for Dunigan that afternoon, either. Trailing by seven points in the second quarter, he was clobbered by defensive end Glenn Kulka. The ball popped loose. Linebacker Doug "Tank" Landry scooped it up and ran in for a Toronto touchdown. Dunigan was down on the field with a concussion, one of many instances of brain trauma he suffered during his career. He watched the rest of the 1987 Grey Cup game in a fog. The Esks rallied for a 38-36 victory in one of the most exciting championship contests ever, thanks in large part to the heroics of Dunigan's replacement, Allen.

His team had won the championship, but for Dunigan it meant little because he had not been able to contribute much.

Heading into the 1988 season, a quarterback controversy was brewing in Edmonton; Allen seemed ready to take over as the Eskimos' starter.

Dunigan shocked fans by announcing he was retiring to try out for baseball's Montreal Expos. He hadn't played baseball since high school, but Montreal was willing to look at him in its minor-league development system.

Reporters in Edmonton suggested this might be a ploy to get a new contract from the Eskimos, but Dunigan insisted he was serious about baseball. He might not have been a two-sport wonder like his contemporary, Bo Jackson, who excelled in both the NFL and Major League Baseball, but he was athletic enough to earn his Expo tryout.

Almost as soon as he reported to Montreal's minor-league facility in Florida, doubts fell over the venture. The Expos said Dunigan was 25 years old. CFL media guides, however, suggested he was 27, and the record-keepers at Louisiana Tech confirmed he had been born in 1960. "I feel like I'm 21," Dunigan insisted to a reporter.

Three weeks after arriving, the would-be left fielder gave up on baseball as a possible career option. After slapping out just five hits in 19 exhibition at-bats, he had been advised he wouldn't even make the Expos' roster in Rookie ball, a rung or two below Class A.

He was still under contract to the Eskimos, but with Allen ready to start, and another promising backup named Tracy Ham heading into his second year, Edmonton made a deal just as training camps were opening: Dunigan and future considerations to the B.C. Lions in exchange for receiver Jim Sandusky plus players to be named later.

Dunigan excelled with the Lions in 1988. The team's offensive co-ordinator, Adam Rita, loved his new quarterback and came up with a simple and appropriate nickname for him. He called him Sgt. Rock after the popular comic-book character, a tough-as-nails soldier. Dunigan returned the love by passing for 26 touchdowns and helping first-year receiver David Williams win the league's most outstanding player award. The Lions advanced to the Grey Cup game, only to lose 22-21 to Winnipeg. That result was sealed when Dunigan's last-minute pass in scoring range was deflected into the arms of the Bombers' Michael Gray.

For the third year in a row, the league's best quarterback had helped his team advance to the big game, but failed to help them win.

Their defence plundered by the Eskimos in the second phase of what became a six-for-two trade, the Lions fell out of contention in 1989. Despite Dunigan leading the league in passing yards, B.C. finished last in the West Division.

Midway through that season, the Lions were purchased by Murray Pezim, a flamboyant stock promoter who said the CFL's days were numbered, and the NFL would have Canadian franchises within three to four years. One of the new owner's first decisions was to hire Joe Kapp, a local legend who had quarterbacked the Lions to their first Grey Cup title in 1964, as general manager.

While these front-office manoeuvres were going on, Dunigan was publicly fighting with the club over his contract. That's when McCarthy let Kuharich talk him into sending six Argos to the Lions in exchange for Dunigan.

The day after that trade was announced, the Argos and Lions worked out a second deal. Toronto sent B.C. the rights to negotiate with college quarterback Major Harris in exchange for James "Quick" Parker, a three-time most outstanding defensive player. The Argos launched a marketing campaign featuring "Slick" (Dunigan) and "Quick" (Parker).

Although Dunigan had two years remaining on his contract, he was determined to renegotiate. Talks with the Argos dragged on for ten weeks, but on the day training camp opened, he signed a new agreement taking him through the 1991 season. He would reportedly be paid between $240,000 and $250,000, with incentive bonuses increasing his potential take-home pay to $300,000. That maintained Dunigan's status as the league's highest-paid player.

On the eve of the 1990 season, Matthews heaped praise on his new quarterback. "I consider myself lucky to have him," said the Argo coach. "The thought of Matt Dunigan coming here was mind-boggling."

Shoot the Lights Out

FOOTBALL COACHING WAS STILL an ultra-conservative profession in 1990. Players suited up in full pads for almost every practice, hit each other hard, and were regularly required to run until they puked. Don Matthews stunned Argo veterans at training camp when he announced that, once final cuts had been made and the roster chosen, only helmets and shoulder pads would be worn during the week. Hitting was for games, not practices.

"You only have so many hits on your body," he told them. "I need you to save them for game day. Training camp ends and we lock the pads up."

Guys who weren't needed on the field for a particular drill during practice were expected to rest, preferably under a shady tree. "If you're not in the play, I don't want you up," Matthews would tell his team. "I want you laying down, off your feet getting the rest you need."

The theory was that with their bodies recuperated from the punishment of the previous game, players would be dying to pound their opponents when they next took the field. "I'd go into games and I'd feel so good.

Hitting people was fun," says offensive tackle Chris Schultz. "Matthews would make you so hungry to physically go after the opponent."

For decades, football coaches had employed large, heavy sleds to help players practise blocking and tackling. After Matthews was hired, equipment manager Danny Webb asked what type of sleds he wanted. "Sleds?" the coach responded incredulously. "Webb, you tell me if there is a team in this league that is made up of sleds. I don't think so. The day we play a team of sleds is the day I use some sleds."

Matthews never asked his starting offence to go hard against his starting defence in practice. "We're not playing the Argos this year," he'd say. "They're not on our schedule."

He could crack up his players even while establishing his place squarely atop the team hierarchy. "This is a dictatorship," he'd say, "and I'm the head dick."

Although he acquired a reputation as the ultimate "player's coach" at each of his many stops around the CFL over three decades (including three separate stints as Toronto's head coach), Matthews was no soft touch. If you played badly, he was sure to let you know. Even if you played well, he was liable to give you a cutting jab.

"We were stretching one time," says Schultz. "I'd just had a great game. He walked by and gave me a look. 'I expected you to play a hell of a lot better.' I was crushed. What did he see that I hadn't seen? Where did I mess up? He knew exactly what he was doing. I was getting a little cocky, and if you get a little cocky, you don't take care of details. He had to bring me down to get me back to where I was. And it was in one sentence."

Matthews was a master psychologist, says quarterback Matt Dunigan. "Pushing the right buttons to challenge you individually in front of the room so you'd be committed and accountable in front of everybody else.

Now it's up to you to go out there and do your job because you just said you could do it in front of everybody."

Rather than drilling his players to death all week, Matthews simply "demanded that you perform," says linebacker Chris Gaines. "How you prepared for it was up to you."

As countless journalists found out, Matthews had an enormous ego. Challenge him and the coach's devilish grin could turn instantly into a chilling death stare. Says Peter Martin, who served as analyst on the team's radio broadcasts for decades: "If you crossed him or tried to question or challenge him, he'd throw it back to you. 'How many Grey Cups have you won?'"

Many players interviewed for this book had nothing but positive things to say about Matthews. But not all of them. Jock Climie, drafted in the first round by the Argonauts in 1990, says Matthews favoured a "pickup-truck-driving, tobacco-chewing, take-the-knees-out-of-the-other-guy type of player." Climie, a smooth receiver who ran precise patterns, was definitely not that type. He fell out of favour almost immediately, and was lost on waivers (to the Ottawa Rough Riders) early in the season.

Individuals who coloured between the lines were of no interest to the "live on the edge" coach, says kicker Lance Chomyc. "He would find the bad boys, the incorrigibles or the difficult-to-deal-with and he would not only support them and encourage them, he'd almost put them on a pedestal. Guys who were late for meetings or missed flights . . . he had all the time in the world [for]. Guys who did pull all the weight, he'd look down his nose at them and couldn't care less."

Matthews was not shy about his compulsion to win, constantly. Even by the exceedingly confident standard of football coaches, he raised the bar for cockiness. He went into every game fully expecting to win. "If you talked to him on the Monday of every week, you'd figure [his team] was going to be 18-and-0, there's no way they can lose," says his agent, Gil Scott.

Never was Matthews' swagger more evident than in the weeks between his appointment as Toronto head coach and the start of the 1990 season. With the Argos building a marketing campaign around the theme of "Big City Football," Matthews repeatedly stated that the team was going to "shoot the lights out." The Argos, he said, were aiming to score more points than any team in the history of Canadian football.

"We'll have a wide-open, exciting offence that will put 40 points on the scoreboard every game," Matthews said. "If we win 38-12, we'll still be disappointed because we won't have achieved the objective of scoring 40 points."

It was a bold statement, especially considering the Argonauts in 1989 had averaged just 20 points a game, worst in the CFL. And the team's best offensive player, running back Gill Fenerty, had jumped to the NFL. Matthews was soon hedging. "I never promised we'd score at least 40 points in every game this season," he said. "Aim high is my motto. But I don't guarantee it. That would be crazy."

He nevertheless held to a goal of *averaging* 40 points a game.

Matthews' confidence was not entirely misplaced, notwithstanding the team's poor showing in 1989. The Argos had some decent weapons in their arsenal, and had obtained a star quarterback in the prime of his career to lead the offence. And Matthews had hired a brilliant offensive strategist to design the plays.

As soon as he agreed to become Toronto's head coach, Matthews called an old pal. Adam Rita had served as his offensive co-ordinator with the B.C. Lions starting in 1983. Together they made two Grey Cup appearances and won the championship in 1985.

An easygoing Hawaiian, Rita relished the offensive creativity allowed in Canadian football. The wider and longer field, unlimited pre-snap motion in the offensive backfield, and three downs created greater impetus to pass the ball regularly.

When Matthews was fired by the Lions late in 1987, Rita stayed on for a year under the new head coach, Larry Donovan. He then took a low-paying job as an assistant coach at the University of British Columbia, a holding pattern until Matthews asked him to serve as mastermind of an offensive eruption in Toronto.

"We need to name your offence," Matthews told him. Rita laughed the suggestion off, saying he needed a better understanding of the team's personnel before he could commit to a brand strategy. But he soon came to accept Matthews' phrase: "Shoot the lights out."

During training camp, Rita coached the Argo offence to operate without a huddle. Dunigan would bark out signals to his mates as they moved directly into position. The next play would begin as soon as possible after the previous play ended.

The so-called "hurry-up offence" had traditionally been used only late in games or first halves by teams trying to score before time expired. Matthews and Rita were determined to roll it out regularly, in all situations. Doing so, they reckoned, would tire out opposing defences and maximize their own scoring opportunities.

Dunigan was salivating at the prospect of a high-octane offence. "We practised hard and put in the time so we could play fast," he says. "The opponent doesn't know what you're doing, and they can't play at the same speed as you're playing. [We're] jabbing you in the face, and the next thing you know it's a right cross, you're staggering and we're in the end zone."

The no-huddle worked like a dream in Toronto's first preseason game. The Argos crushed the Hamilton Tiger-Cats 60-19, reeling off an astonishing 92 offensive plays, about 50 per cent more than teams typically managed. At halftime, veteran linebacker Moen tried to settle down excited young teammates. "It's nothing-nothing, guys," he said.

Matthews heard Moen and took exception. "Fuck that! We're kicking their ass!"

In the first game of the regular season, the Argos ran the no-huddle offence through the entire first half, piling up 20 offensive plays in the first quarter alone. They also introduced one of Rita's other innovations on their first offensive play of that game: the "Ninja formation." Instead of placing the customary five blockers in front of the quarterback (a centre surrounded by two guards and two tackles), the Argos went with an unconventional three-man front. Guards Dan Ferrone and Bob Skemp flanked out to the left, far beyond tackle Chris Schultz. Dunigan took the snap and immediately tossed a pass to Darrell K. Smith, who had lined up behind Ferrone and Skemp. With the two guards chopping down defenders in front of him, Smith gained seven yards before being tackled.

The Ninja formation reappeared from time to time through the rest of the opening game, but the Argos returned to conventional five-man blocking formations for most of the season. The no-huddle approach, however, was implemented regularly, far more frequently than any team had used it in the past.

The team was adapting to Rita's offensive philosophy, but the success of the preseason was not evident once the regular season began. In the season opener, the no-huddle offence was effective at times and the team served up moments of creativity such as the Ninja formation, but the Argonauts trailed from the outset and ended up losing 40-34 to Edmonton.

The Argos then went on the road to face the Winnipeg Blue Bombers, who had knocked Toronto out of the playoffs the previous two years.

This game proved to be a test of Matthews' faith in Dunigan. When the quarterback was acquired from B.C., the head coach had assured him, "If you throw five interceptions, I'm leaving you in." Against the Bombers, Dunigan threw five interceptions. True to his word, Matthews left him in the game. Then Dunigan threw two more picks, tying a league record for the most interceptions thrown in a single game. After the seventh, he ran to the sidelines with a grin on his face.

"Hey, Don, am I going to get a chance to throw eight?"

"Sit your ass down!"

"So seven's the limit," Dunigan says now.

The Bombers beat the Argos. Toronto finally got a win in Week 3, but the result was overshadowed by the first of what became a seemingly endless succession of injuries suffered by Dunigan.

John Congemi started the next four games. Then he, too, got hurt. That left third-stringer Tom Porras, a veteran whose skills as a quarterback were far surpassed by his Elvis Presley impersonation, to start the eighth game of the year, in Edmonton.

Two days before that game, Mike McCarthy earned his entire year's salary. With Porras Toronto's only healthy quarterback, the general manager pulled a fast one on the B.C. Lions. He had noticed that third-year quarterback Rickey Foggie, the Lions' starter when the season began, had fallen down the depth chart. With the emergence of Doug Flutie as the new starter, Foggie had been moved to B.C.'s practice roster and was being converted from quarterback to slotback.

McCarthy called Foggie in the middle of the night, asked if he wanted to come to Toronto and promised he would dress for the Argos' next game. That would mean a game cheque (rather than the smaller stipend paid to practice-roster players), a return to his preferred position of quarterback, and a chance to be reunited with Rita and Dunigan, both of whom had been with the Lions when he turned pro in 1988. Foggie agreed and flew in from Vancouver.

Lions GM Joe Kapp was livid. While practice-roster players were officially free to sign anywhere, teams had traditionally sought permission before scooping one away. The unwritten rule allowed the player's original team to either work out a trade or put the player on its active roster, rather than lose him for nothing. McCarthy had no intention of giving Kapp a chance to keep the quarterback. Better to seek forgiveness than permission, he figured.

Foggie had a single practice with the Argos, then flew with the team to Edmonton. Porras started the game and had an utterly miserable night: three interceptions and two fumbles. With 14 minutes left and the Argos trailing 42-15, Matthews put in Foggie, who completed seven passes for 204 yards and three touchdowns while rushing for 53 more yards. The Argos lost 56-36, but a characteristically cocky Matthews said afterward that he would be more than happy to roll with Foggie as long as Dunigan remained out. The Argos and their fans had just caught their first glimpse of a man who would become a key to their fortunes over the next year and a half.

Dunigan came off the injury list the following week, in time to ignite the most impressive explosion of high-scoring football Canada had ever seen: 68-43 and 49-19 wins over B.C.; 39-16 over Hamilton; 70-18 over Calgary; 60-39 over the Ticats. In that stretch of five games, the Argonauts averaged an unheard-of 57 points.

The first of those games, at home against the Lions, set a record for most points scored by both teams, with Toronto and B.C. combining for 50 points (also a record) in the fourth quarter alone. After the Argos scored a touchdown to go up 68-35 with less than a minute left, Matthews sent Dunigan onto the field to attempt a two-point convert, perhaps the most outrageous attempt to run up the score, ever. "I wanted 70," said Dunigan, the ex-Lion.[4]

After the next game, in Vancouver, disgruntled Lions fans pelted coach Lary Kuharich with garbage as he left the field. "Coach Q" and his boss Kapp were then run out of town by Pezim and replaced by Bob O'Billovich, the longtime Argo head coach whose dismissal ten months earlier had paved the way for Matthews in Toronto.

Dunigan got hurt yet again, which meant Foggie would make his first start for the Argos at home against Hamilton. He erupted with a performance no other quarterback in history has ever been able to match. Foggie threw seven touchdown passes, one short of the CFL record, and rushed for more than a hundred yards. Dave Hodge, calling the game on the Canadian Football Network's TV broadcast, practically begged Matthews to let Foggie try to tie Joe Zuger's touchdown record when Toronto got the ball back in Hamilton territory near the end of the game, but the coach instructed his quarterback to take a knee twice and run out the clock. As the final gun sounded, the ever-smiling Foggie hurled the ball jubilantly into the crowd behind the Argo bench.

* * *

Even though their star quarterback had been out almost half of the time because of injuries, the Argos had become an offensive powerhouse. The primary reason was the play of two guys who had been afterthoughts on the team a year earlier.

---

4   The 68-43 win put the Argos into the record book for the second-most points ever scored by one team. (Montreal holds the record for an 82-14 win over Hamilton in 1956.) Three weeks later, the Argonauts surpassed themselves by putting up 70 points against Calgary in a game that was delayed, and nearly postponed, because large mounds were left under the artificial turf at SkyDome when the field was converted from baseball to football.

Darrell K. Smith and Pinball Clemons were the talk of Canadian football in 1990. Smith scored more touchdowns on pass receptions than any player in history. Clemons racked up more yards than anyone ever had.

When he took over as head coach, Matthews already knew he had something special in Smith. And he made sure the man nicknamed Stymie, because he resembled a young character of that name in the 1930s movie series *Our Gang*, knew it, too.

"I told him every day, when he looked in the mirror, to say, 'One hundred,'" Matthews had said during Argo training camp in 1990. Smith didn't understand at first. "I want you to go for one hundred catches this season," the new coach elaborated. Saying "one hundred" each day, Matthews reckoned, would reinforce the message. Matthews also set aggressive targets of 1,800 yards and 18 touchdowns.

The fifth-year receiver didn't need convincing. Smith, who figured he would have either been traded or demanded a trade had O'Billovich returned as coach, had an unshakeable conviction that he was open on every play. And even when blanketed by a defender or two, he could use his considerable strength and huge hands—bigger than basketball giant Shaquille O'Neal's, one teammate says—to catch the ball.

Smith constantly lobbied his quarterbacks for passes. "Deal me some cards!" he'd demand. "If you want to look good, get me the ball. If you want to win this football game, just focus on me." It sounds self-centred, but Smith genuinely believed he gave the team its best chance to win. "He felt he needed to carry the team on his back," says fellow receiver Jeff Boyd.

Smith responded to Matthews' challenge in 1990 by almost reaching one of the goals, and surpassing the other two. He had 93 receptions, 1,826 yards, and a then-record 20 touchdown catches. He had two games with more than 200 yards receiving, something done previously only by one other Argonaut, Terry Greer. He had four touchdowns in a game against Hamilton "and he was upset that I didn't throw him five," says quarterback Rickey Foggie.

While Matthews had needed no convincing to make full use of Smith, he initially had no idea what to make of Clemons.

Rita had barely settled into his new job with the Argos when Matthews gave him an assignment. Star running back Gill Fenerty had gone to the NFL, and Matthews needed to know if Clemons, the only returning tailback on the roster, was capable of replacing him. The head coach had already told McCarthy: "I don't know if he's good enough; he's so small."

"I want you to look at this guy Pinball Clemons," Matthews told Rita. "He didn't play much on offence last year, and no way I'm wasting a position on a kick returner. Let me know if we need to trade him or cut him or whatever."

Rita walked to the film room and queued up footage from 1989. After watching Clemons return a punt and a kickoff, he shut off the projector and strolled back to the head coach's office.

"That was fast," Matthews said.

"Don, the little guy can play," Rita responded.

He had seen enough to discern that Clemons was uniquely adept at making tacklers miss. "I didn't care that he was too small, I just knew he was a playmaker. He wasn't worried about [his size], so why would I be?"

Even in a league where five-foot-six kick returner Henry "Gizmo" Williams had excelled, Clemons' short stature set him apart. But with a ball in his hands, standing five-foot-five made no difference at all. Pinball ("Pinner" to close friends) constantly wowed teammates and opponents with his ability to bounce away from tackles and squeeze through tiny openings. "It's like trying to catch a chicken," says teammate Chris Gaines. "Almost impossible."

Opponents "were scared of Pinball because he'd embarrass you," says Ken Evraire, who played on kick-coverage units against the Argos. "Oh, great, it's Pinball. I'm going to end up on TSN because he's going to make me look stupid."

Rita designed an offence that could take full advantage of Clemons' elusiveness. Flanked out as a receiver, or running pass patterns out of the backfield, he created a matchup nightmare for defences.

As the Argos' primary offensive weapon in 1990, Clemons set a league record for most total yards in a season with 3,300. He was named the CFL's most outstanding player. In any other year, that award likely would have gone to his 20-touchdown teammate, D.K. Smith.

* * *

There was just one obstacle standing in the way of this sudden juggernaut: the Winnipeg Blue Bombers. A week after Foggie's seven TD passes had helped Toronto rack up a fifth consecutive lopsided victory, the Argos went into Winnipeg Stadium and managed a mere three field goals in a 25-9 loss. The following week, the Bombers won again, 21-16, at SkyDome to clinch first place in the East Division.

A team without much offence, and none of Toronto's razzle-dazzle, the Blue Bombers were built around a defence that terrorized opponents. Winnipeg pressured quarterbacks relentlessly, from unpredictable angles, and stifled receivers' attempts to get open. Toronto played four regular-season games against the Blue Bombers in 1990, losing all four by an aggregate score of 107-65. Against the rest of the league, the Argos averaged 45 points (and won ten of 14 games). Against Winnipeg, Toronto barely managed 16 a game.

After closing out the season with wins of 59-15 and 49-30 sandwiched around a 33-31 loss, the Argonauts were comfortably in second place in the East Division. Despite starting four quarterbacks, the team had broken the CFL scoring record with 689 points, an average of 38.3 per game. Not quite Matthews' prediction of 40, but impressive nonetheless.

When healthy, Dunigan had lived up to his billing. Foggie, an Argonaut only since late August, had been an utter revelation. Despite suiting up for just ten games, and seeing significant playing time in only seven, he had led the team with 21 touchdown passes while rushing for a team-best 674 yards and five more TDs.

Now the playoffs awaited, and a hoped-for rematch with the dreaded Blue Bombers for a shot at going to the Grey Cup game. But to have a crack at playing Winnipeg in the Eastern Final, the Argonauts first had to get past the Ottawa Rough Riders, again with a depleted lineup. Dunigan was unable to play, or even dress for the game. Foggie started and got hurt, leaving after just seven plays. His replacement, Congemi, managed to stay in for eight plays before he, too, got injured.

That forced the ball into the hands of unproven fourth-stringer Willie Gillus, who had arrived in Toronto late in the season as an insurance policy against injuries. Gillus had thrown just nine passes as an Argo, completing just two, both for touchdowns.

Inserted unexpectedly into a do-or-die playoff game, he immediately started forcing the ball deep, to no avail. Matthews called Rita in the spotter's booth to demand that Gillus, whose arm was as strong as any in football, rein it in. Rita ordered Gillus to call a simple short slant pattern to D.K. Smith. Gillus executed the play call, completing an eight-yard pass near the left sideline deep in Argo territory. Smith cut around several defenders and started weaving towards the distant end zone. As he picked up speed past midfield, Gillus appeared on his flank. The quarterback raced the length of the field, throwing blocks along the way, to escort his mate across the goal-line.

"He must have run 220 yards on that play," marvels Congemi. Smith's 99-yard touchdown was the longest pass reception ever recorded by an Argo in the playoffs.

As players and coaches reviewed game film the next day, Rita showed the play over and over. "Look at the hustle," he told his troops. "Look at your quarterback on this play. This is the type of effort we need to win."

Inspired by Gillus's blocking and full-field sprint, and helped considerably by Smith's 99-yard TD and the 364 all-purpose yards racked up by Clemons, the Argos fought from behind for a 34-25 victory.

It was a battered and bruised band of Argonauts that flew to Winnipeg for the Eastern Final. Middle linebacker Chris Gaines, the leader of a tough Argo defence, was not on the plane after blowing out a knee in the semifinal. The offensive leader, Dunigan, was also out, and so were his primary backup Foggie as well as Gillus, who had been injured later in the Ottawa game. Congemi had to start, even though he was nursing a hand injury that left him looking like "I had an egg on the top of my right palm." Porras, who had been released by the team after his abysmal performance in Edmonton and Foggie's arrival, was summoned to serve as the backup QB.

The black cloud that had followed Argo quarterbacks all season showed up again in Winnipeg. On a quarterback sneak, Congemi got hit by a helmet on his injured hand. "It blew up and I couldn't hold the ball."

Offensive tackle Kelvin Pruenster pleaded with Congemi to stay in the game. "You can't leave us in there with Tom," Pruenster said. "You've got to get out there and try." But with Congemi unable to grasp the football, there was no alternative. It was up to Porras, the fifth-string, break-glass-only-in-event-of-emergency quarterback, to try to lead the Argos to the Grey Cup.

Amazingly, it wasn't a completely impossible mission. Toronto's defence kept the Bombers in check, and midway through the fourth quarter, Porras plunged over the goal-line from one yard out for a touchdown that tied the game 17-17.

Then, with less than a minute to play, and overtime looming, the Bombers advanced to midfield. On second down, needing nine yards for a first down and at least 15 yards for a long field-goal attempt, Winnipeg quarterback Tom Burgess sent all six of his backs and receivers out on pass patterns. Toronto's five defensive backs and three linebackers dropped back to cover them.

Some of the defenders turned their backs to the quarterback as they ran alongside the receivers. After all, there was no way Burgess, a slow-as-molasses QB, was going to try to run with the football. Even his own teammates knew that. When he had called a quarterback running play in practice the week before, players on the Bomber defence just laughed. "That's never going to work in a game," cornerback Rod Hill said disdainfully that day.

But now a playoff game was on the line, and suddenly there was no one in the middle of the field. Burgess took off and didn't get tackled until he had gained 31 yards. That set up a chip-shot field goal with no time remaining that gave Winnipeg a hard-fought 20-17 win.

Asked what happened on the play, a few Argos reluctantly point a finger of blame at Harold Hallman, who was playing nose tackle in the centre of the defensive line. Replays show Hallman, trying to shed two blockers, make a fateful decision to slide a step or two to his right. That opened a gap Burgess exploited. "He went the wrong way," McCarthy says bluntly. Hallman, who died in 2005, carried a feeling of guilt with him afterwards, says teammate Keith Castello.

The shoot-the-lights-out season had come to a bitter end, one game—

a few seconds, really—short of the Argonauts' goal of the Grey Cup game. The old cry of "wait until next year" would echo through the ranks of the Argos and their fans.

But for one man, there was to be no next year. After two years as owner of the Argos, Harry Ornest was ready to move on to other things.

Ornest had seen average attendance drop below 32,000, despite the Argos being one of the most exciting CFL teams ever. By the end of the 1990 season, he had grown tired of owning the club, and possibly of going home alone every night to his room in the Sutton Place hotel. With his wife, Ruth, back in Beverly Hills, the owner whiled away lonely evenings reading stacks of newspapers, clipping stories to send to friends.

"I'm getting out of this," he told McCarthy one day before the season ended. "Let's go to a hockey game. I want you to meet somebody."

That somebody was Bruce McNall.

The Three Amigos

THE WAY BRUCE MCNALL describes it, the initial approach was casual. One day in 1990, he bumped into Harry Ornest at the Hollywood Park racetrack in Los Angeles. "You know," Ornest said, "I own a football team in Canada. Toronto Argonauts. I'm trying to sell it."

Both Ornest and McNall belonged to the aging horse track's board of directors. They were also members of an exclusive fraternity of guys who owned clubs in the National Hockey League. Ornest had owned the St. Louis Blues from 1983 to 1986. McNall had become a minority partner in the Los Angeles Kings in 1986, and within two years was the team's sole owner. Now Ornest wondered if McNall might like to add to his stable of sporting investments.

"I had never heard of [the Argos] and had no idea what he was talking about," McNall says. But he knew someone who might have an idea. His hockey team's superstar, Wayne Gretzky, had grown up not far from Toronto. McNall called Gretzky, who was also his partner in a few racehorses.[5]

---

5   They would also team up later to pay $451,000 for an extremely rare piece of sports memorabilia, a mint-condition baseball card from 1909 depicting star player Honus Wagner.

"What do you know about the Toronto Argonauts?" McNall asked.

"Oh my goodness, I know plenty," Gretzky replied. "It's right in my backyard. It was the team I followed when I was a kid. Bruce, there's only one team in Canada to buy: the Toronto Argonauts."

McNall, who also produced motion pictures, next called someone else he knew from Toronto. In his capacity as the Kings' "honorary captain," John Candy regularly attended pre-game dinners McNall hosted at the Forum Club, a private dining room inside the Inglewood arena where the team played. He would sit alongside McNall at the centre of a large, E-shaped table, schmoozing Hollywood celebs such as Mary Hart, Goldie Hawn, Patrick Swayze, and Alan Thicke.

McNall explained to Candy that the Argos might be for sale.

"Are you kidding me?" the actor said. "I love the Argonauts! I can't believe it."

And with that, McNall's story goes, the wheels were set in motion. Not long after the preliminary phone calls, he and Gretzky and Candy introduced themselves as the newest owners of the Toronto Argonauts.

That may or may not be how it all went down. It's reasonably consistent with what McNall said back in 1991, and it's how he still remembers it. Others, though, have different recollections of the particulars.

In another version of the story, Candy was the first to hear that the Argonauts were for sale. "He was always talking about the Argos and telling stories about being a football player in high school," says Roy Mlakar, an executive with the Kings. After hearing elsewhere that Ornest "was going down the tubes," Candy talked to McNall, Mlakar says.

In yet another account, the genesis of the deal was a chance meeting between Gretzky and Ornest on a flight from Los Angeles to Toronto in the summer of 1990. "Dad returned from Toronto telling us that he ran into Wayne Gretzky . . . and they started negotiating on the plane," says Ornest's daughter Cindy.

Gretzky, however, recalls first hearing about the possibility of buying the team from McNall, not Ornest. When McNall asked if he wanted to be part of the deal, Gretzky said he didn't see how he could get involved because of his commitments as a hockey player. Then McNall told him Candy was coming on board. "OK! Of course, I'll do it," the Great One replied.

Regardless of where, when, or by whom the deal was initiated, there is no doubt about how events ultimately unfolded. After a brief period of exploration that didn't include a whole lot of due diligence, McNall and his execs began negotiating with Ornest.

On Feb. 25, 1991, McNall, Candy, and Gretzky, instantly dubbed the "three amigos," ended weeks of speculation and rumour by announcing they had purchased the Argos for a stated price of $5 million. More journalists were in attendance than at any press conference the team had held since the late 1970s.

Candy and Gretzky were thrilled to own 20 per cent of the Argos, McNall says. "Being Canadian, it was a really big deal to them. Especially John, who was a huge Argo fan."

While all three of the owners now lived in Los Angeles, Candy and Gretzky played up their local roots. The actor was raised in the Toronto borough of East York, and had attended games at the old Exhibition Stadium as a kid. He had played on the offensive and defensive lines at Neil McNeil High School, and fantasized about someday suiting up for the Argos.

Gretzky had grown up in Brantford, an hour or so west of Toronto. He had been taken to an Argo game in the mid-1970s when he was being billeted with a family in suburban Oakville during a hockey tournament. "I was so excited to go because I had heard so much about it, and my parents couldn't afford to go to an Argo game." Gretzky remembers watching Granville "Granny" Liggins terrorize opposing quarterbacks from his position on Toronto's defensive line.

McNall and Gretzky made a few awkward stabs at being witty at the press conference, but Candy was in his element. He resurrected one of his SCTV characters, Dr. Tongue, the star of three-dimensional horror films that were never scary—"football in 3D," he hissed. He suggested he himself might suit up for the Argos. And when a banner constructed of team pennants fell from the wall behind the head table, exposing a vintage portrait of 1930s diva Marlene Dietrich, Candy snapped into improv mode: "There she is. Marlene Dietrich is with us. Our silent partner. We were saving this for later."

The announcement of the new ownership group was front-page news, naturally. McNall's slick publicity machine even arranged special coverage in the *Toronto Sun*: Janet Jones, Gretzky's wife who had ended her acting career after she married the hockey star in 1988, appeared on page 3, bedecked in an Argonauts jacket as the newspaper's "Sunshine Girl."

* * *

It was one thing for Ornest and McNall, the new majority owner, to agree on a deal, but before it was official, the CFL's board of governors had to approve the sale. While most governors were giddy at the prospect of household names coming into the troubled league, one was dubious. "Listen," the governor said at a meeting, "maybe we need to do some due diligence on Bruce McNall. We need to make sure this guy is who he says he is."

Everyone else in the room pushed back. "We all said, 'Oh, man, you can't do that,'" says Phil Kershaw, who attended the meeting as president of the Saskatchewan Roughriders. He has a clear memory of the remark but can't recall which governor made it. The feeling in the room was "what if we insult this great man's intelligence and ego by making him prove his financial worth? He'll be very upset. We saw Bruce McNall and all the glamour and glitz that he brought as a salvation during a dark time in the league."

It was indeed a dark time. Less than four years earlier, the Montreal Alouettes had folded on the eve of the 1987 season, turning the CFL into an eight-team league for the first time since the B.C. Lions were formed in 1954. Of the remaining franchises, five were in precarious condition by the time the McNall group arrived.

The Ottawa Rough Riders were on the brink of bankruptcy, and ended up being operated by the league for most of the 1991 season. When Rider players received their paycheques after games that year, they would race to a bank branch near the stadium "to make sure the money was there," says receiver Ken Evraire.

Hamilton Tiger-Cats owner David Braley was desperate to unload his team, which typically drew 11,000 spectators at the 30,000-seat Ivor Wynne Stadium. At training camp, Ticats players practised twice a day but could get their ankles taped only once. "For lunch it was either a ham sub or a tuna sub," remembers receiver Lee Knight.

The Saskatchewan Roughriders were only a few years removed from running a telethon to raise operating capital. The Calgary Stampeders, who avoided folding in 1985 only because of a desperate "Save Our Stamps" campaign, were sinking back into financial peril by 1991. They ended up getting bought late in the season by Larry Ryckman.[6]

---

6   Ryckman himself ran out of money four years later, and failed to meet his contractual obligations to superstar Doug Flutie.

The B.C. Lions were owned in 1991 by Murray Pezim, the braggadocious penny-stock promoter and tireless self-promoter whose fortunes waxed and waned with the success (or lack thereof) of the various ventures he invested in.[7]

Even the comparatively healthy Winnipeg Blue Bombers were $2 million in debt, and pinching pennies everywhere. Star running back Robert Mimbs once walked, in uniform, across the street from the stadium to a department store to buy socks because equipment staff would not issue him a fresh pair. "After a game we were allowed one pop or one beer," says offensive tackle Chris Walby. "You had to sign it out with the equipment guy."

After three consecutive thrilling Grey Cup games with cliff-hanger finishes, the CFL's most recent championship, in Vancouver, had been a disaster. The city was dead during the usually raucous Grey Cup week, and the league had to provide free tickets to thousands of military personnel to fill the stadium. Even with that handout, there were more than 13,000 empty seats at B.C. Place to watch a turgid game in which Winnipeg destroyed Edmonton by 39 points.

It was well known among those who covered the CFL that it was struggling to earn television revenue. When a three-year TV rights deal that paid the league $11 million a year came to an end in 1986, CTV walked away and gave the CFL's other broadcast partner, CBC, all the leverage in subsequent rights negotiations, driving down the price.

---

7   Larry Smith, who became CFL commissioner in 1992, tells a story about Pezim's abrupt departure from the league. "I've only got money for six months and then I'm going to go bankrupt," the Pez told the commish. Two weeks later, Pezim called Smith back. "Kid, I've only got money for three months." Smith noted that he'd recently said he had enough money to keep going for six months. "Yeah, but I'm running out." The next day, Pezim called again. "Hey, kid, I've got a ticket waiting for you at the counter. You've got to come up tomorrow because I'm going bankrupt at noon."

The prevailing sentiment among journalists covering the league was that it was on life support. Halftime shows during CBC telecasts of CFL games regularly focused on the state of emergency at one team or another. At a news conference about one such calamity, a reporter asked point blank: "What would you say to our bosses who sent us here today to cover the death of the Canadian Football League?"

The Toronto Argonauts were by no means aloof from these trends, and the problems dated from long before Harry O got involved. Back in the 1970s, the team had routinely generated front-page headlines by signing American "superstars" like Anthony Davis and Terry Metcalf; it had drawn crowds above 40,000 even for intra-squad scrimmages, and averaged more than 47,000 per game in 1976. But those good times didn't last. Attendance dropped, even when the team was competitive on the field. "The more we won," notes offensive guard Dan Ferrone, who joined the team in 1981, "the less they came."

There are many possible reasons for this strange phenomenon. Some were specific to the Toronto marketplace.

The Toronto Blue Jays baseball club arrived in 1977 and developed into a contender within six seasons. The Jays also marketed their product effectively from Day 1, attracting families and young kids with mascot BJ Birdy, the *OK Blue Jays* jingle, fan-friendly radio broadcasts and the intrinsic charms of a slow-paced game played every day, all summer.

The Argos, meanwhile, virtually ceased marketing efforts after Ralph Sazio signed on as club president in 1981. Sazio believed a winning team was the only requirement; his idea of a good marketing campaign was "tickets on sale now."

The Argos' long-awaited success in 1983, finally winning the Grey Cup after a drought of 31 years, seemed to release a "pressure valve" that had been building over those years. Finally winning the championship gave some fans permission to focus on other pursuits.

The emergence of cable TV in the 1970s brought a multitude of NFL games into Toronto living rooms at the same time as antiquated blackout rules were keeping most Argo games off the local airwaves. NFL telecasts, with a smaller field, larger crowds, and more cameras, had higher production values than CFL broadcasts. NFL salaries rose by the mid-1980s, and the Argos could no longer compete for big-name talent.

Torontonians' perpetual longing for "world-class" status meant baseball games against the New York Yankees or Boston Red Sox had more cachet than football games against the Saskatchewan Roughriders or Winnipeg Blue Bombers.

The increasingly multicultural nature of Toronto meant that a sizeable and increasing proportion of the population had not grown up with "gridiron football," which for all practical purposes is played only in North America. And the ballooning of new entertainment options, from live theatre to a multitude of music venues, created more ways to spend disposable income in Canada's biggest city.

The Toronto Argonauts, in short, were every bit as shambolic as the rest of the CFL in 1990. Yet, suddenly, into this mess came what Michael Landsberg on TSN's *Sportsdesk* called "a life preserver all the way from Hollywood."

"People thought, boy, we've got the motherlode here," says Scott Oake, who as host of *The CFL on CBC* reported constantly on the league's troubles. "They're going to make the CFL relevant again in Toronto. People thought it would be the league's salvation."

"When [the three amigos] showed up and were now going to own the Argos, it took our media profile from close to zero to a hundred almost overnight," says Saskatchewan's Kershaw. "This would provide an aura of glamour and an infusion of interest."

As popular and iconic as Gretzky and Candy were, McNall was seen as the mastermind of the deal, and the key to its potential success. Hence the reluctance to annoy him with uncomfortable questions, never mind that no one knew much about him.

"He was just a guy who is suddenly a zillionaire who popped up out of nowhere," says Cam Cole, a sports columnist for the *Edmonton Journal*.

That might have been reason for suspicions, but McNall instead was viewed as a visionary who had found success with hockey in a non-traditional market. CFL people hoped his magic would rub off on them. Maybe the league, like the L.A. Kings before McNall came along, was just under-exposed, and a little marketing savvy would change its fortunes overnight.

McNall's idea, it was widely believed, was to emulate what he had done with the Kings: a cocktail of sports, celebrity, and glamour. "You create that idea of special people being around, and other people just gravitate," says sportswriter Stephen Brunt. The notion was that "if we sex this up enough and package it in the right way and make it feel of the moment, we can sell this to people, whether or not they have any history with it." It seemed revolutionary. "The idea that glamorous people were excited about the CFL or the Argos," says Brunt, "didn't line up with anything that had gone before. It was the big-time idea of it, rather than the league your dad watched."

Saving the Argonauts and the CFL, in fact, was not McNall's real goal. With control of the Argos came the exclusive right to operate a football team in the two-year-old SkyDome, a state-of-the-art stadium. Contract language suggested it need not be a CFL team.

Journalists at the introductory news conference asked McNall (as they had asked Ornest two years earlier) if he had a plan to bring the National

Football League to Toronto. Like Ornest, McNall said no. He insisted he saw the Argonauts as an undervalued property that could be built up in value the way the Kings had been. And anyway, as owner of a hockey team, he was not eligible to own an NFL franchise under that league's rules.

But in an interview for this book, confirming other statements he has made since selling the Argonauts, McNall owned up to his real intentions. He wanted to put an NFL team into SkyDome. "That was my main thing. I could never say that at the time."

He even engaged in discussions with Art Modell, owner of the Cleveland Browns, about possibly moving that team to Toronto. Modell eventually relocated the Browns to Baltimore, where they became the Ravens.

"I had him pretty much convinced to move to Toronto," McNall says. "Toronto being the largest metropolitan city in North America that didn't have an NFL franchise, I thought that would make a lot of sense."

The plan was scuppered, he says, because NFL owners thought it might damage the Buffalo Bills, located just a couple of hours from Toronto. "Buffalo's a small little dirt town. Toronto's a major city, for God's sake. Modell and I really worked on it for a long time [but] we could never get over that damn hump. I just couldn't overcome the Buffalo issue."

McNall says he never revealed his NFL plan to Candy, whose love of the Argonauts was genuine and dated back decades before his decision to put a million dollars into the team, nor to Gretzky, who had been excited to attend an Argo game as a kid, but otherwise didn't follow football closely. "The minute you say something to a third party, even as close as Wayne and I were, or John and I, you lose control. All they have to do is say something to a Brian Cooper [Gretzky's longtime business partner who became the Argos' chief operating officer] or someone like that and it would get out. So I was keeping this really on the down low. The odds of this happening were not great, and I knew that."

None of that surfaced as McNall settled for Plan B and the three amigos took it upon themselves to save the Argonauts and the CFL. Players and others associated with the Argos were ecstatic. "Uncle Buck [Candy] is going to own us? I couldn't fathom it," says offensive lineman Jim Kardash. "And Wayne Gretzky and Bruce McNall? You couldn't believe it could possibly happen."

Exciting as this news may have been, McNall was shrewd enough to know that no one ever bought a ticket to a sporting match to watch the person sitting in the owner's box. Something even bigger than a life preserver all the way from Hollywood would be needed to make the Argos relevant again. Something on the field.

Rocket Man

BRUCE MCNALL HAD ONE simple suggestion when he met for the first time with Mike McCarthy, general manager of the football team that he and partners John Candy and Wayne Gretzky had just acquired.

Think big.

Over the past four years, McNall had gone from a guy no one had ever heard of, outside the arcane world of ancient-coin collecting, to a big-time sports mogul. After first acquiring a minority stake in the Los Angeles Kings of the National Hockey League, and buying the remaining shares from Jerry Buss to become sole owner, McNall had made the biggest splash imaginable.

It was the summer of 1988, mere days after the hockey superstar Wayne Gretzky married actress Janet Jones in what was billed as "Canada's royal wedding." McNall threw a pile of cash and a few decent players at Edmonton Oilers owner Peter Pocklington in exchange for Gretzky. Just like that, the best hockey player on the planet, maybe the best of all time, and still very much in his prime, was leaving the sport's heartland for Tinseltown, where the only ice that mattered was in cocktail glasses.

That's no exaggeration. One of McNall's predecessors as owner of the Kings, Canadian Jack Kent Cooke, had found out the hard way that hockey was a tough sell in southern California. There were 300,000 expatriate Canadians in L.A., he famously said. "Now I know why they left Canada. They all hate hockey."

For two decades, the Kings had been an afterthought in the highly competitive L.A. sports marketplace. Gretzky's arrival, enhanced by gangsta-appeal black-and-silver uniforms that replaced the dreary purple and gold the team had worn since it arrived in the NHL in 1967, turned hockey into L.A.'s hottest ticket virtually overnight. The Kings were generating a buzz normally reserved for the city's red carpets.[8]

McNall had given Los Angeles what it loves most: a star. *The* star, in fact. The celebrities came out to see Gretzky, even though they had no idea where to sit in a hockey arena. They were used to attending basketball games, where the cool thing was to sit in highly-visible courtside seats. Ice-level seats behind the protective glass in hockey arenas are some of the worst available. "You can't see anything," says sportswriter Stephen Brunt. "But all the movie stars wanted to be around the glass. So [McNall] put them around the glass and they were on camera constantly. Kurt Russell and Goldie Hawn and Tom Hanks and Ronald and Nancy Reagan, all these people with their noses pressed right to the glass."

Gretzky soon stood alongside basketballer Magic Johnson as one of the two faces of sports in the entertainment capital of the world. Thanks in large part to his presence, the NHL dropped a second California franchise

---

8   When he bought a majority interest in the Argos, McNall mused aloud about possibly changing the team's colour scheme from the traditional Oxford Blue and Cambridge Blue to the Kings' black and silver. He said fans would be polled and would get their wish. Nothing ever came of the idea, and both Candy and Gretzky were said to be in favour of retaining the traditional Double Blue look.

in San Jose, to be followed by a third in Anaheim, and still more teams in other warm-weather states, including Florida, Arizona, and Texas. TV revenues rose and hockey, for the first time, assumed a legitimate place among the Big Four professional sports leagues in North America.[9]

That's what could happen when you thought big.

Now the owner of a football team, McNall wasn't interested in slowly and methodically building a winning team, or implementing clever, sustainable marketing strategies to expand the audience, one ticket sale at a time. He was focused on making a gigantic, instantaneous splash.

"Something with pop," he told McCarthy. "A big explosion."

It didn't take the general manager long to come up with the kind of brainwave McNall was sure to love.

Several weeks before McNall and company took possession of the Argonauts, McCarthy had been passing time as he always did on New Year's Day, watching U.S. college football bowl games on TV. As general manager of the Argonauts, McCarthy was responsible for keeping the team stocked with talented players, and holiday-season bowl games featuring the top college teams in the United States were full of those.

New Year's Day was a particular bonanza. The first day of 1991 featured no fewer than eight games, including a matchup many football fans had been anticipating for weeks: the Colorado Buffaloes, top-ranked team in the United States, against the fifth-ranked Notre Dame Fighting Irish, arguably America's most popular college squad, in the Orange Bowl. It was a rematch of a game one year earlier in which the Irish had upset the top-ranked Buffaloes.

---

9   McNall, not coincidentally, profited directly from this. He pocketed half of the $50 million Disney
    Corp. paid to bring the Mighty Ducks of Anaheim into the NHL, a rather generous "finder's fee."

Clinging to a one-point lead with a minute left in the 1991 game, the Buffs almost gave the national championship away thanks to a play that is often described as the greatest touchdown that didn't count. Colorado lined up to punt the ball deep into Notre Dame's end of the field. Standing near his own goal-line, awaiting the kick, was a marvellously talented young man named Raghib Ismail or, as he was known to virtually every sports fan in America because of how fast he could run, the Rocket.

In three years at Notre Dame, Ismail had returned five kickoffs for touchdowns. Twice he had run back two in the same game, including runs of 88 and 92 yards in a 1989 nationally televised showdown between the No. 1-ranked Fighting Irish and the second-ranked Michigan Wolverines.

Precisely one year before the 1991 Orange Bowl, the Rocket had dashed the hearts of Colorado fans with a brilliant touchdown run that helped the Irish upset the top-ranked Buffaloes in the 1990 version of the same bowl game.

Bill Walsh, who as head coach of the San Francisco 49ers had won three Super Bowl titles, described the Rocket as possessing the "fastest functional football speed" he had ever seen. Many players are fast, but Ismail was not just fast, Walsh said. He could also do other things that are needed on a football field: "Stops and starts, lateral movement, making a tackler miss."

Ismail's college career had been marked with a flair for the dramatic. So it came as no surprise to teammates when, in the dying seconds of the 1991 Orange Bowl, with the game on the line, he glanced over at the Notre Dame sideline and gave a thumbs-up gesture. As if to say, "I got this."

Even with Ismail almost the full length of the football field from his opponent's goal-line, allowing such a dangerous returner to receive a punt with a minute left in a one-point game seemed a foolhardy strategy. Yet that's what the Buffaloes did.

Fielding Tom Rouen's punt at his own nine-yard line, the Rocket, thinking to himself, "no matter what, don't go down," blasted off. He shook off one Colorado tackler, then another, and another, eluding half a dozen on his way to the Colorado end zone where he was mobbed by teammates.

The stunning touchdown run would have given Notre Dame the lead with 43 seconds left. Would have, that is, if there hadn't been a clipping penalty against one of Ismail's blockers. The return was negated by the penalty, and the Buffaloes held on to win 10-9.

Watching the game, McCarthy couldn't help but fantasize about adding the Rocket to the already powerful, high-scoring Argonauts. "That's the guy I need," he thought. "Another racehorse."

Signing the runner-up for the Heisman trophy as college football's outstanding player seemed like the longest of long shots, however. If, as expected, Ismail was to leave Notre Dame and turn professional, he would likely be the first player selected in the 1991 NFL draft. The previous two players picked first, quarterbacks Troy Aikman and Jeff George, had signed six-year contracts worth $11.2 million and $15 million, respectively.

The CFL, with a salary cap of $3 million per team and an average salary of $57,500, couldn't possibly compete for the top talent coming out of college.

Could it?

* * *

Once upon a time, the Argonauts and Montreal Alouettes had been able to outbid the NFL for big-name players. Toronto had signed quarterback Joe Theismann and defensive tackle Jim Stillwagon in the early 1970s, running backs Anthony Davis and Terry Metcalf later that decade, and defensive lineman Bruce Clark in 1980. Montreal had shocked the football world by signing Super Bowl-losing quarterback Vince Ferragamo, star receivers James Scott and Billy "White Shoes" Johnson, and two first-round NFL draft picks in 1981. Since then, though, NFL salaries had skyrocketed, and the Canadian league had fallen on increasingly hard times.

But McNall had demanded he think big, so McCarthy figured he had nothing to lose by quietly adding Ismail's name to the Argos' negotiation list, players with whom Toronto had exclusive rights to try to negotiate a CFL contract. Many "neg list" players never sign in the CFL, but some do.

McCarthy called Roy Mlakar, an executive with the Kings who was also doing work for the Argos.

"I've got an idea, although it's a little far-fetched," he said. "There's a guy on our negotiation list who's a game-breaker. He's a big name and it's going to cost us a lot of money. Rocket Ismail. He's the best player in the country. Tell Bruce this is the guy. Here's our big splash."

Mlakar took the idea to McNall. The owner's eyes lit up. "I love it!"

McNall loved the idea so much, in fact, that he couldn't keep it to himself. Mere hours after the GM had planted the seemingly outlandish notion of outbidding the NFL for Ismail, the owner spilled the beans. The Argos were going to try to sign the Rocket, McNall said during intermission of a televised Kings game at home against the Toronto Maple Leafs on March 20. He elaborated to reporters travelling with the Leafs. "We will pursue, fairly actively, bringing him to Canada."

Speaking openly about such matters was standard practice for McNall. As Gretzky, his former star player, business partner, and longtime friend, says: "I tell Bruce he's like a garbage can: step on his foot and his mouth opens."

McCarthy was stunned the news had come out so quickly. "I hadn't talked to Rocket yet. I hadn't talked to (his agents) yet. And I hadn't talked to Bruce at all. My phone rings until two in the morning. This went viral, and this was before the Internet. Everybody's calling me. Every big paper. I'm just bullshitting my way through all the phone calls. 'Well, Bruce is a deal-maker. He brought Wayne to L.A.'"

The frenzy had begun.

* * *

After his third football season at Notre Dame, Ismail had to decide whether to stay for his senior year or enter the NFL draft. When they returned from the Orange Bowl loss to Colorado, he and his Fighting Irish teammates had been stunned to learn of the sudden death of linebacker Chris Zorich's mother. Ismail's father had died when Raghib, the eldest of three sons, was ten years old. He took the death of his teammate's mother as a signal, he later said in a radio interview.

"One of the fears that I had was, 'Oh man, this might happen to me. Here I am, supposed to be the man of the house and I'm supposed to be providing for my family.' The fear of not being able to provide and not having provided yet led me to say, OK, I need to make this decision and become a professional football player."

The Rocket contacted Ralph Wiley, who had written a sensitive, complimentary profile of him for *Sports Illustrated* during his second year at Notre Dame. Wiley recalled Ismail's approach in a later article for ESPN: "My family is destitute. I need to go pro. Will you help me?" Wiley, who died in 2004, wrote that he "wrestled with it for about two seconds," then began assembling a group comprising a half-dozen attorneys, marketing experts and financial advisers: "Team Rocket."

The day after McNall announced his intention to pursue Ismail, McCarthy placed a call to Ed Abrams, one of the lead negotiators on

Team Rocket. Abrams, well aware that the CFL's financial resources were a fraction of the NFL's, was highly skeptical but willing to listen.

McNall's initial public statement that he was prepared to offer $6 million over two years was sufficient to get the attention of Ismail's advisers. But they were also dickering with the New England Patriots, who owned the top NFL pick and were determined to negotiate a contract in advance.

Fortunately for the Argos, at one point during a New England meeting, a Patriots executive made a remark Ismail considered racist and insulting. "That was the final nail in the coffin as far as New England was concerned," Abrams later said.

The Patriots, whose final offer of $10 million over five years had been rejected by Team Rocket, decided to trade the No. 1 pick to the Dallas Cowboys. Soon afterwards, Argo head coach Adam Rita got a call from an old colleague. Bobby Ackles had been general manager of the B.C. Lions in the 1980s, when Rita was an assistant coach there. He was now working in the Cowboys' front office.

"I heard you guys are going to sign the Rocket," Ackles said sarcastically. "What are you going to pay him?"

Rita said he was not privy to financial discussions, "but I'm going to tell you this: you might want to think about trading your first pick. I'm not kidding you. Our owners have enough hair up their ass that they'll get this done."

In early April, members of Team Rocket met with McNall, Mlakar, McCarthy and Suzan Waks, one of McNall's senior financial executives. A few days later, Ismail received a call in his room on campus in South Bend, Indiana: "We have a car downstairs waiting to take you to the airport."

McNall had sent a private jet for him.

"I thought the limo driver didn't know where he was going because he drove on the airport grounds, but past the main terminals," Ismail recalled at a 2011 reunion of the 1991 Argonauts. "We pull up to part of the airport that regular people never saw. It was the part where all these really cool-looking airplanes are. I get out and they escort me to the tarmac and there's a pilot, a co-pilot, and a flight attendant. They're all looking at me."

The jet, about to take the Rocket on a three-city odyssey from Toronto to Las Vegas to Los Angeles, had some amenities that impressed the kid from small-town Pennsylvania. "Back in the day, the highlight of my culinary experience was like, Chef Boyardee. . . . This plane had lobsters . . . all types of food that I never knew existed. They had a spread!"

At the first stop, Ismail was put up in a suite at the hotel attached to SkyDome, shown on the JumboTron at a Blue Jays game, and taken out on the town by quarterback Matt Dunigan, receiver Darrell K. Smith, and running back Mike Clemons.

"If this was a publicity stunt, I wouldn't be here," the Rocket told reporters. Jon Edwards, a member of Team Rocket, told the *Boston Globe*: "Two weeks ago I would have never thought we'd be here. But Bruce McNall came out of the blue. They made us a serious offer and it would be stupid not to look at it."

Ismail and Dunigan were then flown across the continent, first for some quick casino action in Vegas, then to L.A where McNall piled the players into his Bentley and drove to Rodeo Drive in Beverly Hills for a high-end shopping spree. Encouraged to buy anything he wanted, the Rocket filled bags with more than 4,000 dollars' worth of clothing. Dunigan dropped about 6,000 of McNall's dollars on an outfit for his wife.

"Then the next thing, we're at the Great Western Forum," Ismail said in 2011. "The Kings are playing somebody, and I mean it was like opening *People* magazine and seeing all the celebrities that you see on television and in the movies. All of them were just like, 'Hey, Rocket, nice to meet you.' I'm like, wow, this is nuts.

"The next day Mr. McNall takes me to some real exclusive restaurant and just starts giving me his vision with his team called the Toronto Argonauts. So he and John Candy—Snap! Uncle Buck? What? John Candy—and Wayne Gretzky are going to be a part of it. He just starts telling me all this fantastic stuff and I was like, wow."

"If you're willing to listen to us," said McNall, "we're going to make you very happy."

* * *

While Ismail was being courted in L.A., the man who had the original idea to pursue him found himself sidelined. McCarthy sent a hand-written fax to Mlakar: "Is the Rocket deal going down? If it is, I should be there, don't you think? . . . It bothers me. I would like to be informed as to what's going on."

McCarthy negotiated contracts with every Argo player, but McNall had decreed that this negotiation would be handled by Waks, his financial lieutenant, even though she had initially scoffed at the notion of pursuing Ismail. "You're competing with the NFL?" she had said to her boss. "Really?" But she came around to the idea. "You needed something that was really going to ignite the league and change the league, and that was Rocket," Waks says now.

As negotiations heated up, Edwards called Cowboys owner Jerry Jones to see if he would match what was being offered by the Argonauts. He wouldn't.

On Saturday, April 20, Ismail flew to Los Angeles and attended a Kings-Oilers playoff game. While the game was on, Waks and other Argo executives were hammering out the final details of a deal with members of Team Rocket. A 24-page agreement was typed up. Between the first and second periods of the NHL game, Rocket signed the contract.

Waks called a few reporters to break the stunning news. Rick Matsumoto of the *Toronto Star* hopped an early-morning flight to L.A.

A few weeks earlier, Matsumoto had looked for Ismail in South Bend when rumours began surfacing about him signing with the Argos. Finding the Rocket in his dorm room but unwilling to answer any questions, Matsumoto stuck his foot inside the door so it couldn't be closed. Finally, Ismail said he hadn't decided where he was turning pro.

"Would you mind, sir, taking your foot out of the door?" the Rocket asked. The reporter obliged.

Getting off the plane in L.A., Matsumoto high-tailed it to the news conference, which was already under way. At the podium, Ismail saw him enter the room. "Hey, man," he said, "you're the guy who was trying to get into my room."

The contract Ismail agreed to was unprecedented. It promised to pay him at least $18 million US, and potentially as much as $26 million, over four years. He would earn at least $4.5 million US per season; the rest of his teammates combined would be paid $3 million in smaller Canadian dollars (worth about 89 cents US). The Rocket's pay worked out to $250,000 US per *game*; the CFL's minimum salary was $32,000 Cdn for the entire season, or $1,778 per game.

The Rocket, before ever stepping onto a professional football field, had become the highest-paid player in football. Ever.

It was far more than he would have received had he been taken first in the NFL draft, as predicted, and signed with the team that selected him. The man who ended up as the top draft choice in 1991, defensive lineman Russell Maryland, signed with the Cowboys for $8 million over five years.

Super Bowl-winning quarterback Joe Montana was being paid $4 million per season. The best receiver in NFL history, Jerry Rice, was making less than $800,000. Ismail's own boss, Gretzky, had a contract with the Kings that paid him $3 million per season. [10]

McNall and Waks knew a significant premium would have to be paid to lure the Rocket away from the NFL.

"The numbers didn't work, but we did it anyway," Waks admitted after the signing.

One big reason for the premium was that Ismail's opportunities to earn money outside of football by endorsing products would be substantially greater in the NFL. He was already a highly marketable commodity: supremely talented, intelligent, good-looking, with an instantly recognizable and descriptive nickname. He was already well known in a country where football is worshipped from coast to coast. Canada, with a population just one-tenth that of the United States, does not have a tradition of paying athletes big money for endorsements, apart from Gretzky, who has plugged countless products on both sides of the border for decades.

Instead of a straightforward football contract, Waks persuaded Team Rocket to accept an unconventional personal-services arrangement. The Argonauts, and not Ismail, would own the right to negotiate and be paid for his endorsements. The Rocket would get guaranteed money, something the NFL wouldn't offer, and the Argonauts would try to cut deals with, and generate revenue from, companies whose products he

---

10 When speculation he might buy the Argos first surfaced in February 1991, McNall was quoted as saying he had called Montana but "the CFL, with its salary cap, isn't right for a Gretzky-like acquisition." A few months after the sale went through, Candy joked publicly about pursuing Montana. The legendary quarterback himself has subsequently indicated that casual discussions about him possibly jumping from the NFL to the Argos did, in fact, take place.

promoted. Ismail ultimately appeared in ads for Reebok, Pepsi, Ford, and Subway, and was the featured attraction in collectible card sets produced by a new company called AW. But the Argos would never come close to covering Rocket's salary with the endorsement deals they put together.

The Argonauts also expected the signing to generate much higher ticket revenue than the team had in 1990 with its official attendance of 32,000 per game. McNall mused that if the club could sell out the 54,000-seat stadium, the contract would pay for itself. "It's a risk," he said, "but I'm a risk taker, and I think he can put a lot of bodies in the seats."

There was still the matter of the CFL's salary cap, which limited each team to a total expenditure of $3 million on all players combined. While the cap was not yet being rigorously enforced, paying a single player $4.5 million US would make a mockery of the entire concept. But the CFL's commissioner, a former accountant with the retrospectively comical name of Donald Crump, said it would be fine. Ismail would have a standard CFL playing contract in line with what other players were paid; the big money was in the personal-services agreement that paid him to help promote the Argonauts. "It would be like if McNall hired Bob Hope to go out and sell the team for him," Crump said, dating himself immeasurably.

McCarthy sweated over the actual playing contract, which Ismail still hadn't signed less than two weeks before the season was to begin. "I don't care what you pay him, but he ain't playing unless we have a CFL standard players contract," he told Argo executives in Los Angeles. "He won't be allowed on the field."

The playing contract paid $110,000 a season, which alone was sufficient to make Ismail one of the highest-paid receivers in the league. This galled McCarthy, who felt the league minimum would have sufficed, since Rocket was making so much on the personal-services deal. Signing him for the minimum would also have freed $80,000 against the salary cap, money that McCarthy could have given to other players.

Rocket's signing prompted a torrent of reaction on both sides of the border. There was delight from Argo players and coaches happy to add another weapon to an already potent lineup, and some Canadian journalists eager to see the story play out over the season. There was disdain from executives of other CFL teams who feared the financial implications for a struggling league, and some U.S. journalists who seemed to feel betrayed. But the most common reaction was utter astonishment.

"Incredible. Absolutely incredible," wrote Nick Miliokas in the *Regina Leader-Post*: "That's insane. Totally insane."

McNall's splashy L.A. news conference had managed to upstage ESPN's telecast of the NFL draft. That show had opened with what its producers must have known would be a major downer for the audience: the biggest-name player in the draft was suddenly "off the board." Ismail and McNall both appeared on the broadcast, interviewed by Roy Firestone while host Chris Berman and analysts Joe Theismann—himself a former Argonaut from Notre Dame—and Chris Mortensen looked on rather glumly.

Whatever they felt about how Ismail's signing affected the competitive balance in the CFL, most in the league enjoyed ESPN's discomfiture. "I just loved the way the NFL draft was screwed up," said Edmonton general manager Hugh Campbell. "Very sadly and even respectfully, they had to keep explaining what happened to the Rocket."

Added Jim Hunt, the veteran columnist for the *Toronto Sun*: "Watching the NFL and its TV apologists squirm was the next best thing to sex."

The signing was front-page news not just across Canada but in some U.S. outlets, including the *New York Times*, *USA Today*, and *The National*, an ambitious but short-lived sports daily.

USA Today compared the signing to other big-name players who had spurned the NFL in the past to sign with lesser leagues. "Joe Namath did it for the American Football League. Herschel Walker couldn't do it for the USFL. Now Raghib 'Rocket' Ismail takes his shot at making an ailing league healthy."

New York Times columnist Dave Anderson sniffed at Ismail's decision to forgo the NFL: "The Rocket accepted the money instead of the challenge. Now that the Rocket will be running in the obscurity of the Canadian Football League, it's as if he were put into a space capsule that disintegrated. For all practical purposes, he's vanished."

The *Globe and Mail*'s Stephen Brunt countered from the CFL's perspective: "A whole lot of people ought to be dancing in the streets . . . every general manager, every coach and player, every team owner in the CFL. . . . This is a godsend, folks."

Brunt's counterpart at the *Toronto Sun*, Steve Simmons, was more dubious: "One man cannot solve a decade's troubles. . . . Signing Rocket Ismail represents a new beginning for the Argos, another chance to believe in the CFL. But there is still so very far to go."

Two days after Ismail's signing was announced in L.A., he was paraded in front of a massive media throng in a ballroom at the SkyDome hotel. The same journalists who had been limited to one hot dog each by previous Argo owner Harry Ornest were pleased to sample from platters of smoked salmon and flutes of Dom Perignon.[11]

The Rocket showed up at the ballroom in his inimitably geeky manner, wearing a dark blazer, white dress shirt buttoned to the neck, white shorts, white socks, and black loafers. Asked what he planned to spend

---

11 Asked by the *Toronto Star* about the Ismail signing, Harry O said: "If I still had a football club, I'd pee my pants with joy."

all his money on, he replied: "I have some plans on getting some long pants."

More seriously, he repeated for the Canadian media what he had said in Los Angeles. NFL owners treated a player like "a piece of meat," but McNall was different. And he felt more "at peace" in Canada. "I got the feeling that when [Canadians] saw me, they looked past the colour of my skin and saw the person. . . . It was a feeling I hadn't had before."

The racial theme was sincere. Ismail's mother, Fatma, said when her son told her he was going to Canada, "I said, 'Honey, get on that freedom train and let's go.'"

* * *

So just who was this kid on whom unprecedented riches had been bestowed?

Raghib Ramadan Ismail was born November 18, 1969, in Elizabeth, New Jersey, the eldest son of Ibrahim and Fatma. Ibrahim had been born Abraham Bauknight, but changed his name when he converted to Islam. Raghib (which means "desirous to serve his lord," and is pronounced RAH-gibb, not ruh-HEEB as uttered by countless broadcasters over the years) and his younger brothers Qadry and Sulaiman were sent to Islamic school in Newark, where the family lived close to the poverty line.

When Raghib was ten years old, Ibrahim died suddenly from tuberculosis and kidney failure. Three years later, his mother sent the three boys to live with their paternal grandmother in Wilkes-Barre, a small city in northeastern Pennsylvania, two hours north of Philadelphia. "I told them either they go to their grandmother's or there wouldn't be enough to eat," Fatma told the *Washington Post.* She remained in Newark, working a variety of low-paying jobs, before rejoining her sons in Wilkes-Barre a few years later.

Raghib has often described feeling a sense of responsibility for the family even before he hit his teenage years. After his father died, "the boy part of my life was gone," he said in 1991. His brother Qadry, one year younger, said Raghib "took over the leadership responsibilities in the family. He was leader of our household."

The boys' grandmother was not Muslim, and took them to her Assemblies of God Christian church. Raghib, who eventually attended Notre Dame, the most famous Roman Catholic university in the United States, told *Maclean's* magazine after signing with the Argonauts that he considered himself non-denominational. He has since described himself as a devout Christian.

The Ismail boys initially had difficulty fitting in in Wilkes-Barre, a city that has seen a slow but steady population decline over the past century as the coal mines it was built around were abandoned. The predominantly Caucasian community did not have many residents with Islamic names.

Things began to change when Raghib attended Meyers High School. While learning how to sprint, he burst out of the starting blocks so quickly that the track coach told his fellow athletes the young man looked like a rocket. The nickname stuck.

Starting high school at a slender 130 pounds, Ismail scored 76 touchdowns in four years at Meyers, including 35 as a senior and six in his final game.

A prize recruit at Notre Dame, Ismail burst onto the college football scene as a freshman with two kickoff-return touchdowns in one game against Rice. He ended his college career, by which time he had bulked up to 175 pounds on a five-foot-ten frame, with 4,187 all-purpose yards for an average gain of 15.3 yards per touch. Ismail's 15 touchdowns as a collegian had an average length of 62 yards.

As one of the highest-profile players on a team that won the national championship his first year and was among the top-ranked squads in the nation the following two years, the Rocket received marriage proposals in the mail, and had students he didn't know, and often their parents, knocking on the door of his dorm room. He signed autographs on the way to class. But unlike most college football stars getting ready to turn pro, he continued to attend classes until the semester ended. (He would return to Notre Dame to further his studies in the off-season after joining the Argonauts.)

With nearly 2.3 million residents, and a couple million more in the suburbs, North America's fourth-largest city dwarfed Wilkes-Barre, population 47,000, and the college town of South Bend where he had lived for three school years.

Toronto's seemingly endless boom in condominium construction was still a few years away. Most of the downtown skyscrapers were office towers, not residences. The imposing circular roof of SkyDome could still be seen from the far western edge of the Gardiner Expressway, with no condo buildings blocking the view. But even with fewer towers than today, Toronto was still a massive metropolis, and Rocket was on his own.

Fatma visited frequently but continued to live with Sulaiman in northern Pennsylvania. Qadry, the middle brother who was also a gifted football player, headed back to upstate New York for his third year at Syracuse University.[12]

---

12 Qadry "the Missile" Ismail, a wide receiver like the Rocket, played ten seasons in the National Football League, one more than his brother. Their career NFL statistics are very similar: Raghib caught 363 passes for 5,295 yards and 28 touchdowns; Qadry had 353 receptions for 5,137 yards and 33 TDs. Youngest brother Sulaiman played briefly in the Arena Football League. He was nicknamed "the Bomb." Fatma Ismail sometimes called herself "the Launching Pad."

Ismail moved into a spacious high-rise apartment a few blocks east of SkyDome, in the southernmost part of the downtown core. It was sparsely furnished, with few personal touches or attempts at decorating other than a Pepsi dispensing machine that could be operated without coins.

The Argonauts team that entered the 1991 season was full of veterans, with just two first-year players, Ismail and slotback J.P. Izquierdo, playing regularly. At 21, Ismail was younger than every teammate except Izquierdo. More than a dozen players were over 30. Many Argonauts had wives. Quite a few had kids. With the league's average salary below $60,000, most players held down jobs in the off-season. A few worked year-round, somehow juggling work commitments with the demands of pro football.[13]

Then there was the Rocket, reluctant to accept, let alone embrace, his stature as one of the highest-profile athletes in the city. When teammates would invite him out, he would decline, saying, "I don't want to do that because all the people are around."

"Wherever he went, there was a crowd," says teammate Rodney Harding. "He could never be himself. Everybody wanted his autograph."

Ismail liked the city well enough, but there was one aspect of life in Toronto that really grated on him, a small but noticeable difference between fast-food restaurants on either side of the border.

"I would go to sub shops and they would have straws that weren't wrapped in paper," he said a few years later. "That sucks. I hated that. I don't want someone touching a straw that I'm going to drink through. But other than that, I loved it up there. . . . That was a real cool city."

---

13 One of these was lineman/long snapper Blaine Schmidt, who ran three phone stores when cell phones were still in their infancy. He outfitted owner John Candy with a phone, assigning it a number appropriate to one of the actor's most popular movie characters: 416-606-BUCK.

Most Argonauts interviewed for this book said they found Ismail to be a humble, respectful teammate. But apart from Carl Brazley, Ismail's roommate on road trips, and Pinball Clemons, his locker mate, no one got to really know him.

"He didn't have a lot of friends," remembers Steve McCoy, the team's assistant equipment manager. "He didn't have anybody he was tied to, because of that generation gap. He didn't even know what to do or where to go. He would just sit in the locker room all afternoon. He'd always ask those elementary questions. What should I eat tonight? Where do I go? What do I do?

"On campus, you're with kids your own age and they're just kind of hanging out with you. Toronto was kind of looking at him like this American football hero and it was pretty daunting for him. He was just on his own. . . . The poor kid, it was too much too soon."

Ismail once said he hadn't wanted to worry his mother or brothers about his adjustment to life in a big city. Keeping any anxiety he felt to himself, he would "go to my apartment and lay down and just think—for hours."

Gus Heningburg, who became Ismail's business manager after the player disbanded the large group of advisers known as Team Rocket, says that in the Rocket's first year in Toronto, "all he did was eat pizza. It's easy enough to order pizza. You don't have to leave your room and face the world."

In *Glory Days*, a documentary about the 1991 season commissioned by the Argonauts, there is a stark scene of the Rocket in his spartan apartment, with a direct view of SkyDome to the west. Wearing short shorts and an oversized hoodie, he stretches out on a recliner, lazily watching a Notre Dame football game on TV.

"I remember how big the place was, and how little he seemed in the place," says Jocelyne Meinert, who assisted film producer David Mitchell on the shoot. "I would have thought some of his family would be up there with him, but he was all by himself. Where were his friends? Who were Rocket's friends in the city?"

Mitchell recalls that after the brief shoot, Ismail "basically asked us if we wanted to hang out. It seemed to me at the time that he was kind of lonely. I almost felt like we should stay and hang out with him."

Barely noticeable in that scene is a second person: a kid who appeared to be in his early teens, sprawled on a sofa. Knowing almost no one his own age in town, Ismail befriended two young Torontonians, according to a cover story in *Sport* magazine.

The story says he met 12-year-old Quincy Warner and 16-year-old Carl Hoyte, both of whom lived in subsidized housing, after an Argo practice. He offered to drive them home and hang out with them on one condition—they had to stay in school and stay out of trouble. Hoyte had been told: "Here's the deal. You stay in school, be a good kid, and I'll be your big brother. You drop out of school, you're on your own."

The Rocket was like "a stranger in a strange land," the *Globe's* Brunt says now. "I don't think he really understood what he was walking into. The contrast: this swirl around the glamour of Bruce McNall and private jets, and suddenly you're in [training camp in] Guelph playing with guys who played for McMaster [University]. He must have wondered where the hell he was."

The quaint atmosphere at camp in Guelph was just one of the changes Rocket had to navigate. At Notre Dame, one of the ways players were catered to was never having to handle their own equipment bag. But with the Argos, each player was expected to pack their own shoes, helmets, and shoulder pads before out-of-town games. On his first road trip, Ismail left the locker room without packing his stuff. The team arrived in Vancouver to find no equipment bag for the Rocket. "What do you mean, pack my stuff?" Ismail asked. "At Notre Dame, you never touched your bags. Why would I think we do it in the pros?" A call was made to Toronto and the gear was shipped out on the next flight.

There may have been good reason for Rocket's reticence to be out in public. His well-publicized riches made him a natural target for shady characters.

Before Ismail's rookie season began, McCarthy asked a police officer acquaintance to look into the background of a guy who was hanging around the wealthy rookie at training camp. The cop's hand-written report documented the 21-year-old man's interactions with the justice system: fraud, use of stolen credit cards, obstruction of justice and other criminal charges.

McCarthy summoned Rocket to his office and showed him the report. "Your mother wouldn't want this guy hanging around with you," he told the rookie.

Even though he had come from a sleepy small town, Ismail was aware of the potential for a young man to take a crooked path. For a profile in the *Toronto Star*, he made reporter Judy Steed listen to a recording of KRS-One rapping about kids being forced into crime because of America's racism. "You understand?" he asked her. "That could have been me. . . . In poor communities, you see the drug dealers who have all these great, glamorous things, and it looks like the only way out."

Ismail had found another way out, and was using some of the money from his Argo contract to buy his mother "glamorous things," including a Mercedes. He was also having a house built for her.

That was one aspect of the Rocket, and it was real. But many of those interviewed for this book about Ismail and his time in Toronto used the same word: "kid."

Teammate Kelvin Pruenster noted the detail about the house in Steed's feature, and quizzed Rocket about it in the training room.

"How many square feet?"

"Oh man, I don't know," said Ismail. "It's large. All I know is it's large. It's a large house."

"That was just Rocket the kid," says Pruenster. "He had no idea. He couldn't give you any details about her house except that it was really large."

Barely out of his teens, Ismail wore a plastic digital wristwatch and liked to play video games, listen to hip-hop music and, especially, to sleep.

Stories abound about Ismail's propensity for sleep. "He was like a light," says Waks. "Either on or off. On was excited. Off was fast asleep. Literally. He sat down in a chair and he was asleep."

Argo executives Scott Carmichael, David Watkins, and Bret Gallagher each went to Ismail's apartment on occasion to pick him up for appointments arranged by the organization. Gallagher and Carmichael were given keys to the apartment. Watkins, who did not have a key, had to call ahead. One morning when he and the Rocket were scheduled for a blitz of radio stations. Watkins called repeatedly as he drove downtown, but Rocket didn't pick up.

"I get to the front lobby of his condo, still no answer. I wake the super up. We go and we're knocking on his door, still no answer. Open the door, still no answer. Go to his bedroom and bang on the door, still no answer. Open the bedroom door and he's asleep. Slept through everything. It was probably the only time we asked him to do those morning radio things. He just liked to sleep too much."

Carmichael let himself in one day when Rocket could not be reached and seemed to be missing. "The alarm is blaring. I walk into his bedroom, he's not moving. I thought something was wrong. I literally had to shake him [awake]. 'Rocket! Dude! You've got to get up.'"

No other player received such attention from the organization, of course. The executives who had pinned so much on Rocket's marketability allowed him—and in some cases required him—to miss practices and other team activities. They also kept a tight lid on who had access to him.

Mike Levenseller, in charge of the team's receivers and kick returners in 1991, was the coach in position to provide the most guidance to Ismail. Levenseller's desire to help the rookie develop his football skills butted up against team brass's determination to shelter him.

"I need to get a hold of Rocket, and nobody's got his phone number except the McNall group. They wouldn't give it to me," the assistant coach says. "Who's more important in his life at this moment than the guy that's going to be [coaching] him as a receiver and on special teams? He's so vital to what we do, and they won't let me have his phone number."

It bothered Levenseller that Ismail's love of sleep would make him late for team meetings. "How do you allow that to go on, which is what the McNall group wanted us to do?" the coach wondered. "One day I'd had it. Rocket walks into our special-teams meeting late. I said, 'Rocket, if you're late one more time they're going to fire me because I am going to kick your ass.' He was never late again, and he became more professional. It just took some growing up."

Central to the effort to help Ismail grow up was the choice of his roommate for road games. Head coach Adam Rita assigned that job to Brazley, a ten-year veteran defensive back.

"Anybody would have been a good roommate for Rocket on our team, but the guy who was best suited was Carl Brazley," Rita says. "Great sense of humour. Straightforward. Honest. If you didn't like what he was going to say, don't listen. And he was a positive guy. Almost like a father figure, a big brother figure."

Brazley, who didn't pay attention to college football, had never heard of Ismail before he signed with the Argos. The defensive back's mom called to tell him she'd heard "you guys just signed some big guy. Y'all got the Bullet or the Torpedo or something."

Once Brazley found out who the Rocket was, he became the mentor the rookie needed. "It was like your classmate in elementary school," says head trainer Kevin Duguay. "This is going to be your little friend—walking with hands together to make sure they don't get lost."

At the 20-year reunion of the 1991 Argonauts, Ismail seemed to acknowledge he hadn't been prepared for the demands that accompanied his status as the highest-paid player in football, and that teammates like Brazley had helped him cope.

"I felt like I was always fighting, and I felt like I was always trying to like defend all, and I felt like I didn't have the tools that were adequate to defend myself. I didn't know how to.

"I got the cultivating from the locker room, which was a blessing. Coach Rita, probably the best thing that he did was put me in a locker next to Pinball and [make] Carl Brazley my roomie. It was like they were the shelter from the storm."

The Candy Man

HE WAS THE GUY pacing nervously on the sideline, sweating over every play. The guy trotting onto the field, against protocol, to tend to an injured player. The guy who swept the floor of the locker room, and was often the last to leave, long after the players had cleared out. The guy who never said "no" to anyone who wanted a moment (or ten) of his time. The guy who, more than any other club owner in a century and a half of Toronto football, genuinely loved the Argonauts.

John Candy was all of the above, and so much more, during the three years in which he held a minority ownership stake in the Argos.

Offered a piece of the action by his friend Bruce McNall, Candy paid a million dollars for 20 per cent, and brought far more than a million bucks' worth of value to the franchise and the entire Canadian Football League.

Thanks in large part to Candy, fan interest exploded not only in Toronto but across the league. The Ottawa Rough Riders franchise was saved from bankruptcy, and the league found new partners and, more importantly, new money in the United States.

Nice work from a Toronto kid whose rise to global acclaim, mostly for playing lovable losers on TV and in the movies, never got in the way of his abiding passion for his city's football club.

On his first visit to the team's office after the ownership change, Candy met with a small group of employees who had no idea whether they still had jobs. "It's all going to change for the better," Candy reassured them. "We're family, family, family."

He immediately started establishing relationships with the Argo players, as well. "Hey, you're Carl Brazley," Candy said to the defensive back. "Man, you're great."

Candy called guard Dan Ferrone: "I know you're one of the captains and I want to tell you, I'm so excited to be a part of your team." Later, when Ferrone suggested it would be nice to have a cappuccino after practice, Candy had a cappuccino machine installed in the locker room.

Offensive tackle Kelvin Pruenster introduced himself on the first day of training camp in 1991. "Kelvin, of course I know who you are," a beaming Candy replied. The new boss was "like your fan instead of the other way around," Pruenster says. "He was just thrilled to be part of the guys."

Countless others had a similar experience.

An offensive lineman during his high school days, Candy naturally gravitated to members of that position group. But he also hung around with the quarterbacks and the defensive linemen, spending "quality time," in fact, with almost every player on the roster.

Linebacker Prentiss Wright, a reserve who played only a couple of games in 1991, was popular among teammates for raps featuring his nickname: "It was Big P!" In the locker room when Candy was around, teammates would chant, "It was J.C.!" Candy would then perform a version of Wright's rap.

When he was in California between games, Candy frequently called equipment manager Danny Webb at home to inquire about the health of injured players and muse about the next game. While players warmed up on the field, Candy, "smoking like a chimney," would pace nervously in the locker room, talking strategy with Webb. "This is a big game," he'd say. "Someone's got to step up."

Candy's nervousness was exactly what many hard-core fans experience. He lived and died on every play, and yelled at referees when calls went against the Argos. "It wasn't just for show," says kicker Lance Chomyc. "He knew what calls to argue."

If a play went bad, he'd sag, says tackle Chris Schultz. When the team lost, Candy was devastated. "You can't fake that."

His co-owner Wayne Gretzky says Candy loved the Argos unconditionally. "He loved the players; he loved the coaches and the trainers."

Candy was so smitten that he frequently treated large groups of players to dinner and drinks, and even invited some to his farmhouse in Queensville, north of Toronto, where he would cook for them. Gretzky tried to tamp down his partner's enthusiasm: "John, there's a hundred players. We can't have a dinner every night."

To Candy, family mattered more than anything. A devoted husband and father, he always put his family first, says daughter Jennifer. But he also considered the Argos family, and the team ranked second, well ahead of his Hollywood career. "At that time in his life," adds son Christopher, "he had a cartoon show, a huge acting career, a radio show, and he was producing films. All top-level stuff, but it was pretty obvious that he really loved what he was doing with the Argos."

The Argos naturally became intertwined with Candy's family life. Jennifer and Christopher, along with many cousins and friends, were driven down from Queensville to each home game during the summer months, watching from a private SkyDome box their dad spent hundreds of thousands of dollars renovating. To celebrate the birthday of Candy's wife, Rose, the extended family had an annual "Rose Bowl" game at the farm. Kids and grownups suited up in Argo jerseys and played for either Jen's Mighty Unicorns or Chris's Terminators. Candy played nose guard, counted steamboats and rushed Pruenster, who played quarterback.

* * *

John Franklin Candy was born in Newmarket, north of Toronto, on Halloween in 1950. He grew up in Toronto's working-class Danforth community and attended Neil McNeil High School, where he suited up for the football team. A tall, husky lad, he played centre and other positions along the offensive line and dreamed of someday playing for the Argos. "I wanted to be like you," he once told Pinball Clemons. A serious knee injury ended that hope. "I lost a kneecap," he often said years later.

With football off the table, the naturally hilarious young man with the ultra-expressive face turned to acting. He landed roles in a few television commercials before joining Chicago's Second City, a theatre specializing in improvisational comedy. He was among the group that started a Second City branch in Toronto in the mid-1970s, and achieved low-key fame on a televised sketch show called SCTV that portrayed the programs and personalities of a local TV station in the fictional town of Melonville.

The cast initially included seven brilliant talents: Eugene Levy, Catherine O'Hara, Dave Thomas, Andrea Martin, Joe Flaherty, Harold Ramis, and Candy. Apart from Ramis, who as head writer had less screen time than the others, each developed a series of memorable characters, and none moreso than Candy. He created Melonville's eccentric mayor,

Tommy Shanks; horror-show host Doctor Tongue; fishin' musician Gil Fisher; sycophantic talk-show sidekick William B. Williams; polka king Yosh Shmenge; and his most brilliant creation: the hard-drinking, monogrammed-robe-wearing playboy, Johnny LaRue, who hosted man-on-the-street interview segments on *Street Beef*.

SCTV, which had begun as a low-budget production on Ontario's Global TV network, eventually landed a late-night weekend slot on NBC. It received 15 Emmy nominations and two wins, both for writing, with Candy among the team of writers.

After receiving favourable reviews for supporting roles in two movies, *Stripes* and *Splash*, Candy moved wife Rose and young children Jennifer and Christopher to Los Angeles in 1986. His Hollywood career ignited the following year thanks to star turns in *Spaceballs* and *Planes, Trains and Automobiles*. *Uncle Buck*, perhaps his most popular role, followed in 1989.

Candy became one of the highest-paid actors in show business, often receiving more than a million dollars for a top-billed role. He didn't always choose films wisely, starring or playing small parts in many duds. But his appearance on screen, often as a buffoon with a big heart, was invariably appreciated by audiences. In a career that eventually spanned 40 films, Candy could draw laughs with nothing more than a slyly cocked eyebrow.

SCTV castmates called Candy "Johnny Toronto." While firmly ensconced in Hollywood, his roots remained deep in his hometown. He brought his young family home each summer to Queensville. That made getting involved in the Argonauts logistically convenient, although it required putting his acting career on hold—which he did for virtually all of 1991.

When Candy bought into the Argos, he immediately knew "it would be the perfect use of his celebrity, goodwill, and public persona, as well as his capital," says longtime friend Dan Aykroyd. "He got it right away. He was all in on this."

Candy was full of ideas for promoting the team, sometimes calling Argos executive Suzan Waks in the middle of the night to excitedly run a new scheme past her. Gretzky said Candy always had "about two hundred marketing plans and schemes going." Bret Gallagher heard some of them soon after meeting Candy for the first time.

Gallagher had happened to bump into an acquaintance, Brian Cooper, in downtown Toronto. Cooper had just been hired by the new owners as the Argos' executive vice-president. One of his priorities was staffing up the organization. Chatting on the street, Cooper offered Gallagher a job in promotions and marketing. Gallagher, working in TV production, had aspirations of moving into the world of film. After mulling over the fact that one of McNall's companies had produced successful motion pictures, including *War Games* and *Mr. Mom*, he called Cooper and accepted the offer.

Cooper told Gallagher the Argos had booked Candy to appear on the youth-oriented MuchMusic TV network, and "the only one he wants to talk to is your brother." Bret Gallagher's brother Dan was a bandanna-wearing game-show host and veejay on Much. With long, curly blond hair that sometimes took the form of a mullet, he was often compared to Candy because of his rotund shape and wise-cracking persona.

Bret called Dan, who raced to the Much studios to interview one of his heroes. There, Bret introduced himself to Candy as an Argo employee.

"You work for us?" Candy asked.

"Yeah," said Bret. "I got hired like two hours ago. And Dan's my brother."

Candy seemed bowled over by the coincidence. After the interview ended, he invited Bret to join him in a waiting limousine. Gallagher's head was exploding. "What am I doing here?" he wondered.

The limo dropped the pair off at the Four Seasons hotel, Candy's "home" whenever he was in Toronto. In the hotel bar, Candy started talking "a million miles an hour" about his ideas for promoting the Argonauts. Gallagher scribbled notes while the pair talked deep into the night.

A day or two later, Gallagher and Candy headed to the airport for a flight to Ottawa. Gallagher had not flown much in his life and was boggled to board a private Gulfstream jet that had previously been used by Chrysler executive Lee Iacocca.

Candy's next stop after Ottawa was Vancouver. Candy made it clear that Gallagher was to join him. "I've got to go to work," Gallagher insisted. "No, no," Candy replied. "This *is* work. This is what we do."

After the Vancouver news conference, the Gulfstream flew Candy to Los Angeles. Gallagher hopped a commercial flight to Toronto, where he met with Cooper, the man who had just hired him. "You're his guy," Cooper said. "He wants everything to flow through you. But you've still got to do your other job."

Gallagher's other job was director of promotions for the Argonauts. That made him responsible for halftime entertainment as well as the team's ad campaigns. But in many ways his biggest role was as Candy's majordomo. Everywhere Candy went around the CFL in 1991, Gallagher was by his side.

Candy, Gallagher, and sometimes Cooper flew (or drove, in the case of Hamilton) to every city the Argos visited in 1991. McNall was also present on occasion, and once or twice Gretzky made an appearance, but this was the John Candy show. Candy knew, says Gallagher, "that promotion of the games was his end of the bargain. He knew to create the hysteria and the circus to get that turnstile going."

Candy and Gallagher would arrive in town two days before a game. After a night in the hotel bar—"I've never seen anyone party as hard as John Candy did," says Saskatchewan Roughriders president Phil Kershaw—they would drag themselves out of bed at 4:30, hop into a limo and make the rounds of every radio station and every breakfast-television show in town. "Buy tickets, buy tickets," Candy kept repeating.

Behind the scenes, Candy lobbied the home team's executives, usually successfully, to lift the local TV blackout of the next night's contest. "Why not give people a chance to see the game?" he asked in the *Calgary Herald.* "Why not give them the option and they see that it is fun and maybe they'll go down?"

Candy's efforts, and the Argos' decision to televise all of their 1991 home games in the Toronto market, were the beginning of the end to a decades-old policy that prevented fans from seeing their team play at home unless they bought tickets.

As exciting a brand of football as the Argonauts played, as star-laden as they were with Rocket Ismail, Matt Dunigan, Pinball Clemons and D.K. Smith, Candy was the primary attraction in 1991. "When John started coming down the tunnel [at a stadium], you would hear this roar as people saw him coming in," says Pruenster. "The whole stadium would erupt. The Canadian love of John Candy was way more than any kind of rivalry that might be going on in the game."

Candy would keep an eye on the game while kibbitzing with spectators, and occasionally high-fiving members of the Argonauts. Sometimes he got swept up in local traditions, like in Edmonton when he went for a ride around the stadium on the miniature fire truck that was a fixture at Eskimos games. Gretzky saw this on TV and called Candy, afraid his partner had put himself at risk. "Don't worry, Wayne, I'm OK," Candy assured him.

At the same game in Edmonton, two members of the Argonauts were injured on a single play. With medical staff attending to one of them, Candy said to equipment manager Danny Webb, "Let's go." The pair ran onto the field to carry the injured Brazley off. This prompted a stern lecture from Argo brass about the ramifications if Brazley had been seriously injured.

Through all the road trips, Candy got to know more and more members of the Argonauts. A handful got especially close to him when he got the brainwave, after an exciting early-season win in Regina, to fly a few players home on his private jet. Paul Masotti, Andrew Murray, and Lance Chomyc got the word: "You're not flying home with us tomorrow. You're flying home with Candy."

Gallagher asked what food they would like catered for the flight. Perogies, one of Candy's favourite dishes, were ordered, but that barely scratched the surface of the flight's offerings. Candy broke the ice on board by ordering a double shot of his usual rum and Diet Coke. "The size of a pint glass, cut crystal, gold fittings, everything," says Murray. "The flight attendant is coming out with 15 different forks and knives. Which ones do we use to eat the Hollywood star food? We [normally] ate Kraft Dinner and sandwiches and pizza.

"All John wanted to talk about was what was it like to play in the CFL, because that was his dream. All we wanted John to do was regurgitate all of his skits from Second City. He did every Second City skit—everything." It was a dream for "three Canadian boys who grew up watching SCTV and knew all the characters," adds Chomyc. "We're doing the voices along with him because we remember these sketches."

Hours of frivolity later, the jet landed in Toronto. The Argo players disembarked on the tarmac at a part of Pearson airport that caters to charter flights, without a clue how to get to their cars. It was just as well because they were in no condition to drive anyway.

The Candy that Argo players, and thousands of fans throughout 1991, were personally exposed to was the antithesis of a guarded, egotistical celebrity. He was shy, humble, genuinely interested in others. "A lot of times you meet celebrities and maybe for their own self-preservation they have a mask, or they put a wall up," says Waks. "You're only going to get superficial. That was not John. He was genuine."

"When you were with him," adds Clemons, "it was like there was no one else in the world. He gave you his undivided attention. He would ask you real questions. He wanted to know about you. He was just so incredibly kind and human and loving. One of the greatest human beings I've ever met."

Kelly Ryback, who spent years wearing the costume of one of the Winnipeg Blue Bombers' two mascots, introduced himself in street clothes to Candy at the 1991 Grey Cup. "Hi, I'm Buzz, the mascot," he said. Candy's response: "You're doing a great job."

Jo-Anne Polak, general manager of the Ottawa Rough Riders, recalls going to the hotel gift shop during a CFL governors meeting. A woman working there pulled out an "autograph book that was probably 30 years old" and asked Polak if she could get the actor's signature. Polak returned to the meeting and asked Candy to sign the book. "We can do better than that," he whispered.

Polak led Candy to the gift shop. The store clerk nearly fainted.

"It was the greatest moment of her life," Polak says. "He stayed there for almost an hour and a half. She had him calling her mother, her daughter. He sat behind the cash selling stuff. People would come in to buy a newspaper, and then it was absolute shock. He just loved being able to do that. It wasn't about him; it was that he got a chance to make all these people happy. That was John Candy."

Candy signed thousands of autographs in 1991, including hundreds at a preseason fundraising event in Ottawa. "It was just, 'Uncle Buck!

Uncle Buck!' He stayed until the very last person in the building got an autograph."

Ironically for a man who exchanged cordial conversation with virtually everyone he encountered one-on-one, Candy was shy, and prone to severe anxiety attacks. While he was able to handle being the centre of attention at games and other CFL events, he tried to avoid being spotted when out in public.

"I called him the one-person Beatles in Toronto," says Bob Crane Jr., son of the *Hogan's Heroes* star of the same name. Crane worked for Candy in many capacities, and was with him on most of his forays around the CFL. "We couldn't go anywhere without people coming up to him. You could not hide him."

Once, while Crane was in California, Pruenster, who had become Candy's personal trainer, filled in as his bodyguard/assistant on a movie shoot in Calgary. The six-foot-three Candy's weight fluctuated between 275 and 350 pounds, but even at his slimmest, he was a big man. Pruenster, who stood six-foot-six and weighed close to 300 pounds, would position himself to block people from seeing his friend.

"If we walked in formation towards people, nobody could see him," Pruenster says. "He stayed off my shoulder on a diagonal. He was a big man, but with a big winter coat I could block him out. I was like a walking wall."

With time on his hands one day, Candy told Pruenster he wanted to personally buy gifts for Rose and the kids, rather than delegate the task to an assistant, as usual. Pruenster figured it was possible. It was mid-day on a weekday, so shopping centres would be empty. "As long as we get out of the mall between 2:30 and 3, before the school day ends, we'll be fine," he said.

The pair went to a shopping centre. Candy wore glasses and a hat, trying to look less conspicuous. Pruenster started regretting his decision when a store clerk screamed, "Oh, my God, it's John Candy!" Nobody heard her, though, and Candy began shopping. He told Pruenster he was having a fantastic time. "Do you know how long it's been since I could do this?"

Unbeknownst to the pair, Calgary's schools closed early that day because of a winter storm. Shortly after noon, "it looks almost like an avalanche of kids pouring into the entrances. There's thousands of kids and people in this mall, and we're trapped in this store."

Pruenster desperately summoned their car, but before they could get out of the store, "some 14-year-old girls see him, and screaming starts. Everyone in the mall hears it and their heads all swing around. And then everyone starts screaming: 'John Candy!' Hundreds of high-school kids. We're in this little shop and they're like 20, 30, 50 feet thick.

"John's trying to be nice because they're little kids. We're stuck. The crowds are getting worse and worse. They have their pens and papers out, pulling on his jacket. Some of them are crying, they're so excited. John looks at me completely panicked. We just started shoving through people and kids."

Pruenster found a security guard who escorted them to the mall's exit. Pruenster got chewed out later by Crane, who would never have allowed Candy to make such an outing. "What started out as a great thing, with John getting his gifts, turned into that," Pruenster says with chagrin.

* * *

Candy's boyish enthusiasm around the Argos tended to overshadow the serious role he played on the team and, indeed, in the CFL. One of Candy's first official acts as part-owner of the Argonauts was to attend a governors' meeting in Regina. It began at 7 a.m. in a hotel meeting room. Candy, as usual, had been out late the night before, drinking and smoking in the hotel bar, surrounded by fans. But he was on time for the meeting, and stunned by the breakfast offering: rolled slices of salami and roast beef.

"I didn't know when you came to these meetings, you get cold cuts for breakfast," he told his fellow CFL executives. "This is fantastic. Is this a Regina thing? Is this a CFL thing?" (Candy offered a somewhat more jaundiced recollection several months later when he met with reporters during Grey Cup week. "There was warm Diet Pepsi on this bare wooden table, and rolled ham and rolled roast beef," he said. "I thought, what the hell is this? . . . Where is the real meeting? Then they said, 'We'd like to welcome the McNall group' and I realized, oh, my God, this is it.")

Candy sat through ten hours of discussions and surprised executives of the other teams with the depth of his commitment, as well as by flicking rolled-up pieces of paper at the heads of unsuspecting governors. "The funny man, it turned out, was dead serious about Canadian football," wrote journalist Stephen Brunt the following November. "[He] was as in love with the game and respectful of its traditions as any of the [governors]. But he also had ideas—big, shake-off-the-cobwebs ideas—and in a few short months his point of view would become the league's point of view."

The biggest idea was to expand the CFL. Candy and McNall wanted the league to grow beyond eight teams, and ideally beyond Canada. Candy volunteered to become head of a committee to explore the possibility of expansion. Asked a month later how he had ended up as the committee's chair, he joked, "I was last in the room." But the day he took on the role, he was bullish on the notion of expansion: "We have to explore it; it's the future of the league." He dismissed opponents to a U.S. rollout as "bleeding-heart nationalists who fight for the Canadian game but never buy a ticket to see it."

That wasn't the only time Candy demonstrated an acid tongue. At the CFL awards show before the 1991 Grey Cup, Candy made a surprise appearance on stage, carrying a sign bearing the phone number for Argo tickets. Bantering with host Dan Gallagher, he said: "There's a few media people that I would like to see eat a lot of crow. And I'll cook it."

One of those media people was likely John MacKinnon of the *Ottawa Citizen*. When MacKinnon asked what qualified the actor to be placed in charge of expansion, Candy fired back. "It's called show *business*, you know," he told the columnist. "It is a *business*."

Just as crucial to the CFL's future was Candy's role in saving the Ottawa franchise. On one of his early promotional trips to the city, Candy had been informed by Polak, the Riders' general manager, that her club's ownership consortium of small-business investors was about to walk away from mounting debt.

"I'm going to help you out," Candy assured her. "I'm going to be there to help you."

Three weeks after the season opened, the ownership group pulled the plug. Polak, who had stashed things required to stage a game in the trunk of her car, in case door locks were ever changed, swung into action. The league officially took over operation of the team, but Polak was doing most of the work. Candy was by her side at each step. "I was feeling completely under siege," she says, "and he came to help me and help the league."

The biggest thing he did was find a buyer for the Rough Riders. After reading about the McNall group's expansion dream, Bernie Glieberman and his son, Lonie, had become interested in putting a franchise in their hometown of Detroit, Michigan. Lonie, a 26-year-old, had fallen in love with Canadian football by watching games beamed across the river by Canadian TV stations.

"We don't know when expansion is going to happen," Lonie was told by CFL commissioner Donald Crump, "but Hamilton is available."

Glieberman started thinking about buying the Tiger-Cats, another failing franchise, and moving it to Detroit. He attended several Ticats games and began discussions with David Braley, the Ticats' owner. Word of this got back to Candy, who called Lonie.

"Why aren't you guys looking at buying Ottawa?" Candy asked.

"The league office directed us towards Hamilton," Glieberman replied.

Candy was exasperated. Why weren't league executives working harder to find a buyer for the Rough Riders? he wondered. "We're paying the bills for Ottawa. All the teams are."

Glieberman told Candy his goal was to own an American team.

"We're going to expand to the U.S., and we'll grant you an option for Detroit if you guys will take Ottawa," Candy replied. "Ottawa is a great market, it's a beautiful city with a lot of history."

Bernie Glieberman flew to California a few days later to meet with Candy. "My dad was a little skeptical of it," Lonie says, "but John Candy really sold him. He came back a much different guy towards the CFL. John had really inspired him on what this league could be, what the opportunities were and how it was really undervalued. From there, we had no more talks about buying Hamilton."

The Gliebermans' purchase of the Riders was negotiated with the McNall group, not the league. "We met at Bruce McNall's office several times. We started going to Argo games and meeting people in Toronto. The league office [had little involvement] with the whole Ottawa purchase."[14]

---

14 Candy and McNall eventually got their way on expansion. The Sacramento Gold Miners joined in 1993; by 1995 the league had five teams south of the border. Expansion came to an end in 1996 when the 1995 Grey Cup champion Baltimore Stallions were forced to leave town after the NFL's Cleveland Browns moved to Baltimore and became the Ravens. The other American

In Wayne Gretzky's eyes, there's no question about it. Without John Candy, there might be no Canadian Football League today.

"He's a Canadian icon that people idolized and loved, and he went to every game. He genuinely loved every bit of it. John Candy put his heart and soul not only into a city but into a country. He would rather go to Saskatchewan to an Argo-Roughrider game than do *Uncle Buck 2*. That's how much he loved it.

"He single-handedly, not playing it down, kind of saved the CFL. For a guy who never played a game, he was just as important to the CFL as [star players such as] Russ Jackson and Leon McQuay and Tom Wilkinson. That's how important John was to the league."

teams fell by the wayside at the same time, including a franchise in Shreveport, Louisiana, that the Gliebermans had formed after selling the Rough Riders. While most CFL fans view expansion as a failed experiment, a more measured perspective would suggest it gave the CFL two things it desperately needed to survive in the mid-1990s: an infusion of money from franchise fees, and time to sort out a number of serious financial problems.

Launched

AFTER ALL THE HYPE of the previous months, from the surprising purchase by the McNall group to the stunning signing of Rocket Ismail, it only made sense that the Toronto Argonauts would have a splashy opening to their 1991 training camp.

Usually, the first day of camp is attended by a handful of diehard fans, two or three newspaper reporters, a couple of TV crews, and maybe a columnist or two. But there was nothing usual about the 1991 Argos.

On a scorchingly hot June 7 at the University of Guelph, an hour's drive west of Toronto, team owners Bruce McNall, Wayne Gretzky, and John Candy posed for pictures in a pseudo-football formation, with one-time offensive lineman Candy, flanked by Gretzky and Ismail, hunched over to snap the football to McNall.

Gretzky and the Rocket, casually dressed in t-shirts suitable for the heat, tossed a football back and forth. McNall and Candy sweated the day out in expensive suits. Or rather, Candy sweated it out. David Watkins, the Argos' director of public relations, has a vivid memory of Candy drenched with perspiration. "I thought he was going to expire right there." McNall, says *Toronto Sun* columnist Steve Simmons, "didn't sweat a drop. It was like he was made of something different than everyone else."

About 75 journalists from Canada and the United States, roughly one for every player on the Argos' training-camp roster, gathered with team officials, invited guests, and hangers-on under a large marquee tent. Gretzky's wife, Janet Jones, mingled with attendees while their two-year-old daughter, future Instagram sex symbol Paulina, horsed around in an Argo helmet.

The hundreds of fans in attendance were kept a safe distance from Ismail and the other celebrities by security guards and police officers. Members of the team's recently formed fan club, the Friends of the Argonauts, turned the day into a celebration, packing lobster and Champagne for the hour-long bus ride to Guelph. The whole day felt more like a movie premiere than a football camp.

The day after the grand opening, 75 players got down to the business of trying to earn a spot on the Argonauts. All of them were eager to catch the eye and win the approval of a new head coach.

Months before camp opened, while Harry Ornest was secretly negotiating to sell the Argonauts, Don Matthews had launched a power play. He and general manager Mike McCarthy had mostly stayed out of each other's way in 1990, but neither wanted to be anything other than top dog. Matthews also had other aspirations.

Word leaked to the press that after signing as Argo coach, Matthews had submitted his resumé to the World League of American Football, which was to start operations in the spring of 1991. Summoned to a meeting with Ornest, the Don demanded full control of football operations. Ornest said No. Matthews resigned and signed on as head coach of the World League's Orlando Thunder.

McCarthy, now secure in his position, immediately promoted assistant coach Adam Rita. An even-tempered Hawaiian who stayed out of backroom politics and got along well with just about everyone, Rita had declined Matthews' offer to join him in Orlando.

Matthews' departure did not mean the end of shooting the lights out. Although Rita was a much lower-key personality than his predecessor, the 46th head coach in the 118 years of the Argonauts was the mastermind of the innovative offence in 1990. He was eager to continue working with quarterbacks Matt Dunigan and Rickey Foggie and offensive stars Pinball Clemons and Darrell K. Smith. Imagine his joy a few weeks later when the arsenal was expanded with the addition of Rocket Ismail.

The Rocket was one of more than two dozen rookies on the training-camp roster. Only a handful had a real chance of making the team. This was a veteran-laden squad; the only significant members of the 1990 Argonauts who weren't in camp in 1991 were receiver Jeff Boyd, who had retired, and quarterback John Congemi.

After starting 1990 as Matt Dunigan's primary backup, Congemi had dropped a peg with Rickey Foggie's arrival, and had been traded to Ottawa shortly after the McNall group's purchase was announced the following February. Learning he had been traded "was a gut punch," says Congemi. "I was never more disappointed because I knew how good we were and how good we could be."[15]

For the same reason, everyone in camp was desperate to make the team. Even among seemingly secure veterans, the prevailing attitude was "please, God, don't get me cut," says Kevin Duguay who, as head trainer, helped each player through a pre-camp medical examination.

Football activity began as it always does during training camp: once

---

15 Neither Congemi nor Boyd was done with the Argos, though. Boyd rejoined the team after camp ended, lured back from California to give the team one more veteran receiver. Congemi would return to the Argos in 1992, and also played a surprising behind-the-scenes role in the team's 1991 success (more about that later).

players pass their medicals, each is required to run 40 yards while coaches with stopwatches record their times.

Although football players seldom sprint 40 yards in a straight line, untouched, during games, the 40 is a time-worn tradition. General managers and coaches scrutinize results carefully, eager to learn if veterans have gotten slower or (in rare cases) faster since the previous season, and to see how newcomers stack up against the holdovers.

For the large men who line up along the line of scrimmage, a 40 time under five seconds is considered fast. For smaller, leaner players in the so-called "skill positions" (running backs, receivers and defensive backs), a time above 4.5 seconds is considered mediocre. Any time below 4.4 is exceptionally fast.

In 1991, there was only one 40-yard time that anyone really cared about. How fast would the Rocket run? "For all of training camp it was the Rocket show," says Watkins, but especially on this day.

Ismail, who took the field late after attending a photo session, was the last to run. Even after the rest of the afternoon's on-field activities ended, everybody hung around to watch. The Rocket seemed bewildered by the attention. "Why are they all watching me?" he asked equipment assistant Jason Colero. Well, Colero told him, "they think this is what you're getting paid to do."

Rita instructed his star prospect to warm up properly. "I want to see you sweat," he told the Rocket. "Don't run until you work up a sweat. I don't give a shit how many press guys are here, or all these other yo-yos are here."

Ismail followed instructions, loosening up for nearly 25 minutes. An impatient McCarthy tried to hurry him along: "Are you warmed up yet?" Rita told his boss to shut up. "He's warmed up when he tells me he's warmed up."

Finally, the Rocket pronounced himself ready. At least eight coaches and helpers stood poised to click their stopwatches on and then off. A hush fell over the field.

The Rocket got into his stance, heard the "Go" signal and blasted off. The hush continued. Ismail was so smooth, so gazelle-like, he made virtually no sound as he ran. "It was like a whisper," marvels defensive lineman Leonard Johnson.

"If I had closed my eyes, I would have never heard him run past me," adds assistant coach Dennis Meyer. "His feet were so light, I couldn't hear it."

Reaching the end of the line, 40 yards from the starting point, Ismail turned around. "How did I do?" he demanded.

Coaches stared at their watches in disbelief. Rita, looking at his own watch, started laughing.

"What did you get, Coach?" players demanded.

"He was damn fast," the coach replied. "Why do we have to know?"

Cornerback Ed Berry pressed Rita to say what time he had recorded.

"Four-point-blur," the coach replied.

"Blur?" asked Berry.

"Yeah. Blur."

Finally, the agreed-on, official verdict: 4.21 seconds, almost certainly the fastest time recorded by an Argo, ever.[16]

"We've got the guy!" an assistant coach whooped. "We've got the guy that can run!"

Ismail, incredibly, was unhappy. "Aw, man, that's so bad. I want to run another one."

---

16 Electronic timing, started by hand, stopped electronically, is considered more accurate than manual timing using stopwatches. Since the NFL went to electronic timing at its annual scouting combine of college prospects in 1999, just 16 players have had a time recorded below 4.3 seconds; none has been as fast as 4.21.

Rita was having none of it. "Enough!" he said. "The next time you're running, you're running for a touchdown."

McCarthy speculated Ismail might be able to improve upon his world-class time. "Dude!" Rita snarled. "He's already fast enough! He pulls a muscle, your ass is fired."

The Rocket did, in fact, pull a muscle soon after, a quadriceps. No one's ass got fired as a result, but Ismail's absence from on-field activity stretched through the remainder of camp. He sat out both preseason contests and eventually headed to Los Angeles for a few days while some teammates began to gripe about the star rookie receiving special treatment.

Rumours began circulating that Ismail would be held out of the Argos season opener in Ottawa to boost ticket sales for the following week's home opener in Toronto. After the McNall group purchased the Argos, McCarthy had tried to get the league to change the schedule so Toronto would open the year at SkyDome. He failed.

While he had indeed injured the quad, Rocket almost certainly could have played in Week 1, but that would have prevented the McNall group from squeezing maximum value out of his debut. To no one's surprise, McCarthy and the Argo brass decided to hold the Rocket out of the lineup for the game in Ottawa.

The Ottawa Rough Riders, coming off a rough decade, with a dwindling, disenchanted fanbase, had initially hoped Ismail's coming-out party would help them sell out the 30,000-seat Lansdowne Park. But general manager Jo-Anne Polak was savvy enough not to count on it. "If I were them, I would never play him in Ottawa," she says now. "I would wait and play him in Toronto." Twenty-three thousand spectators ended up attending the game anyway, a good but not great crowd by Rider standards.

After his controversial sojourn in L.A., Ismail had flown to Ottawa by private jet on the day of the opening game. Even though he wasn't playing that night, he had to endure a media availability session, speaking for ten minutes to more than 40 reporters and photographers.

This was too much for veteran *Toronto Sun* columnist Jim Hunt to bear. "No one in the hundred years we've been playing Canadian football has ever met the press as often as the Rocket," he wrote. "I don't know how the rest of the media feel, but this reporter has gone to his last Rocket press conference, at least until he scores the winning touchdown in the Grey Cup."

The most expensive player in football history stood on the sideline throughout the opening game in a garish paisley dress shirt buttoned to the neck, watching his teammates dismantle the Rough Riders. The game was just a dress rehearsal, conveniently staged far off-Broadway, with a star temporarily replaced by an understudy.

* * *

Just before the game in Ottawa, Argonauts players got more evidence that 1991 was going to be a season like no other when Bruce McNall came into the locker room and made an announcement: "Guys, we need to generate some excitement here. If you score a touchdown, throw the ball in the stands. And I'm giving a hundred dollars for every touchdown we score tonight . . . cash."

Rita sidled up to McNall. "You do realize that we're the No. 1 offensive team in the league? All-time? You might want to reconsider because you're going to be paying out a lot of money, and these guys aren't going to be embarrassed to take it."

McNall just grinned.

The first touchdown was scored by Darrell K. Smith, who promptly fired the ball into the stands. The Argos added two more touchdowns, and won 35-18.

The score was lopsided, but it was a tough game. Dunigan took a pounding, and at one point was deliberately poked in the eye by Ottawa linebacker Jeff Braswell.

"My whole game was to try and get them mad and frustrated, because it's hard to play when you're mad and frustrated," Braswell says. "So yeah, I took a poke at his eye. I wasn't going at his eye initially; I was just making sure he knew he was going to be in for a long game."

Dunigan endured several hellacious hits from Rough Rider defenders, not to mention a gouged eyeball, but kept bouncing up. "The next morning," says team executive Greg Campbell, who had travelled to Ottawa for the game, "he's got black eyes, and he's got a cane, and he's hobbling around like he's 85 years old. I'm like, what happened?"

"You know what," Dunigan replied. "I took a few hits. I was so hyped last night. It was so much fun."

A big part of the fun was returning to the locker room after the game and opening envelopes stuffed with hundred-dollar bills. It wasn't just the guys who scored touchdowns who got the bonuses—it was everyone.

"I'm thinking, I've got to score because I want a hundred dollars," says Boyd, who had ended his brief retirement just in time for the Ottawa game, and did score a touchdown. "I didn't realize that anytime anybody scores, everybody gets a hundred dollars."

Players couldn't believe it. "Is this really happening?" wondered Dunigan. "Is this real money? Is this *Candid Camera*?"

The cash pushed an already amped-up locker room into overdrive. "The buzz was already there," says defensive end Brian Warren, "and now you put some American presidents [hundred-dollar bills] in there as well . . . it was euphoric."

Off-book bonuses had started with McNall's other team, the Los Angeles Kings, at the behest of his star player, Gretzky. "These are bounties that are not supposed to be there," McNall says. "It's outside the salary cap . . . just to make it fun for them, a game within a game. What I found with the Kings was that when I would do little things like that, they would go through a wall for me. And that's what happened with the CFL guys. These poor guys are not exactly making a lot of money, so a few hundred dollars to them was really meaningful."

Ismail, of course, was making a lot of money and did not need any more hundred-dollar bills, although he rarely had more than 40 dollars in his pocket. "He's been bumming money from me," road-game roommate Carl Brazley told a reporter in 1991.

The Argos' owners had another surprise in store for the players. As a big shipment of boxes arrived one day, McNall approached equipment manager Danny Webb and his assistant, Steve McCoy. "These are for the guys, could you put them in their lockers?"

The boxes contained melton-and-leather jackets bearing a big letter A on the front, "Toronto Argonauts" on the back, and personalized uniform numbers on the sleeves. They had been manufactured by Candy's friends at the Roots clothing company, and were similar to jackets worn by McNall, Candy, and Gretzky on the day their purchase of the team had been announced. Every player received one, even those who arrived late in the season. So did other team employees.

The jackets sparked jealousy around the league. Rumours suggested "dollars were just spilling out of the bathtub" in Toronto, says David Bovell, who played for the penurious Winnipeg Blue Bombers before joining the Argos late in 1991. Added Chris Walby of the Bombers: "We were seeing these guys with jackets, getting treated liked frigging kings. We're not getting that."

To this day, virtually every Argonaut interviewed for this book still has the jacket.

* * *

While John Candy basked in the adulation of a crowd buzzing with anticipation before his team's home opener, Raghib Ismail was a bundle of nerves in the Argo locker room. Mike Clemons tried to calm his young teammate.

"Relax, dude," said the Pinball. "Just do what we practised."

"This kid's going to drop the ball because he is so scared right now," thought McCoy, the assistant equipment manager who witnessed "this coach/fatherly/big brother-type moment" between Ismail, the second-youngest player on the Argos at 21, and the 26-year-old Clemons.

The Argos won the coin toss and elected to receive the opening kickoff. That meant Ismail would be going onto the field for the game's first play, and might be required to catch and return the kick. Back came the nerves.

"Dude, relax!" Pinball implored. "Catch the ball. Don't worry about it. Go fast."

Then Clemons dropped a nugget of new information: "They're going to kick it to you."

Ismail's eyes widened. "Seriously?"

"Yeah, they're going to kick it to you. They're going to test you."

Indeed, the Hamilton Tiger-Cats had made no secret that they would rather see what the Rocket could do than kick to Clemons, who, with his uncanny ability to bounce off would-be tacklers, had set a league record for all-purpose yards in 1990. Ticats kicker Paul Osbaldiston promised to kick to the Rocket "until he proves he's better or even as good as Clemons."

The kicker known as Ozzy was true to his word. He sent the game's opening kickoff directly to Ismail near the right sideline at the south end of SkyDome. As the crowd buzzed in anticipation, the Rocket caught the ball at the 10-yard line, circled back to the six, zipped diagonally to the 20 and slipped through an attempted tackle before being brought down at the 23.

The first man to tackle Rocket Ismail (salary $4.5 million US, or $250,000 per game) as a professional was Hamilton fullback Ernie Schramayr (salary $40,000 Cdn, or $2,222 per game). "Everybody wanted a piece of him," Schramayr says.

After the 17-yard return, Ismail stood on the sideline for the Argos' first few offensive possessions. He had dressed for the game as Toronto's "designated import," which meant, under the CFL's byzantine rules on how many Americans could be in the lineup, that he was not among the 12 starters on offence but could replace another American player on the unit at any time.

When the Ticats' first two possessions went nowhere, the Rocket ran onto the field with the punt-return unit. However, instead of lining up deep alongside Clemons as a returner, he stationed himself on the left side of the line of scrimmage. When the ball was snapped, he raced towards Osbaldiston, aiming to get there in time to block the kick. Twice he ran into Hamilton's Ken Evraire, who had set up behind the line as a blocking back. The second time, Evraire pushed his shoulder into Ismail, sending the lithe speedster flying. "That's a six-million-dollar man on a suicide squad," colour analyst Joe Galat exclaimed on CBC's broadcast.

Evraire, whose 1991 salary was $55,000, had been surprised to spot Ismail on the line of scrimmage rather than deep downfield alongside Clemons. "I think, OK, he's not as dangerous here as he would be back there. He closed the gap on me so quick. We collided and he rolled. I gave him sort of an elbow to the chest. I remember thinking, 'I just hit Rocket.'"

A lot of relatively underpaid Ticats seemed determined to hit the exorbitantly paid youngster. On the first pass thrown in his direction,

Ismail was rocked on a helmet-to-helmet shot by safety Todd Wiseman, the type of hit against a defenceless receiver that would almost certainly be penalized in today's more safety-conscious game.

Later, after he busted loose for a long gain that nearly resulted in a touchdown, a Hamilton player slammed into Ismail after he had already been tackled on the sideline, a late hit that closely resembled Ticat Angelo Mosca's infamous shot on B.C.'s Willie Fleming in the 1963 Grey Cup game. The hit prompted an infuriated McCarthy to write to CFL commissioner Donald Crump: "He was clearly down and a player pounced on him. . . . We cannot emphasize enough the immense value of Ismail, not only to the Toronto franchise, but also the CFL in general."

Rotating with veteran receivers Boyd and Trumaine Johnson, Ismail finally made an offensive play in the second quarter, not long after Dunigan had left the game with another in a string of injuries. Dunigan's replacement, Ricky Foggie, fired a deep pass up the right side of the field. The Rocket slowed to adjust to the ball's trajectory, then pulled it out of the air. The crowd roared.

Ismail's mother, sporting a No. 25 jersey in the style worn by the Argos in 1989 and '90, whooped with delight in a skybox as her son completed the 38-yard gain.

Another Ticats possession stalled. Argo assistant coach Mike Levenseller had something different in store this time. In the huddle before Hamilton's punt, Ismail didn't fully hear the play call, he said years later. "I just saw Pinball smiling at me and making the 'I wanna give the ball to you' gesture."

The Rocket lined up again on the line of scrimmage. As Osbaldiston received the snap, Ismail took a quick step towards the punter, then turned and began racing back towards Clemons. "Rocket can make up a lot of ground," says Levenseller, who devised the strategy to have Ismail rush the kicker on the first two punts, then head for Clemons on the third. "He goes blowing by everybody."

Evraire, who had become accustomed to blocking an onrushing Rocket in the backfield, saw his man suddenly running in the other direction. While no one else on the Ticats' coverage unit noticed, Evraire discerned that a reverse was in the works. He made a frantic effort to catch up to Ismail.

"He starts to pick up speed. He's looping around, making his way around the punt coverage to Pinball. I flew across the field, [guessing] what the angle's going to be. I've got to get where he's going to be."

Clemons caught the punt near the left sideline, waited until would-be tacklers converged on him, then handed the ball to the Rocket, who circled behind him and headed to the right. It was a brilliantly executed exchange.

"He was flying," says Evraire. "I grabbed him by the facemask, almost tore his head off."

Ismail's head spun sideways, but he shook off Evraire's facemask tug, which drew a penalty flag, and raced up the field, displaying speed that had rarely, if ever, been seen on a Canadian football field. He was finally dragged down at the Hamilton five-yard line.

The rest of the game passed quickly, with the Argos never threatened by Hamilton en route to a 41-18 thrashing. Each time Ismail touched the ball—seven times in all, for 213 all-purpose yards—the crowd came alive. Even his shortest gains, 14 yards on a punt return and 17 on a kickoff return, were thrilling to witness. On one of these, he showed off his extraordinary balance, touching his hand down twice to stay on his feet and spin away from tacklers.

The reviews of his performance were, as they say in Hollywood, boffo.

The *Ottawa Citizen's* Lynn McAuley was rapturous, albeit metaphor-happy. "A 73-yard punt return that looked like a jog for a bus; a pass reception that nestled in his hands as sweet as a baby . . . a 24-yard kickoff return where he zigged and zagged smooth as water through a sluice. . . . He took six tacklers for 17 yards, throwing off the great big men as you would throw off old bedclothes."

Hunt, the *Toronto Sun* columnist who had vowed never to attend another Ismail news conference, now predicted the Rocket's time in Toronto would be short. "The guy is just too good for the Canadian Football League. . . . So what if he's only going to be up here a couple of years? It's going to be a ball while it lasts."

Deer in the Headlights

HEY KID, SIGN HERE and we'll make you the richest player in the history of your sport. All you have to do in return is move to a foreign country and persuade its largest metropolis to start loving that sport again, after years of barely paying attention to it. You're up for becoming the Wayne Gretzky of Canadian football, ain't ya, kid? Easy-peasy, right?

Not so easy, as it turned out, for a 21-year-old kid still working towards his college degree and barely three years removed from living a quiet life in a nondescript small town.

From the moment Rocket Ismail signed with the Toronto Argonauts, it was no secret what the plan was for him. He was expected to do for Canadian football in Toronto, and, to some extent, all across Canada, what Wayne Gretzky had done for hockey in southern California and indeed much of the U.S. Sun Belt.

Paying top dollar to import a world-beating talent in Gretzky had worked brilliantly for his Los Angeles Kings, so Bruce McNall saw no reason he couldn't repeat the feat in Toronto with the Argos. And who better than a player sensational enough to have "Rocket" as his nickname?

McNall was so confident and proud of the plan that he spelled it out to none other than Gretzky's father, Walter, at a Kings game. This account was related years later by Wayne Gretzky, who, as a minority owner of the Argonauts, presumably signed off on the plan himself.

"You know I signed Rocket Ismail to play for the Argos," McNall told Walter Gretzky. "I want him to be sort of the Wayne Gretzky of the CFL and do for the Argos and the league what Wayne's doing for the Kings."

Walter, a plain-spoken telephone installer whose tutelage on a backyard ice rink is widely credited for his eldest son's unparalleled hockey prowess, had an immediate response for McNall: "There's only one Wayne Gretzky."

After the game, a somewhat chagrined McNall related that conversation to Walter's son. "Geez, I don't know if I did a good thing or a bad thing," he told Wayne.

McNall now has no problem agreeing there was only one Wayne Gretzky. But Rocket "was the closest we could come at that time."

Not close enough, unfortunately.

* * *

Rocket Ismail had managed to pass the test of his initial appearance before two huge media throngs after his signing in April 1991. He had come across as charming and enthusiastic in both Los Angeles and Toronto.

But by the time he made his next appearance before cameras, at the opening of training camp in Guelph six weeks later, he already seemed to be feeling the pressure that accompanied his outlandish contract. "This is making me more nervous," the Rocket told some of the journalists on hand for his debut. "I can take care of myself on the field. This kind of throws you back a little bit."

Within a couple of days, the demands on Ismail's time from the media were clearly starting to grate. A *Canadian Press* report by Doug Smith described Ismail making a CBS crew from Buffalo wait three hours for an interview. He also met a group of waiting journalists with exasperation: "What could you possibly want to ask me now?"

"He gave the reporters the five minutes he promised," Smith wrote, "almost to the second."

One could almost sympathize with the kid, given the level of scrutiny he was coming under. Everything about him generated comment—even his clothing. Ismail's idiosyncratic apparel at his introductory Toronto news conference had been celebrated as indicative of a free-spirited young man. Now reporters were asking questions about his sartorial choices. What was the significance of *Button Your Fly*, a slogan emblazoned on his shirt? Why did he wear a T-shirt to a banquet for fans at SkyDome? Ismail found it annoying.

"As we go along, I'm becoming more accustomed to things, and becoming more a part of everything," he said. "But it's hard, man."

It was hard, but it was part of the deal. The massive personal-services contract Ismail had signed with McNall Sports Entertainment required him to do more than just play football. He was expected to promote the Argonauts and work closely with sponsors. That was why he jetted down to L.A. a few days before the team's season opener: to attend a photo shoot for AW's inaugural set of CFL collectible cards, to appear at a sports collectibles show, and to make an appearance on Arsenio Hall's late-night TV talk show.

All of these responsibilities, plus the removal of his wisdom teeth, and a pulled quadriceps muscle, kept him off the football field for a couple of weeks. When the regular season began, Rocket had barely run any pass patterns or fielded any practice kicks. That the rookie had yet to develop professional-grade work habits, the *Toronto Star* reported, only made matters worse: "Players say he has been late for strategy sessions, missed team meals, fallen asleep at meetings and generally not made an effort to be part of the club."

Some of his teammates complained of what seemed to be a different set of rules and standards for the rookie. "No one is saying he's dogging it or milking his injury, we're just saying it's time for him to step up now," said D.K. Smith. "If he's going to be part of this, now's the time for him to show us what he can do. . . . This isn't Notre Dame. This is the big time, whether he believes it or not".

Ismail did have his defenders. One sports columnist thought it was ridiculous that the Argonauts were being criticized for Ismail's visit to L.A. "He appears on a major television show instead of sitting in his hotel room. This is wrong?" wrote Jim Proudfoot in the *Star*.

> *Or is it a step forward for the CFL, awarding it prominence nobody ever dared dream of before McNall came along? C'mon, this is what we talked about when McNall, John Candy and Wayne Gretzky bought the Argos. They were going to enliven the CFL, make it sparkle. And now, when what was predicted actually begins to take place, we're hearing, "tsk, tut" instead of "way to go."*

General manager Mike McCarthy insisted Ismail's decampment to southern California was no big deal, and read his players the riot act: "This isn't about you guys. We're going to have the most popularity of any frigging football team in North America." Ismail was in L.A., McCarthy insisted, "talking business" with owners McNall, Gretzky, and Candy.

Indeed, there was a business purpose for the trip, beyond promoting the Argos in the U.S. After the team's first preseason game, Rocket had breakfast with Wayne Gretzky. They discussed his problems with the media and his attitude in general. When Ismail failed to demonstrate the requisite improvement, the bosses decided a more formal lecture was needed.

The media's view was that further discussions were entirely warranted. "It's time for the big sit-down, time to have that little conversation," wrote Steve Simmons in the *Sun*. "Time to grab the Rocket by the scruff of the neck and read him the riot act. Like, kid, we've paid you all this money, and we've been nice to you, we've been patient, SO WHAT THE HELL IS GOING ON HERE?"

In retrospect, it seems almost astonishing that such a conversation should have been needed. But executives from the 1991 Argos now freely acknowledge that in their zeal to make a huge splash by signing Ismail, the organization had failed to do any due diligence on whether he would be as comfortable selling football in Toronto as Gretzky had been selling hockey in California.

Gretzky himself confirms that he and Candy were, to their considerable dismay, required to provide Ismail with what amounted to remedial media training.

"I have to have you guys sit down with Rocket and talk to him about dealing with the media," McNall told his fellow owners. So Candy and Gretzky had "the big sit-down" with him.

"Rocket, we've got to sell the game and we need you to talk to the media," Candy said.

"John, I'm not a bad guy and I'm not trying to shrug off the media," Ismail said. "I don't know how to deal with the media. I'm not trying to hide. I'm not trying to be a bad guy. I just don't know how to deal with it because I've never done it. Guys, I've never talked to the media, really."

"It was the most amazing thing I have ever heard in my life," Gretzky says now. "I remember my heart dropping, going, 'oh my God.' I'll never forget John and I looking at each other, going, 'Oh, man.'"

"Oh my gosh, this wasn't in the profile," Gretzky later told McNall.

The owners assumed that because Ismail had played at Notre Dame, he must have had a lot of experience talking to reporters.

"But he had never talked to the media one-on-one," Gretzky says he was told by the Rocket. "This poor kid is 21 years old and never really talked to the media. He had no idea. He had no comprehension.

"We just took it for granted. It was totally overlooked by everyone. It was an oversight [assuming] that he could sort of stand up and try to sell the game and sell tickets. That wasn't him."

Telling his bosses he had "never talked to the media one-on-one" was not entirely accurate, and in retrospect it's clear McNall and his executives should have done more research. Warning signs were missed. It was not simply a matter of training Ismail on how to deal with the media. He had done that. He just didn't enjoy it.

The Rocket wasn't completely sheltered during his three years as a media darling at Notre Dame. John Heisler, who was sports information director at the university during Ismail's time there, says reporters were regularly granted one-on-one and group access to the team's star players. Ismail had been interviewed before, and more than once.

But after Ismail had been "fabulous" at a media day before the Fiesta Bowl in his freshman year, "he got a little bit gun-shy in terms of the media," Heisler says.

"I remember having conversations with him and trying to explain that we weren't trying to take hours out of his time every single day. We were trying to manage the situation with him, as we were with all of our players, and trying to make sure their life was as normal and as routine as it could be, and still deal with the media requests that we had. I don't know if he felt comfortable thinking that he would be the spokesman for the program."

The school hired Kathleen Hessert, who has built a successful career coaching executives, celebrities, and athletes on how to speak to journalists, to conduct media training sessions. Ismail participated, Heisler says, but "I'm not sure he needed a whole lot of help. He was really good at it— when he wanted to do it. At times it was just a matter of convincing him that it was important to us and important to our program and we weren't trying to ruin his life every day."

If that paints a picture of a player not suited to becoming the focal point of an entire league, so did a report in *Football Digest* published before Ismail signed with the Argonauts. "As the adulation from fans and attention from media escalated [at Notre Dame], Ismail became more elusive," Bill Bilinski wrote. "He has skipped news conferences and told reporters he considers such affairs 'an infringement' on his time. He also doesn't suffer the repetition of questions well. 'If I said something [before], I feel like can't they just look it up?' he once said."

Ismail didn't attend media day before his final college game, the 1991 Orange Bowl. According to *Sports Illustrated*, he attended one news conference that week and told journalists he resented being there.

Heisler recalls hearing "after the fact" about an incident when the Rocket "was so disinterested in speaking with [journalists] that he had the student managers hide him in a laundry cart with uniforms and other stuff. They were wheeling this cart back to our main administrative building where the football offices were."

A lesson had been learned. Several individuals associated with the Argonauts say Ismail and the team's equipment staff sometimes used laundry carts to spirit him away from unsuspecting reporters during his time in Toronto.

Having failed to spot the red flags initially, the Argonauts' management belatedly moved to protect Ismail and zealously control his interactions with journalists. Suzan Waks, McNall's most trusted senior executive, gave blunt marching orders to Scott Carmichael, who had overseen Gretzky's media relations for the Kings: "You've got to go there . . . and manage Rocket."

Carmichael couldn't be in Toronto all the time, though. Day-to-day management of Ismail was assigned to David Watkins, who was rehired to handle media relations after holding that job with the team in the early 1980s. Watkins was told his job was to shadow the Rocket whenever media might be present.

Ismail watched the first game of the season from the sideline in Ottawa, then went into the Argo locker room at Lansdowne Park. Standing outside the locker room in the old stadium, Watkins was approached by Carmichael.

"What are you doing?" Carmichael asked.

"I'm waiting for the guys to finish up their interviews," Watkins responded.

"Well, who's with Rocket?" Carmichael shot back.

"The guy didn't even play in the game, yet I'm supposed to go to him," Watkins says now. "From then on, I knew that was clear. Los Angeles [head office] put him on a pedestal. The expectation was you were not too far from their prize investment.

"I was asked by Los Angeles to stay next to Rocket, and when the questions started getting troublesome or too much for him, I was to break it off. 'Rocket, you've got to do so-and-so.' Don't put the athlete in a position to have to break things off, because that leaves a bad impression. Be the bad guy. Get him out of there."

Dave Naylor of the *Globe and Mail* saw the results first-hand: "They would cut off interviews with him when scrums were still going. Sometimes Rocket would look at us and go, 'Sorry guys, I was good still answering things.'"

In one instance, Global TV's Don Martin lit into Watkins: "You didn't cut *us* off. You cut *him* off."

Try as they might to shape his media environment, one thing the Argos couldn't control was what came out of Ismail's mouth, and sometimes he didn't help his own cause. Less than two months into his rookie season, he was asked in Edmonton if he was earning his pay. He looked from reporter to reporter and said: "I'm doing it right now."

Naylor recalls arriving at Rocket's locker for an interview. Before he could ask a question, he overheard Ismail talking with his locker mate, Pinball Clemons.

"What are you doing tonight?" Clemons asked.

"Getting the heck out of here as fast as I can," Ismail answered. He seemed to have deliberately said it loudly enough for the reporter to hear the disdainful remark.

"You always had the sense he had only so much patience for this," says Naylor. Rocket's approach seemed to be, "I'm a football player, not a public-relations ambassador."

Which might be fine for most players, even in a city where football was only the third-biggest sport. But it wasn't fine for a guy who was paid $110,000 a year to play football, and $4.5 million to sell football to the masses.

Later in the season, after Ismail "overslept" and missed an important media availability, Cam Cole wrote in the *Edmonton Journal*: "All he's giving back [for his salary] is what he does on the field. Off it, he gives nothing. Cares nothing for the Canadian Football League, does nothing to promote it. A second of his precious time seems to be too rare a gift to present to the TV cameras and newspapers that carry the CFL's story to its fans. . . . Nobody is asking for miracles. But an effort would be nice."

Looking back, McNall and his colleagues acknowledge it was a mistake to think Ismail might be "the Wayne Gretzky of Canadian football."

"Rocket's a shy guy, not an outward guy," says McNall. "Wayne's shy, too, but he knew the media and he understood it because he had been doing it since he was 11 years old."

Ismail and Gretzky "are worlds apart," says Carmichael. "Wayne has been followed . . . with media and everything else from such a young age. And by then he was a 14-year NHL veteran and had basically seen everything in his life. Rocket was a young pup. He was just so overwhelmed by it all. His reaction was to kind of draw in. I think it was all overwhelming to Rocket, all the attention."

Both Watkins and Carmichael use the same phrase to describe the Rocket, and it has nothing to do with Gretzky. The Rocket, they say, was a deer in the headlights.

* * *

Ironically, Ismail endeared himself to teammates by doing something that ran counter to ownership's determination to make him the Wayne Gretzky of Canadian football. When cornered by reporters, he would routinely talk up his fellow players and portray himself as just one of 37 guys. "Talk to anyone else but me," he would say.

"He wanted team," says Bret Gallagher, who worked as Candy's right-hand man. "Not me—team. He loved pushing Pinball out. 'Let those guys get the exposure.' He knew what they were paying him for. He just didn't want to be the guy, the face of a franchise."[17]

Watkins says he never sensed any animosity from teammates "because I think they realized he was their future, in terms of greater revenues for the team." That point was made repeatedly by players interviewed for this book. Even those who earned less money for an entire season than Ismail was paid to play a single quarter of one game felt his presence in Toronto could only be a good thing for the league and its players. Some noted that by bearing the publicity burden, Ismail took pressure off everyone else.

"Wherever we went, there was Rocket, the face of the team," says quarterback Matt Dunigan. "And here was this group of talented, veteran players that had no worries in the world. Didn't have media or microphones shoved up their ass, asking them stupid questions 24/7. We were just jacking around having a good time going and playing football. Rocket was doing all the dirty work.

"That kid, what he had to overcome and handle as a 21-year-old: not only the face of the franchise but he had really taken the Canadian Football League and put it on a different level. Everybody's watching him, every step, [even] if he's coming out of his hotel room or going shopping. Weight of the world and the league on your shoulders at such a young age."

---

17 For a guy who wanted desperately to fit in and be inconspicuous, Ismail faced some challenges beyond his control. Not only were all eyes trained on him at every game; CBC's isolation cameras were constantly pointed in his direction. And, like the leader of the Tour de France cycling race wearing a distinctive yellow jersey, Ismail's Argo jersey was different from everyone else's. Long after the team's uniform order for the season had arrived, senior management dictated that the Rocket wear a new shirt each game. Equipment manager Danny Webb was unable to find a supplier that could match the Argos' number font. Ismail's No. 25 jerseys had numbers that were significantly larger, and differently shaped, than everyone else's. "The ugly duckling shirt" drove Webb crazy.

And the weight of the world was about to get heavier. It was time to see if the highest-paid player in football history could help his team win a championship.

The Argonaut Twist

EVEN WITH ALL THE HYPE surrounding the new celebrity owners and their hyper-expensive Rocket, the Argonauts knew they needed to build a stronger brand presence in Toronto's crowded sports/entertainment marketplace. Who better to lead that effort than Johnny Toronto?

John Candy threw himself into the task with gusto. In addition to making the rounds of radio and TV stations for interviews talking up the team and hawking tickets, the team's minority owner made commercials for both platforms, including memorable TV spots filmed outside the Colosseum in Rome.

Candy also came up with the idea for what became the Argos' theme song in 1991. He had recently filmed a brief cameo in a video promoting a song called *The Wilbury Twist* by the Traveling Wilburys, the "supergroup" side project of four rock legends: Bob Dylan, George Harrison, Tom Petty, and ELO founder Jeff Lynne. (Founding member Roy Orbison had died two years earlier.)

In the *Wilbury Twist* video, Candy appears as an underwear-clad man who involuntarily follows instructions delineated in the song's opening lyrics: "You put your hand on your head/Put your foot in the air/Then you hop around the room/In your underwear."

Around the time the song was released, communications executive David Watkins, promotions director Bret Gallagher and Candy were brainstorming ways to generate publicity for the Argos.

Someone suggested a theme song. Candy's eyes lit up.

"How about *The Argonaut Twist*?" he said. "Let's get the rights to that!"

Candy had Harrison, one of the three surviving members of the Beatles, in his Rolodex.

"I'm up in Toronto and the team I own, the Argos, we want to use a little bit of *The Wilbury Twist* and do a little commercial," he told Harrison. "Can we do it?"

Candy handed the phone to Gallagher, who gulped as he suddenly found himself negotiating with a member of the most popular and influential group in music history.

"We're not going to use your version," Gallagher assured the ex-Beatle. "We're going to create it ourselves."

"Sure, anything for John," Harrison replied. "Go right ahead."

By the time the 1991 season started, *The Argonaut Twist* had been recorded. The remake changed "room" to "dome" and added Argo-centric lyrics: "Rocket's gonna fly/Right across the field/He's gonna make you scream/'Cuz you're on his team." A video featuring Torontonians dancing and mugging was played regularly on the JumboTron at SkyDome.

"We would never have been able to do that without John," says Gallagher. "We had no budget, but John opened a lot of doors."

The lack of a budget didn't deter Candy. "He's coming up with one great creative idea after the other that'd cost like a gazillion dollars," says Brian Cooper, the team's chief operating officer. For a 30-second TV spot, Candy insisted on hiring Chris Columbus to direct. Columbus had directed the box-office hit *Home Alone*, in which Candy played a small but memorable part, and would go on to acclaim as director of the first two Harry Potter films. "John just thought it was all on the menu," says Cooper, who had to tell his new boss that the budget didn't allow Hollywood-level productions for each piece of the marketing campaign.

The Argonaut Twist and the resurrection of the Blues Brothers at the home opener were not the only times the 1991 Argos intersected with popular music. In a video produced that year to promote his record *Nothing at All*, Canadian hip-hop pioneer Maestro Fresh-Wes sported an Argo jersey bearing Rocket Ismail's number, 25. At the 1991 CFL player awards gala, Maestro performed a CFL-themed rap that had the tuxedo-clad Ismail boogieing in his front-row seat to lines like, "When Rocket got a late hit everybody said, 'Oh!' But he came back cuz he's a tough mutha."

Rap also featured in a weekly routine led by Chris Gaines, a middle linebacker with a menacing glower who had joined the Argos in late 1989. He was an inspirational leader on the Toronto defence.

One of the team's rituals, established by head coach Don Matthews before he left, was to require whichever player led stretching drills at practice to perform in some way. Gaines was called on one day. No one knew that this intense-looking white man with a deep southern drawl, nicknamed "Jethro" in homage to a character on the *Beverly Hillbillies* TV series, was also an aficionado of rap music. It was still a relatively new art form in the early 1990s, but "I grew up on rap," Gaines says. "Kurtis Blow, Grandmaster Flash, Whodini, Sugarhill Gang—I bought every rap album that came out."

Gaines also had a way with words. "I got something for y'all," he told his teammates. "It's called the New Jack." He made up a catchy rhyme on the spot, something with a punchline along the lines of: "You're a wretch. So you better get ready 'cuz now we're gonna stretch."

"We fell out laughing," says teammate Carl Brazley. "We were no good after that. The coaches couldn't even keep a straight face."

Soon the linebacker with the Tennessee twang was doing his rap before every game, blurting out clever rhymes that often related in some way to the upcoming game, while leading teammates, at least the less-self-conscious ones, into a series of one-upmanship dance moves and gymnastics.

The raps became interactive, with responses that egged on the performers. As stretching turned into dancing and in some cases back-flips, rhythmic chants erupted: "Go Jethro, go Jethro, go! Go Jethro, go Jethro, go!"

The entertainers on the team loved it. Ismail, generally diffident in public and around journalists, was among the most enthusiastic participants. One time, he and some teammates unveiled a routine in which they imitated an offensive play, with everyone running the entire play in synchronized slow motion, forward and then backwards, as if game film were being rewound to show it a second time.

While a few players hung back—Chris Schultz found the whole spectacle "ridiculous"—most took part with glee. Head coach Adam Rita—who did an awkward "funky chicken" dance during one New Jack session—justified the ritual as "a way for them to loosen up a bit, a way to express their different talents. Who knew that [fullback] Kevin Smellie could do a full backflip? I said, 'Apparently we're not using him enough.'"

Adding to the weekly frivolity was Gaines' backup at middle linebacker, Prentiss Wright. Even hard-core fans of the 1991 Argonauts would have been hard-pressed to identify Wright, who played just two games that season, but many players, and Rita, singled him out as a key component of the team's camaraderie. Like Gaines, he was a self-styled rapper. His routine began with teammates calling out his nickname and adding the sound of drums. "It was Big P . . . boom-boom . . . boom-boom . . . boom." Wright would burst out of a locker where he had been hiding and throw down a rap.

Still more of the team's goofy showmanship spilled onto television in the form of *The Home Boys Report*. Produced for TSN by defensive back Carl Brazley and shown at halftime on some telecasts, *Home Boys* featured shades-wearing characters named Jerome Love, played by former Argo Doran Major, and Bennie Feelgood: Pinball Clemons, looking and acting nothing like the polished and dynamic public speaker he was to become.

Sprawled on broken lawn chairs in junk-strewn warehouses or on train tracks, the pair riffed on life from a "homey" perspective while bantering with guests like Wally Zatylny of the Hamilton Tiger-Cats and Joe Carter of the Toronto Blue Jays. Reporter Paul Hunter of the *Toronto Star* made an appearance on one segment, gamely playing straight man. "I think I was the whitest guy they could find. I remember them talking jive talk; they were completely amused that I had no idea what they were talking about."

Bennie and Jerome fed themselves fried chicken eaten out of a cardboard "Box of Bird," and served up occasional nuggets of "news," such as a rumour that pop singer Madonna was considering marrying former Argo coach Bob O'Billovich.

The show's standard sign-off was lifted straight from *The Simpsons*, which had just begun its three-decade run as TV's greatest cartoon program: "Smell you later."

The Home Boys also gave Ismail a chance to bust some rhymes. His appearance amounted to a hip-hop public-service announcement: "I was lucky cuz I never did the hard time/I stayed in school, away from the drugs and crime/So heed my words and don't be a fool/Life is more than a good time after school/Have a dream and a master plan/Stay clear of drugs, and life'll be just grand."

* * *

All the off-field hoopla and frivolity didn't hinder the Argos on the field. The tone was set by Rita, the offensive mastermind who had gleefully said, "We've got a lot more lights to shoot out," when he took over as head coach.

Rita had the enjoyable but delicate task of sharing the offensive wealth. Pinball Clemons (3,300 all-purpose yards) and Darrell K. Smith (20 receiving touchdowns) had been the leading weapons in 1990. But now there was also the Rocket to feature, as well as Jeff Boyd, who had surpassed 1,000 yards five times in his first eight seasons as a pro. Canadian receivers Paul Masotti and Andrew Murray also wanted the ball thrown their way. It seemed there couldn't possibly be enough "touches" to keep every player happy.

Masotti recalls bugging Rita for more action. That prompted a blunt reality check about the team's pecking order. Rita approached a small whiteboard, took a marker in hand and wrote the players' numbers in priority order, starting at the top.

"This is who gets the ball on our team: No. 25 [Ismail], No. 31 [Clemons], No. 1 [Smith]." Rita then looked at Masotti and Murray and the other backs and receivers. "This is where you get the ball." He then wrote their numbers—86 (Murray), 88 (Masotti) and the others'—on the bricks, below the whiteboard.

While the Rocket was at the top of that hierarchy, Smith remained the most dangerous weapon in the Argos' passing attack—and the most flamboyant.

Smith, whose middle name was Karland, had begun calling himself Darrell K. in 1990. Ridiculed by some teammates for apparent pomposity ("Oh, Mr. Important is using the 'K' now"), he hauled a few of them up

127

to the Argo front office and pulled out his first contract to prove he had signed his name Darrell K. Smith as far back as 1986. In 1991, he added the first two initials to the nameplate on the back of his jersey, suiting up as D.K. Smith.

Smith's flashiness extended to gobs of bling off the field: rings, earrings, gaudy gold chains, expensive mirrored sunglasses. He drove a shiny white Mercedes-Benz 300E with dark tinted glass (uncommon back then) and a teeth-rattling sound system. Cops were only too eager to pull over a Black man bombing around in a ride like that. One night, Smith said, he got pulled over three times.

"I've been called a pimp, a drug dealer, things like that," he told the *Toronto Sun*. "People see you wearing a hat, wearing the shades, wearing all the gold, and they immediately stereotype you. If that's what they want to think about me, I don't care."

In 1991, Smith was pulled over by police, and found himself surrounded by six cruisers and 12 officers. A couple of them tried to remove his illegal radar detector, damaging the Benz. Stung by the bad publicity the incident generated as evidence of racial profiling, the police force invited Smith to accompany officers on patrol and fire a pistol at their shooting range. He told reporters he was not anti-police, "I'm pro the community."

He also remained a pro's pro. D.K. scored Toronto's first touchdown of the season, and the first in its home opener a week later. He had five games in 1991 with more than 100 yards, and fell just short in two others, ending the year with 73 receptions for 1,399 yards (99 more than the Rocket) and nine TDs.

On September 7, 1991, against Hamilton at SkyDome, Smith grabbed eight passes for 183 yards. A 33-yard reception in the second quarter moved him past Terry Greer as the Argonauts' all-time leading receiver. Greer, whose record of 6,817 yards had been achieved over six seasons, was on the sideline to congratulate Smith, who had arrived in Toronto just after Greer departed for the NFL in 1986.

At halftime, Greer told CBC's Scott Oake that Smith had visited him in Memphis and promised to break the record. "I said, 'Sure, we'll see about that,'" the legendary receiver said with a grin. "And he did it."

In contrast to the quietly confident Greer, Smith was exuberant and cocky. When he scored a touchdown in SkyDome, he often ran along the eastern side of the stadium, behind the Argo bench, flailing his arms to fire up fans. "They can't stop me!" he'd yell. Before games, he would go to a quiet area outside the locker room and let out an enormous yell— almost a primal scream. "Everyone knew what it meant," Pinball Clemons said years later. "It was Darrell's way of saying it's time to play."

After his own astonishingly productive season in 1990, Clemons would have had every reason to be upset when the Argos handed Ismail $4.5 million a year. Pinball had entered the 1990 season with a contract worth $57,000. After a brief stint on the practice roster early that year (during which he rebuffed an offer to jump to the Tiger-Cats), he negotiated a slight raise, signing a three-year deal for $65,000 per season. Bonuses earned as the league's most outstanding player raised his total 1990 take-home to $85,000—good money for a non-quarterback, but a fraction of what Ismail would be paid.

Clemons hired Canadian football's most prominent agent, Gil Scott, to renegotiate his contract. Three decades later, Scott is still offended by the salary disparity. "Clemons was getting shafted. This is the guy who's the face of your franchise."

Reports leaked to the press suggested the Pinball was demanding up to $1.7 million over two seasons. Clemons now says that amount is news to him, but he always believed Ismail's arrival would increase his own value as a player. "From a business standpoint, I understood he was not going to hurt me. I'm not going to get a million dollars or even half a million dollars, but I'm going to do better than I am now."

After briefly considering holding out, Clemons reported to camp and signed a contract that made him the league's highest-paid running back at more than $100,000 a season.

In the 1991 season opener in Ottawa, with Ismail on the sidelines in street clothes and the Argos leading by just two points in the fourth quarter, Clemons showed again why he had been named the league's most outstanding player a year earlier.

The Pinball caught a punt deep in his own end. Ottawa receiver Jock Climie raced downfield to make the tackle. "I remember going to wrap [him up] and then I'm on the ground and I have no idea where he's gone. I roll over and see him sprinting down the field. He'd gone by me like I wasn't even there." Clemons raced 93 yards before running out of gas just short of the Ottawa goal-line. The ensuing touchdown gave Toronto a comfortable lead it never relinquished.

He outdid that three weeks later. With all eyes on the Rocket, who had yet to score a touchdown, Clemons raced 93 yards on another punt return, this time scoring a TD before nearly 54,000 spectators at B.C. Place stadium.

Two weeks after that, he delighted 36,000 fans at SkyDome by scoring a touchdown and handing the ball to his mother in the stands behind the Toronto bench. That was followed by two more special post-TD deliveries that day, to his sister, Kelli, and his future wife, Diane Lee.[18]

18 The 62-10 demolition of Saskatchewan prompted the Roughriders to fire head coach John Gregory and replace him with none other than Don Matthews, back in the CFL after one short season in the World League. Gregory, meanwhile, took over as Hamilton head coach in time for the annual Labour Day Classic against Toronto, which ended up as the Argos' only ugly effort of 1991: a 48-24 loss to the previously winless Ticats.

* * *

The man whose job it was to get all the talent involved in the offence was Dunigan, back for his second year as the Argos' quarterback. But as had happened in 1990, the charismatic leader couldn't stay healthy.

Just a few minutes into the second game of the season, Dunigan limped off the field with a calf injury that kept him out of the lineup for the next four games—to be replaced, as usual, by Foggie. This was becoming an all-too-familiar pattern.

From the moment he'd arrived in Canada in 1983, Dunigan had seemed to relish crashing into defenders. Quarterbacks are taught that when carrying the ball, they should drop to the ground and slide before being hit by a defender. A quarterback-turned-ball-carrier who chooses to slide cannot be aggressively tackled without the tackler being penalized. All the defender has to do is touch a sliding quarterback to end the play.

Dunigan never wanted any part of that sliding crap. Known as a "linebacker playing quarterback," he'd just as soon lower his head and ram his shoulder, or the crown of his helmet, straight into the nearest defender.

"Matt played like he was ten feet tall and he was bullet-proof," says Brian Warren, a teammate of Dunigan with both the Eskimos and Argos. "He would stick his head in there." Joe Faragalli, Dunigan's head coach with the 1987 Edmonton Eskimos, once said he'd regularly yell at the QB, "Slide! Slide! But I knew I was wasting my breath. If he thought he could get an extra yard by running over a couple of guys, that's what he'd try to do."

Dunigan's seeming penchant for punishment sometimes left him wounded, although he also suffered more than his share of fluky injuries, such as deep muscle pulls and tears, that had little or nothing to do with contact. In 1990 he had been knocked out of the Argo lineup three times; the last injury left him unable to suit up for the playoff game that could have sent Toronto to the Grey Cup. Images of a despondent Dunigan on the Toronto bench after suffering another injury were published and broadcast all too frequently.

After missing four games in 1991, Dunigan returned to the lineup and got through three full games unscathed. But early in a mid-September contest in Calgary, the jinx struck again. He got sacked and suffered a separated right (throwing) shoulder. Done again, this time for six games.

It a halftime interview on TSN, Dunigan seemed bewildered by his seemingly endless run of injuries. "It's been one of them things," he said with a sardonic smile. "I think someone's put a curse on me. Anybody that's been watching the last couple of years has got to know what I'm feeling right now. It's part of the game—you accept it; you don't try to understand it."

Dunigan's injury, as deflating as it was for him, wasn't even the biggest story to emerge from that game in Calgary. On a day when a faux rocket bearing the Argos' logo was exploded on the field before the game, the real Rocket got "blowed up real good," to borrow the catchphrase of a John Candy *SCTV* character, Billy Sol Hurok.

While returning a punt, the Rocket was tackled by Paul Clatney. As he fell to the ground, Calgary linebacker Dan Wicklum barrelled in. Wicklum's helmet pounded into Clatney while the full force of his body slammed into Ismail's head. An official threw a flag into the air; Wicklum was penalized for spearing. Ismail stayed down, kneeling, with his head pressed into the turf.

Escorted to the Argo sideline, the Rocket at first looked woozy. Then he sat down and keeled over. Team doctor Mike Ford asked Ismail what day it was. His response: "Calgary."

Before the Rocket was taken by cart to the locker room, TSN's Gord Miller reported that he had "just got worse and worse on the sideline. . . . He kept getting groggier and groggier." Ismail had suffered a severe concussion. He spent the rest of the game in the locker room, distraught and vomiting, and eventually was taken to hospital for observation.

"I didn't see a thing," Ismail said later. "All I know is I was down, getting ready to get back up, and something hit me in the head with a sledgehammer."

Clatney, who had roomed with Wicklum when they were both rookies with the Winnipeg Blue Bombers a few years earlier, admits that while he didn't know his teammate's intent, the hit looked like a blatant attempt to injure. "It was an extremely late hit."

Wicklum, whose father played four seasons for the Argonauts in the 1960s, declined to be interviewed for this book. In comments at the time, he denied any intent to injure. "It's only an issue because he makes so much cash," he said. "I didn't go extra hard. I saw him out of the corner of my eye and launched myself. It was a late hit. If it was intent to injure, they would have thrown me out of the game."

Argo brass were furious that their star attraction had been targeted so viciously, and demanded severe punishment. "I want that guy out of the league," fumed general manager Mike McCarthy.

Coincidentally, the hit happened the day after Argo co-owner Wayne Gretzky was plastered into the boards from behind in the 1991 Canada Cup. Gretzky, who suffered a back injury that caused him to miss the final game of the tournament, told reporters he was "more upset about the hit on the Rocket than the hit on me. That guy should be suspended for four or five games. Fans in the CFL are paying good money to see the Rocket play, and the players should realize he is a meal ticket. Guys like [Wicklum] better wake up."

CFL commissioner Donald Crump buckled under pressure from the Argonauts by sending a letter to all teams warning against going after the league's "marquee" players. Players around the league took issue with an apparent double standard. "So we're allowed to spear a guy who's making 40,000, but not a guy who's making 400,000?" asked Edmonton's Brett Williams.

Ismail, who had strived to mesh with teammates receiving a fraction of his salary, told a reporter: "I'm already uncomfortable. I don't need a situation to separate me more."

* * *

Although the Argos were in first place all season after starting the year with three consecutive wins, football managers and coaches are never satisfied with their personnel. McCarthy was always ready to upgrade, no matter how well his team was performing. That injuries were threatening to derail a potential championship season only made him more eager.

Coming out of the game in Calgary, the Argos were not only dealing with Dunigan's shoulder injury and Ismail's concussion. Their two other American wide receivers, Jeff Boyd and Trumaine Johnson, both suffered injuries as well.

Boyd hurt his leg at the end of a play in which he scored an 85-yard touchdown. "I got into the end zone, went to turn sideways and tore my hamstring." After the game, he broke the news to Rita: "I can't help the team anymore. I want to, but there's nothing left."

McCarthy got on the phone and quickly worked out a trade with Edmonton. In exchange for a draft pick, he obtained wide receiver David Williams, who had developed great chemistry with Dunigan, Foggie, and Rita when they were all with the B.C. Lions in 1988, a year when Williams was named the CFL's most outstanding player. He also happened to be among the league leaders in touchdown catches in 1991.

Williams, who had clashed throughout the season with Edmonton head coach Ron Lancaster, got called to a meeting with Lancaster and general manager Hugh Campbell. "We traded you," Lancaster said. "Do you want to know why?"

Williams said he didn't care. "Who did you trade me to?" Told it was the Argonauts, he started laughing. "Dunigan, Adam Rita, my boy Foggie, Darrell K. Smith, Pinball, Rocket. OK!"

The Eskimos were about to head to Toronto to take on the Argos. Lancaster and Campbell likely presumed Williams could not possibly absorb the Toronto offensive system in just three days. But it was basically the same system he had played under Rita with the Lions. Even the terminology was familiar. Assimilating enough information to play immediately would be no problem.

Lining up on Toronto's first play from scrimmage, Foggie glanced at Williams and nodded: a signal to run a deep streak up the left sideline. Despite having his right arm grabbed by a defender, Williams reached up with his left hand and snared the ball for a 33-yard reception right in front of the Edmonton bench. As Lancaster looked on, Williams muttered to him, "This is going to be a long fucking day."

For the Eskimos and Lancaster, it was. Williams caught five passes for 124 yards and two touchdowns as his new mates hammered his old team 47-28.

For Boyd, it was a bittersweet turn of events. Lured out of retirement on the eve of the season opener, he had arrived in Ottawa just in time to get swept up in the Argo circus. Now he would spend the last two months of his career watching rather than being in the centre ring. "You see all the guys you played with in the circus, and you're not really a part of it."

Still, Boyd was honoured to be asked by Rita to mentor the Rocket.

And he understood what a difference-maker Williams could be. "Dave was an extremely long guy who was confident, someone that Matt didn't have to think about. If anything broke down, he could just throw it up high to Dave, and Dave would make a play for him. For that team at that time, he was the perfect addition."

McCarthy kept tinkering. David Bovell had been Winnipeg's top rookie in 1990, starting at safety on a ferocious defence that helped the Bombers win the Grey Cup. A dispute with GM Cal Murphy led to him being released late in the 1991 season. McCarthy immediately added him to the Argos' practice roster. Bovell drove 20 straight hours to get to Toronto and was activated for the team's second-last game of the season.

Football can be a cruel business, and Bovell's arrival is evidence of that. He moved directly into the starting lineup, supplanting Chris Munford, who was demoted to the practice roster for the rest of the year after starting 15 games including the season opener, when he intercepted three passes.

Asked how they felt about a player losing his job so late in what was becoming a magical journey, almost every Argonaut interviewed for this book expressed personal regret for Munford, but support for the decision. Munford was a smart defensive back, capable of covering receivers and making timely interceptions. Bovell, though, was an assassin. Here's what some teammates and opponents said about him:

> *"He could lay the wood. He'd make guys nervous."*
>
> *"When he came in, we had a dynamic of intimidation that we didn't have before."*
>
> *"There was not a safety that was more feared than him. You knew if he ever lined you up, you weren't going to play again."*
>
> *"He knocked some dicks off."*

Bovell was brought in for one purpose: to make opposing receivers afraid to venture into the middle of Toronto's defence. With all-stars and veterans at the other four positions in the secondary, the Argos were tough to throw against. But the middle, where stars like Calgary's Allen Pitts tended to roam, had seemed vulnerable. That changed with the arrival of Bovell.

Munford politely declined to be interviewed for this book. Bovell says he believes the Argos would have continued winning had Munford remained the starting safety. "If I had the opportunity to pick me or him, I would pick me, too. But I don't think it was necessary. That just points back to the brutal world of [football]—we're all mercenary."

There was one other late-season addition, a guy who had been one of the most polarizing figures in the league. Jeff Braswell had been a star linebacker in B.C., with a reputation for late hits, dirty play, and barking—literally barking like a dog—at opponents. He had been one of the six players sent to Edmonton to complete the trade that moved Dunigan to the Lions in 1988. Despite enormous talent, he was never accepted during his two years in Edmonton. Media members and fans constantly griped that his over-the-edge style was not "the Eskimo way."

Traded to Ottawa in February 1991, he lasted just three games, long enough to poke Dunigan in the eye during the season opener. Despite that dirty play four months earlier, Braswell was embraced by his new teammates, including Dunigan. He played two games late in the season, allowing Gaines time to heal some injuries before the playoffs, and became an enthusiastic cheerleader on the sideline.

Braswell, who had been working as a roofer in Florida when he got the call from McCarthy, arrived eager to find out whether all the hype about the Rocket was warranted. In practice, Ismail made a catch and Braswell went to tackle him.

"See ya! Wouldn't want to be ya!" the Rocket called out as he flew past.

"It was like standing on the side of a highway and a car just whizzes by," says Braswell. "He was gone. I couldn't catch him. You can't hit what you can't catch."

Braswell learned what the rest of the CFL had already discovered. Ismail had become a force on offence as well as kick returns. After making just four receptions in the first four games, the Rocket emerged by season's end as one of the most dynamic weapons in the league. He finished the season with 64 receptions for 1,300 yards, a superb average of 20.3 yards per catch. His 2,959 all-purpose yards were the second-most in league history at that point, surpassed only by the 3,300 recorded by teammate Pinball Clemons a year earlier.

Rita's offence was slightly less productive than it had been in 1990, despite the addition of the Rocket. The Argonauts scored 42 fewer points than the year before, averaging just under 36 per game. They fell more than 400 yards short of the previous year's combined rushing and passing totals. The defence posted almost identical statistics to the previous year, surrendering 12 fewer points and racking up about the same number of interceptions and quarterback sacks. But it all added up to 13 wins, three more than in 1990, and a comfortable first-place finish.

There was just one more hurdle to climb to get to the Grey Cup. The Argonauts had to find a way to get past their nemeses, the Winnipeg Blue Bombers.

Blitzkrieg

I T HAD ALL COME DOWN TO THIS. All the money poured into the bank account of a shy young man who could outrun a gazelle. All the pre-game dancing and jiving and hijinks. All the hype. All the excitement. All the Hollywood magic.

For nine months, everything had been building towards November 17, 1991. This was to be the day when John Candy, Wayne Gretzky, and Bruce McNall would be rewarded for buying the Toronto Argonauts and thinking big, when longtime fans of the Canadian Football League team, after seeing their ranks dwindle steadily for nearly a decade, would experience the euphoria of a big game against bitter rivals in a home stadium jammed with 50,000 bellowing fanatics. Sixty minutes of football to decide which team was going to the Grey Cup, with just one thing standing in Toronto's way.

The Winnipeg Blue Bombers, the team that had killed the Argonauts' hopes of getting to the championship game for three consecutive years. The team that had shockingly ripped apart a 14-win Argos squad in a 1988 playoff game. The team that in 1990 had found an improbable, last-second way to knock the highest-scoring team of all time out of the Grey Cup chase.

Yes, those Blue Bombers, whose players had to buy their own socks, and had to plunk their own coins into a machine to get a soda in the locker room. Those Bombers were coming to Toronto to meet the team with a cappuccino machine in the locker room, a massage therapist, fancy team-issued jackets, and periodic hundred-dollar-bill handouts.

The two teams flat-out hated each other. They fought, they scrapped, they trash-talked. Now they were meeting in the East Division final, with the winner earning the right to compete for the ultimate prize, the Grey Cup.

That Toronto and Winnipeg would meet in the CFL playoffs had seemed inevitable throughout the 1991 season. Hardly traditional rivals (although they did square off in the Grey Cup six times between 1937 and 1950), the two teams had been inextricably linked since the eve of the 1987 season. That's when the Montreal Alouettes suddenly folded, and their scheduled game the next day against Winnipeg was immediately changed to a contest between the Argos and the Bombers. With Montreal gone, the CFL, contrary to elementary geography, made Winnipeg a permanent member of the East Division.

Once in the East, the Bombers met the Argos in the playoffs four years in a row, with the winner advancing to the Grey Cup in all but one of those years. In 1987, the Argos shocked the Bombers 19-3 at Winnipeg Stadium. The Bombers reversed the outcome the following year, upsetting the heavily favoured Argonauts 29-11 in the last game ever played at Exhibition Stadium. In 1989, neither team was any good, but both still made the playoffs, with Winnipeg prevailing 30-7 in the first playoff game at SkyDome. Toronto and Winnipeg clashed in the Eastern Final again in 1990, when Winnipeg's immobile quarterback Tom Burgess stunningly ran far enough to set up a game-winning field goal.

And now the two teams were facing off again in the 1991 Eastern Final. The Argos were loaded with stars on offence: quarterbacks Matt Dunigan and Rickey Foggie, running back Pinball Clemons, receivers Darrell K. Smith and David Williams, and receiver/kick returner Rocket Ismail. The Bombers were built around a superb defence led by aggressive linebackers Greg Battle, James "Wild" West, and the extremely talkative Tyrone Jones.

The animosity between the franchises was real and intense. The wealthy ownership of the Argonauts galled members of the community-owned Bombers. The Argos were fed up with getting knocked out of the playoffs every year by Winnipeg.

"We were jealous because they had the resources and it looked like they had fun," West says. "They had John Candy and Rocket Ismail. Rocket was making more money than the whole team combined. We wanted to be sure to beat their balloon down."

Trash talk, from Jones and a few other Bombers, was a constant feature of games between the two teams. "They talked from the time they got into the stadium," says Toronto's Willie Gillus. "They screamed across the line of scrimmage all during the game. They never stopped." Adds John Congemi: "You could hear those guys before you saw them."

The first game between the Argos and Bombers at SkyDome in 1991 featured a fight, in *preseason*. Toronto offensive linemen Chris Schultz and Bob Skemp were ejected along with Winnipeg's Jones and Battle.

The regular-season games between the clubs were similarly nasty. Toronto's Mike Campbell remembers nearly coming to blows with Jones. "I can't stop you guys from fighting," referee Jake Ireland told them, "so I'm just going to back out of here."

Jones (who died of brain cancer in 2008) actually entered the Argo locker room after a game in 1991, ostensibly to ask Ismail for an autograph.

"What the fuck is he doing in here?" said Schultz, glaring.

Offensive tackle Kelvin Pruenster rose to confront Jones. Pruenster stood six-foot-six, Schultz six-foot-eight; each weighed close to 300 pounds. Jones, a six-footer who played at around 220 pounds, showed no sign of being intimidated.

"Hey, big man, don't be eyeballing me or I'll . . ." he told Schultz with a threatening tone.

"That goes double for you," he warned Pruenster.

Jones, who left that day without any punches being thrown, was also at the centre of another confrontation. When the teams met in October at SkyDome, the Argonauts decided it was time to put an end to an annoying Jones ritual. During warmups before each game, he would lead a contingent of Bombers in a jog around the entire field, intruding into the opposing team's warmup space. "Most of the time he was running his mouth," admits West. "If nobody responded, we just kept on running. We didn't stop. We didn't get into faces with anybody. It was just a friendly warmup."

Friendly or not, the Argos would not stand for it any more. Defensive end Brian Warren made clear that the Bombers would no longer be allowed to cross the midfield stripe without consequences.

"Boys, saddle up," Warren told them. "We're going. Whether we get thrown out of the game right now . . . you don't come to my house like that. You don't pee around my kitchen. Don't you ever cross this line again."[19]

Warren "just went off on them," says cornerback Ed Berry. "He stood up and everybody else just jumped in. I thought, this is going to be good, we're going to smash these guys."

---

19 Warren had a peculiar way of gauging his teammates' intensity. He would ask them, Is your pee hot? "We had a lot of guys that understood how to get their pee hot."

"I guess they felt we invaded their territory," says West. "So there was a little rumble there."

Jones, West, and cornerback Less Browne spent the week before the Eastern Final asserting that "the poor little" Bombers would knock off the pampered "fat cats" from Toronto. Jones brashly predicted the vaunted Toronto offence would score no more than 11 points.

A crowd of 50,380 turned out to see if he could back that up. It was Toronto's largest crowd since 1983, and more than double what the Argos had drawn in their two previous playoff games at SkyDome.

While a few Bombers players had flapped their gums all week, the Argos mostly went about their own business with quiet determination. Sure, their usual cockiness was evident during the final walk-through the day before the game, when the team performed its customary "New Jack" ritual of rapping, dancing and back-flipping. But for the most part they let the Bombers do the talking.

And when the teams returned to their locker rooms after pre-game warmups before the Eastern Final, the ordinarily boisterous Argos were dead silent.

"You could hear the clock going tick, tick, tick," says Schultz. "I've never had a moment where guys were relying on each other more than that. We had taken so much crap for so long from these guys. The intensity in that locker room, the determination."

When it came time for introductions, Toronto's players ran onto the field as a group, helmets held aloft in an expression of solidarity and resolve. They then immediately began making the Bombers eat their words.

On Toronto's first play from scrimmage, the Winnipeg defence ignored individual assignments to set a "smash-mouth" tone. "Hit you in the face in the beginning and see if they could rattle you," says Pruenster. "But everybody was ready for this. We just pushed back. Guys were getting in their faces, and I think they realized really quick that their normal intimidation stuff wasn't going to rattle us."

Just back in action after a shoulder injury that had cost him six games, Dunigan calmly marched his team to an opening-drive touchdown, a 12-yard pass to David Williams just two minutes into the game.

The Argo defence came out playing as recklessly and aggressively as the Bombers had. With a weak passing attack, Winnipeg needed to establish a running game. Fullback Warren Hudson was swarmed by a half-dozen defenders on the first play, and Robert Mimbs, the league's leading rusher, couldn't get beyond four yards on the next. "You're about to have a rough day, partner!" linebacker Darryl Ford yelled at Mimbs. "You're about to have a bad experience!"

Dunigan, his normally long, wavy, and sometimes bleached-blonde locks shorn into a buzz cut that seemed to declare "I mean business," completed four consecutive passes, ending a drive with a six-yard TD toss to Smith that gave Toronto a 14-0 lead. As he ran back to the sideline afterwards, the excitable quarterback leapt into the stands behind the Argo bench, high-fiving a group of spectators.

McNall, Candy, and Gretzky gazed down from the skybox level as their prized investment got into the act. Fielding a Blue Bomber punt off a bounce at his own 35, Ismail shook off an initial tackler, circled back to the 30, bounced off teammate J.P. Izquierdo, then sprang to his right while a phalanx of Argo blockers mowed down pursuing Bombers. As he reached the far sideline near midfield, the Rocket cut back to his left and accelerated into high gear, racing for a 75-yard touchdown that gave Toronto a 22-0 lead just 11 minutes into the game.

"The Rocket," wrote veteran *Toronto Star* columnist Milt Dunnell, "took more U-turns and detours than a drunk in a demolition derby."

The Argo offence, meanwhile, was getting help from an unlikely source. John Congemi was up in the spotter's booth, telling Rita what he was seeing. Congemi, an Argo quarterback from 1987 to 1990 who had been traded before the 1991 season, had just completed his contract with the Ottawa Rough Riders.

"I was done with Ottawa," Congemi says. "I had a one-year deal, and I was going to move on. . . . I was going to try and help my guys beat the guys that gave us so many headaches over the last four, five years."

By halftime, the lead was up to 33-3, an enormous cushion over the offensively challenged Bombers. The trash-talking continued, although the Argos were celebrating so much they barely noticed. By the fourth quarter, even the motormouth Jones had been silenced.

"I'd never seen Tyrone Jones shut up. I'd never seen West shut up," says Schultz. "All those idiots, they were silent. When that game was totally out of hand, they didn't say a word."

Receiver Jeff Boyd, who had begun his career as a Bomber before joining the Argos, says this was "probably the first game I ever watched with Winnipeg where they had no chance of winning. I've seen them have bad games and still the defence kept them in it. But in that game, they had no chance of winning." As the final score, 42-3, attested.

With time ticking down and the Argos holding a gigantic lead, Candy left his skybox and headed down to field level. He asked for a helmet, and was handed Kevin Smellie's. Basking in the joy of the exuberant crowd, Candy stared into the stands and slowly raised the helmet above his head. The stadium went from a roar to utter madness.

It was all coming together perfectly for the Argos. They were going to the Grey Cup. It couldn't have been scripted any better in Hollywood. Except . . .

The injury curse that had plagued Dunigan throughout his two years in Toronto struck again. Driving the Argonauts into Winnipeg territory late in the first half, the quarterback rolled out and threw a pass, releasing the ball just as defensive end Quency Williams slammed him to the turf. The full weight of Williams landed on Dunigan's right upper torso.

While Lance Chomyc kicked a field goal to extend the Argo lead, Foggie began warming up on the Argo sideline. Dunigan would finish the game standing forlornly on the Argo sideline, wearing his game jersey without shoulder pads.

As brilliant as Foggie had often been as Dunigan's replacement over the past year and a half, the hearts of many Argo fans sank. They were bitterly accustomed to this pattern. The Argos' high-powered offence would be rolling up yards and piling up points, "shooting the lights out," then the man pulling the trigger would come off the field limping or sit morosely on the bench clutching some part of his body.

It had happened no fewer than five times in the two years since he joined Toronto at the start of 1990. Strained knee ligaments. A pulled calf muscle. A separated shoulder. The CFL's highest-paid player (until his contract was dwarfed by Ismail's) had suited up for just 16 of 36 regular-season games with the Argos, and had missed big portions of five he started due to injury. He had also been unable to play in either of the team's two playoff games in 1990, one of them the wrenching last-second loss to the Bombers.

Now Dunigan appeared to be injured heading into the Grey Cup, where he'd endured another streak of misfortune. Nothing had gone according to plan in any of the three consecutive appearances he'd made in the title match with his previous teams. In 1986, he and his Edmonton Eskimos had been steamrolled by a ferocious Hamilton pass rush. A year later, Dunigan suffered a concussion that put him out of the championship game. In 1988, Dunigan's B.C. Lions were in position to score the game-winning points, until his pass was deflected at the line of scrimmage and intercepted.

So Dunigan's personal tally was three Grey Cups played, two haunting defeats, and one victory that he did not feel especially part of.

"I treasure that '87 ring," he wrote in his biography. "But quarterbacks *lead*. Until I could start, complete, take the final snap and kneel to let the clock run out with the ball in my hand, the Grey Cup was a job unfinished."

Winterpeg

CAL MURPHY HAD A DREAM. The general manager of the Winnipeg Blue Bombers longed for his city to stage the Grey Cup.

The CFL had traditionally rotated the game among its three largest cities—Toronto, Montreal and Vancouver—and played it in smaller centres only on rare occasions. But Murphy thought Winnipeg deserved a shot, especially now that Montreal was out of the league. If the Bombers could replace the Alouettes in the CFL East, why not as a Grey Cup host, too?

Harry Ornest, still the owner of the Argos in 1989, considered the notion of staging the league's showpiece event outdoors in Winnipeg's 33,000-seat stadium ridiculous. A native of Edmonton, Harry O knew how cold it can get on the prairies at the end of November. Why risk the elements when the league could play its final indoors in Vancouver, at 60,000-seat B.C. Place Stadium? Or at Toronto's new SkyDome with its retractable roof and 54,000 seats? Everyone would be comfortable, and the CFL would maximize its revenue.

But Murphy wasn't one to give up easily, and he had an argument that was difficult to refute. Every other city except tiny Regina had staged the Grey Cup: Ottawa (1967 and '88), Hamilton (1972), Calgary (1975) and Edmonton (1984). It was finally Winnipeg's turn, Murphy maintained. Besides, the Grey Cups in Edmonton and Calgary had been played in extremely chilly conditions, without any real problems. A woman even ran onto the field naked during the opening ceremony in Calgary—how uncomfortable could it have been?

And so the CFL awarded Winnipeg the 1991 Grey Cup, conditionally, early in 1989. Ornest, who had just joined the league's board of governors as new owner of the Argonauts, immediately began working behind the scenes to get the decision overturned. "Unless they fulfil a financial commitment which will equal the revenues that we can generate in the SkyDome or in Vancouver, they won't get the votes," he predicted.

Murphy, naturally, fought back and, unlike the newcomer Ornest, he had a lot of support around the league, especially in his fellow prairie city, Regina. A savvy political operator, he rallied the governors around a mutual suspicion of Canada's largest city. "Somebody in Toronto is looking at his own interest," he said.

When it came to the final vote, Murphy triumphed. Winnipeg would host the 1991 Grey Cup.

While thrilled that his city would be Canada's centre of attention for one day, Murphy lamented that Winnipeg Football Club (the not-for-profit entity that owned the Bombers) would get nothing itself out of the Grey Cup. Revenue would flow to the league, even though most tickets would be sold in the Manitoba capital. He and Ken Houssin, the Blue Bombers' treasurer, discussed this one day over lunch at Rae and Jerry's Steak House.

"You know this thing is going to sell out," Murphy said. "I'm convinced of it."

"What we should do," Houssin replied, "is buy all the tickets and scalp them."

It was said as a joke. But Murphy, whose traditionalist nature had made him one of the last holdouts against signing other teams' free agents or allowing female journalists into locker rooms, seized on it as an idea that might actually work. What if the Bombers bought all the tickets from the CFL (including 19,000 for benches erected temporarily in the end zones), then sold them for higher prices? The league would get guaranteed revenue, and the Bombers could turn a profit.

Rough calculations suggested there was potential to clear up to $4 million in ticket sales, even after other costs were factored in. If the league agreed to sell the 50,000 seats for $3 million, the football club could wipe out much of its million-dollar debt.

The club's executive embraced the concept, and the league was game to try it as well. But there was one big hurdle. The Bombers would have to take on all the risk. A team "owned" by hundreds of community members, and already in debt, could dig a deeper hole for itself. Furthermore, the club didn't have the money to pay up front for the tickets, and no bank was interested in floating a loan for so uncertain a venture.

Murphy came up with another creative idea: ask Winnipeg Enterprises Corporation, the municipal agency that operated the city's football stadium, to guarantee the payment to the league. The initial answer was no.

Houssin pleaded with WEC representatives: "This is a tragedy. We're going to leave a million dollars on the table, which we really need."

Murphy, Houssin, and other executives pushed hard, offering the corporation parking revenue and a big portion of food and drink revenue from the game. In the end, WEC agreed. The 1991 Grey Cup game would be staged for the first time with a revenue guarantee to the league, and the potential for profit (or loss) shifted to the host city.

As expected, the vast majority of tickets, which cost $107 in the grandstands and $70 in the end-zone bleachers, were sold in and around Winnipeg. That was the good news. The bad news was that the defending champion Blue Bombers were crushed by the Argonauts in the Eastern Final, and Winnipeg lost the chance to watch its team play the Grey Cup at home.

When the Argos arrived in town on Tuesday during Grey Cup week, they discovered that virtually everyone in town was against them. Usually, a host city will support its divisional representative in the final, but Winnipeg had never truly felt like an Eastern team, and the city had learned to hate the Argos since joining the division. Winnipeggers weren't especially partial to the Western representative, the Calgary Stampeders, either, but the Alberta team was easier to cheer for than a bunch of big-name Hollywood types trying to buy a championship by signing Rocket Ismail to a huge contract.

Argo fan club members who walked in the Grey Cup parade the day before the game were pelted with garbage. "Old women were coming up and spitting on us," says Lori Bursey, who led a contingent of five dozen Argos boosters to Winnipeg. "I've never seen so much venom coming from any city. They were just nasty."

At that parade, and in hotel lobbies around town, a chant was heard frequently. "I don't know but I've been told. Rocket is afraid of the cold."

The only thing that kept anti-Argo sentiment in Winnipeg from unanimity was the presence of the one person even the most ardent Toronto hater couldn't get mad at: John Candy.

While his co-owners Bruce McNall and Wayne Gretzky didn't arrive in town until game day, the popular actor made the rounds all week. He hosted relatives and friends at Alycia's restaurant, and frequented the Palomino Club, the scene of the week's most raucous Grey Cup parties.

Candy at first tried to party inconspicuously at the Palomino, sometimes called the Palimony because of its reputation for debauchery, with friends like CBC's Brian Williams and actress Cynthia Dale. "We'll come in through the back door, enter through the kitchen because I don't want to create a scene," he told them. But being seated in a roped-off area couldn't stop one of the world's most recognizable humans from being spotted, and Candy's generosity didn't help matters.

"Buy the house a round," he said to a Palomino server. The club's manager came over to make certain he knew what he was doing: "Mr. Candy, there's 600 people here."

"Then you better hurry," Candy replied.

The disc jockey got on the mic: "John Candy just bought the house a round."

The place erupted, and Candy kept the party going all week.

"I don't think he slept," says Williams.

Argo players were overjoyed to be assigned to the Winnipeg Stadium locker room normally used by the Bombers. Some players raced to claim the lockers that ordinarily belonged to motormouth Tyrone Jones and his linebacking partner, James West. "There was nothing we could do about it," says West. "We would have done the same thing."

Some Bombers took part in festivities during Grey Cup week. Not West or Jones. "We were distraught. We didn't hang out; we didn't go anywhere. We were watching TV and looking at all the celebrations and what was going on in the city, and we were in a bad state of mind."[20]

---

20 Jones and West did attend the Grey Cup, with sideline passes. Jones trash-talked the Argos constantly, until league officials told Bombers GM Cal Murphy to get the pair off the field.

John E. Sokolowski

Sweet Home Toronto: Co-owner John Candy had hundreds of schemes to promote the Argonauts. The first was an opening-night performance by his friend Dan Aykroyd and the Elwood Blues Revue.

Harry Ornest owned the Argos for only two years, long enough to earn the perpetual enmity of fans for replacing the team's beloved boat logo with a dull ARGOS script.

Silvia Pecota, Toronto Sun/Postmedia

Jamie Campbell

Majority owner Bruce McNall encouraged his executives to "think big." What could be bigger than signing college superstar Rocket Ismail, who arrived in Toronto with his mother, Fatma?

ne Gretzky arrives in Toronto with daughter Paulina for the Argos' home opener.

Ken Gigliotti, Winnipeg Free Press

Everywhere the Argos went, John Candy was sure to go. Before the 1991 Grey Cup, he hammed it up with defensive back, and *Home Boys Report* producer, Carl Brazley.

John E. Sokolowski

Who better to run Adam Rita's sophisticated offence than the CFL's highest-paid, longest-serving quarterback? If only Matt Dunigan could stay healthy...

Rocket Ismail's astonishing speed caused headaches for the defensive backs assigned to cover him.

Jamie Campbell

John E. Sokolowski

General manager Mike McCarthy, the "god of football," kept upgrading his already stacked roster until the final days of the 1991 season.

Lori Bursey

Unlike most head coaches, "happy Hawaiian" Adam Rita was always ready to crack a smile.

Walter Tychnowitz, Edmonton Sun/Postmedia

John Candy might have been the only owner in CFL history to help an injured player (Carl Brazley) off the field during a game.

John E. Sokolowski

Deal me some cards: Receiver Darrell K. Smith always wanted the ball, and erupted with primal screams before games.

Jamie Campbell

Mike "Pinball" Clemons was the CFL's most outstanding player in 1990, and remained a deadly weapon even after the Rocket was added to the arsenal.

With a trip to the Grey Cup assured, John Candy sent 50,000 spectators at SkyDome into a frenzy with a raised-helmet salute late in the Eastern Final.

John E. Sokolowski

John E. Sokolowski

John Candy made a surprise appearance on stage at the 1991 CFL Player Awards, telling Dan Gallagher there were some journalists he hoped would eat crow: "and I'll cook it."

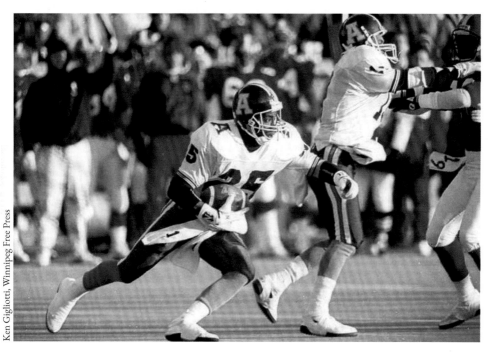

Ken Gigliotti, Winnipeg Free Press

Rocket Ismail embarks on the record-setting, 87-yard kickoff return late in the game that clinched the Grey Cup for the Argos.

The Rocket's touchdown, and the frozen can of beer that almost hit him as he was about to cross the goal-line, were immortalized in a custom-made action figure created by Chris Karwandy.

Frozen beer cans were also featured in a Calgary Sun editorial cartoon by Dave Elston.

Co-captains Don Moen and Dan Ferrone accept the Grey Cup trophy in bone-chillingly cold Winnipeg Stadium.

Rickey Foggie, Adam Rita, and Willie Gillus whoop it up in the moments after the Argos won the championship.

Chris Schwarz, Maclean's/Postmedia

As a kid, John Candy dreamt of playing for the Argonauts. Rocket Ismail had no idea what the Grey Cup meant to Canadians — but he learned.

John E. Sokolowski

Co-owner Wayne Gretzky, next to offensive lineman Blaine Schmidt, became one of a handful of individuals with their name on both the Grey Cup and the Stanley Cup.

John E. Sokolowski

The "three amigos," Wayne Gretzky, Bruce McNall and John Candy, brought the Grey Cup — and the craziest season in football history — to Toronto.

* * *

The one burning question on the minds of Toronto Argonauts fans all week as the team prepared for the Grey Cup was this: would Matt Dunigan be able to play?

The smart money said he wouldn't. Dunigan had suffered a debilitating injury in the area of his throwing (right) shoulder during the Eastern Final. He had just returned from a separated right shoulder that forced him to sit out six games near the end of the season. Team doctor Robert Jackson told reporters the quarterback had aggravated the shoulder separation, with no new damage, but that was not the full story. Dunigan had actually suffered two or three small fractures of the clavicle, or collarbone.

The quarterback insisted all week that he would not miss the Grey Cup. "Sure, I can play," he said. "They could cut this sucker off and I'd play." And he went through session after session with doctors and trainers during Grey Cup week. "He was going through hell," says punter Hank Ilesic, who shared a hotel room with the quarterback. "Matt was probably getting treatment three times a day. They would even do treatments in the [hotel] room. He'd be wrapped up all night. He was exhausted, both physically and mentally."

The quarterback attended his team's daily workouts with his arm wrapped in a sling. Although he led the daily meetings of members of the offence, his practice-field participation was limited to offering encouragement and advice to teammates. Backup quarterback Rickey Foggie took all of the first-team snaps. It seemed highly unlikely that Dunigan could play without having thrown a single pass all week.

He just winked at teammates who wondered if he'd be able to play. "I'm all right," he'd say. "I'll try, and see what I can do."

Some Argos thought he was crazy to even consider the idea. "One shoulder was like two feet lower than the other," says Carl Brazley. "You might want to wait."

The night before the big game, as fans and media swirled through the raucous Sheraton hotel where the Argos were staying, a small contingent gathered secretly in the hotel ballroom under a cone of silence. Among them were GM Mike McCarthy, equipment manager Danny Webb, head trainer Kevin Duguay, and three doctors, including Robert Jackson.

Dr. Jackson, who had worked with the Argonauts for 15 years, was an orthopedic surgeon renowned world-wide as a pioneer in developing and perfecting arthroscopy. The surgical technique inserts a tiny camera to help surgeons see, diagnose and treat injuries to ligaments, cartilage, and other interior body parts. Making only a small incision reduces trauma and speeds healing.

Whether or not Dunigan could play through his collarbone injury would be Jackson's decision.

"We were looking at his pain," says Duguay. "We were looking at his level of function and thinking, Lord, why could it not be his non-throwing arm? It wasn't a complete break. If this was broken, he ain't playing. There's too much risk of a bone impaling inside."

Jackson's expert opinion was that because the fractures were not right on the joint, it should be possible for Dunigan to throw. It would cause excruciating pain, but that could be mitigated temporarily with the nerve-numbing anesthetics Marcaine and Xylocaine. Dunigan would also need a shot of adrenaline to, in effect, "wake up" the anesthetized area.

With the game fast approaching, head coach Adam Rita had told the doctors he needed a decision. Dunigan wasn't the only person affected, after all. If he were to play, Foggie's expectation of starting at quarterback in the Grey Cup would be shattered.

Rita was adamant that Dunigan's wife and parents sign off on any decision to let him play. "I'm not going to be the guy responsible for ending his career. This is a game. Not as important as the guy's career."

Accounts of exactly what went down in the ballroom vary among participants. Dunigan remembers being injected with painkillers before he attempted to throw, but Duguay insists that for ethical reasons, the doctors had to first see whether throwing was even possible. "The night before the game, there were no pharmaceuticals," he maintains. "Functionally I've got to see, and Matt's got to know, 'I can throw the ball. I can't throw a lob. I have to throw a dart.'"

At first Dunigan could barely propel the ball a few feet. "I couldn't move my arm," he says.

Gradually the joint loosened up and he was able to throw closer to his usual velocity. "A little more zip and a little more zip," says Duguay. "Then he starts throwing some heat on the ball."

After ten minutes of increasingly hard and accurate passes, everyone in the room had seen enough. Jackson assured Dunigan he could play without causing any long-term damage. "We can fix whatever happens," the doctor insisted.

Based on the pain he felt as he threw, Dunigan was skeptical. Long-term damage seemed a distinct possibility. But his ambition to start, finish, and win a Grey Cup was overwhelming. The final decision was easy.

"OK," Dunigan told the group. "Let's rock 'n' roll."

Now Rita had to break the news to Foggie, who had led the Argonauts to many victories in relief of Dunigan since he joined the team in August of 1990.

"What do you mean?" an incredulous Foggie asked his coach. "The guy's got a broken collarbone! He can't play."

Rita explained that Dunigan had secretly tested his arm. "Matt's getting up there in age and in his career. He's getting banged up a lot. This might be his last opportunity to win a Grey Cup. If he can play, I'm telling you he's going to play."

"If it was me in that position, would you have done the same thing?" Foggie asked.

"Yeah," Rita said.

"OK, I'm with you, Coach."

"That's all he had to say," Foggie says now. "If it were anybody other than Adam Rita, there's no way to tell how I would have reacted. But Adam was such a father figure to me. Whatever he was going to say, it was good with me."

Still, it was a sad conversation. "He got us to where we were at because Matty was hurt," Rita says of Foggie. "He was our starting quarterback when we ended the year, and he sat so Matt could play. Ultimate team player."

One of the few individuals outside the inner circle who found out about Dunigan's return was Rick Matsumoto, Argos beat reporter for the *Toronto Star*. He had been tipped off about the ballroom escapade. In the Sheraton hotel, he encountered Foggie, who had "this sour look on his face." Matsumoto snagged a brief quote from the backup quarterback: "That's the way it is. That's the system. If we win the Grey Cup, I'll be all right."

Most of Dunigan's teammates did not find out until game day. "That morning when we came in, he had his normal Dunigan swagger on," says Willie Gillus. "He was walking around with that intense look on his face. I knew there was no way they could keep him out of that football game."

The only way Dunigan was going to be held off the field, says Mike Campbell, "was to lock him up or put him in handcuffs."

Most Argonauts interviewed for this book support the decision to play Dunigan, although a handful suggest Foggie had earned the right to start. But it's clear that having one of the CFL's strongest leaders on the field provided additional motivation to an already supremely confident group. "The others look around and it's like, 'I've got Patton in the lineup. We're not going to lose,'" says Duguay.

Although Matsumoto's story in the Sunday *Star* spilled the beans, the identity of Toronto's starter still hadn't been officially announced when CBC went on the air 90 minutes before kickoff. The Stampeders were kept guessing as long as possible.[21]

Even the producer of a documentary the Argonauts had commissioned was not told right away. David Mitchell, who'd had inside access to the team throughout the year, was planning to put a wireless microphone on the Argo quarterback. "We were in the dressing room taking the radio mic off Rickey Foggie and putting it on Matt Dunigan at the very last minute. I felt like, 'Oh, man, this sucks.' But [Foggie] took it in stride."

In warmups, Dunigan's throws were weak and off-target. "Matt bounced the ball about ten feet from me," says David Williams. "It took two bounces before it got to me. You think, holy shit, the ball is going to hang or wobble. Matt could [normally] throw a ball through a hole. But there weren't any balls flying through holes."

Wobbly warmup tosses or not, Dunigan was playing. So was Pinball Clemons, who had limped around on crutches all week after suffering a

---

21 Staying mum about Dunigan was not the only way the Argos played mind games on the Stamps. It was the West Division team's turn to wear home uniforms, but McCarthy insisted the Argos' road uniforms had mistakenly been shipped overseas, so the team would have to wear its blue home jerseys. Stampeder brass spent a lot of psychic energy getting worked up into a fury over this. Argo equipment manager Danny Webb and his assistant, Steve McCoy, watched a TV report about the issue in their hotel room; McCoy was sitting on a bag full of white jerseys at the time. The team wore the road uniforms, as scheduled.

painful "turf-toe" injury in the Eastern Final. In the Grey Cup, Clemons barely touched the ball: three carries, one reception, one kickoff return and two punt returns. But the Stamps didn't know how badly he was hurt, and as one of the league's most dangerous players, he served a valuable purpose as a decoy. Calgary assigned its best defensive back, Darryl Hall, to shadow the Pinball all day.

* * *

When she learned the Grey Cup was going to be played in Winnipeg, Suzan Waks was aghast. "Open air? In the middle of winter? In Winnipeg?"

She was part of the group that boarded the Los Angeles Kings' jet for an early-morning flight to Winnipeg on Grey Cup Sunday. With her were McNall, Gretzky, family members, team executives, and a handful of celebrities, including actors Martin Short and Alan Thicke. Some were not dressed appropriately for a game to be played in temperatures well below zero.

One of them, Rod Martin, a retired Oakland Raider, showed up at the airport in jeans, shoes, no socks, and a light jacket. "Rod, we're going to Winnipeg," said Argos executive Roy Mlakar, who knew Martin from pickup basketball.

"I played on a frozen tundra field" in the NFL, Martin scoffed. "What do you mean, cold?"

Five hours later, the pilot got on the intercom as the booze-soaked jet made its final approach into Winnipeg. It was 70 degrees Fahrenheit in L.A., he said, and minus-30 at their destination. "We have a 100-degree swing."

After landing, the group boarded limos for Winnipeg Stadium. They saw people streaming towards the facility in thick parkas, snowmobile suits, heavy boots, and balaclavas. "Dressed like it's Alaska," Waks recalls. Many were clutching slabs of Styrofoam or cardboard, to be placed under their rear ends or feet to insulate against the cold.

Someone had set up comfortably heated trailers at field level for use by bigwigs. Martin, who had "played on a frozen tundra field," ensconced himself in one of these after ten minutes, and never left.

McNall, wearing a leather coat and a big toque, went back and forth between the trailers and the field. "I have no idea how the players could play," he says. "I had no clue as to what cold was."

Candy and Gretzky, having grown up in Canada, were dressed appropriately for the conditions. Standing on the sideline, they also added liquid insulation. Candy approached Argo head coach Adam Rita, who looked like the Michelin man in a heavy parka, balaclava and toque.

"Coach, you look pretty cold," Candy said. "You want some coffee?" He opened his coat to reveal a flask of alcohol. "I've got some anti-freeze in here."

Rita declined. "John, I've got to coach this game."

Some Argo fans from Toronto, who perhaps should have known better, were also underdressed. Bursey recalls showing up to the game in her "little Toronto fashion boots and this little, short jacket." A fanatic who seldom misses a play, she seriously considered returning to her hotel during the game. "At halftime, I can barely move. I'm crying. I didn't know it could get that cold. I had no idea."

Bursey took her "fashion boots" off in a bathroom and attempted to warm her feet under an electric hand dryer. Another who tried that was Diane Lee, the future wife of Argo star Pinball Clemons; she had flown up from her home in Florida. Her feet were stinging. "You didn't want to put your shoes back on because you knew it would hurt. The gloves I had,

I might as well not have worn any gloves because they didn't do anything at all. I thought, who watches football in the wintertime, with this cold?"

If watching was tough, especially for those unprepared for the deep freeze, playing was something else altogether.

Had the game been played a week earlier, conditions would have been unseasonably pleasant. It was a relatively balmy five degrees Celsius (41 Fahrenheit) on the Monday before the game. But a cold front moved into southern Manitoba, and it got colder and colder as the week went on.

Some Argonauts practised in shorts, determined to show that even though they played home games in a climate-controlled dome, they were not afraid of bad weather. Brian Warren and Darrell K. Smith posed with bare chests for a newspaper photo, saying, "We're ready to fight butt naked."

By game day, however, even tough, normally bare-armed offensive linemen were trying to minimize their exposure. Receiver David Williams recalls peeking at the field before kickoff. There was nobody warming up. "That's when you know it's cold, when there's no player on either team on the field."

When players were instructed to warm up, says cornerback Ed Berry, "I ran out and ran right back into the locker room. 'I'm good! I'll stretch in here.'"

* * *

As game time approached, Rocket Ismail seemed to grasp how important the Grey Cup is to Canadians, including his homegrown teammates. "I'm jealous of you right now," he told Paul Masotti.

"You're jealous of me?" Masotti replied. "You're making four million dollars."

The Rocket elaborated. "I wish I felt like you did. This is part of you. You're going to go win the national championship. You're going to live here when we win, and I'm going to be down in the states."

In the locker room moments before the game, another American seized the moment to say a few words. Chris Gaines had fired up teammates the day before with his customary rhyme at the end of the on-field walk-through: "I've told you before/and I'm telling you again/Sunday against Calgary/I guarantee we're gonna win."

But this wasn't another "New Jack" call-and-response rap. These words were from the heart.

"This is serious," said Jethro, bringing a sudden hush to the room. "This is my last game. I wanted to play this game forever, but this is it. I'm going to leave it all out on the field. I want you guys to, as well. We've got the team to do it. Let's do it for each other. Let's finish this thing off. Let's make it special."

After conferring with the team's medical staff late in the season, Gaines had made the wrenching decision to retire. He was just 26 years old, but accumulated damage from four or five broken ankles over the years meant that if he continued playing, he would soon be unable to walk without a cane. "The longer you play," Dr. Jackson had told him, "the more damage you'll do."

Gaines regularly played through pain that would have felled many others. "We'd see him during the week, purple," says Carl Brazley. Teammates couldn't believe he was even walking. "No, no, I got it," he'd reply. "I'm going to be all right. We've got to strap it up."

But the medical advice couldn't be ignored. Gaines had taken a few days to reflect upon it, finally concluding that being able to live a normal life with his family was more important than football. It was a grim reality for a man who had become the heart and soul of the Argonauts, not only for his pre-game raps but also his superb play at the centre of a defence loaded with stars. He was the epitome of a CFL middle linebacker, able to pound running backs into the ground, drop adeptly into pass coverage, and chase down ball carriers from sideline to sideline. And with hair shaved down to the wood and a scary scowl, he was one mean-looking dude.

Before the Eastern Final, Gaines had turned his head into an inspirational banner. He had a barber shave everything short and use a razor to cut in lightning bolts that pointed to a word: WIN.

"When Chris made that speech, man, that fired everybody up," Gillus says. "We could not wait to get on that field. It went from 32 below zero to a warm, balmy day for the players in that locker room. We didn't feel the cold. That speech from Chris Gaines gave us heat and warmth and the ability to go out and fight."

Gillus may have been exaggerating slightly regarding the cold.

Gaines' retirement announcement wasn't the only thing that fired up the Argonauts before the game. The introduction of the team's starting defence featured the most intimidating entry imaginable.

When player introductions before big games began in the 1960s, they were stilted, serious, sometimes almost sombre. Each player would jog to a specific spot on the field, stop, smile (or scowl) while his name was announced, then trot off to join his mates and wait for the next player to follow the same drill.

By the 1980s, players no longer had to stop and pose, but they still ran on as their names were announced. That's what fans saw when the Calgary Stampeders were introduced at the 1991 Grey Cup. The starting members of the Stamps' offence, from centre Doug Davies to quarterback Danny Barrett, took turns running between two lines of snowsuit-clad cheerleaders while annoyingly repetitive, brassy music echoed through the stadium and on TV monitors.

When it came to the Argonauts' turn, the anti-Toronto sentiment started cascading from the Winnipeg Stadium stands. Defensive end Brian Warren was announced first. Instead of jogging onto the field, Warren popped off his helmet, raised it over his head, and began walking, slowly. His breath created big clouds of steam in the bitterly cold sunshine. His brow was furrowed, his grim visage leaving no doubt about his serious purpose.

Boos got louder when defensive tackle Harold Hallman followed. Helmet raised, Hallman sauntered casually past the cheerleaders, slowly trailing Warren. Defensive tackle Rodney Harding came next, pointing to the large white "A" on his helmet, turning to make sure everyone in the stadium saw the gesture.

Raising the helmets, says Harding, was intended to show the Stampeders that they would be hit, hard, all afternoon. The sentiment, Warren adds, was "let's take it up over the edge. Put your hat up and say I'm going to feed you this all day."

Vitriol was cascading from the stands, the boos of 50,000 spectators easily drowning out the cheers of the handful of Argo fans in attendance. "They were booing us so loud, the turf was shaking," says Mike Campbell.

The funereal procession continued through the remaining members of the Argo defence. "It's really hard to walk out there because you're so jacked," says linebacker Don Moen. "You're used to bolting, and now you're going super-slow."

After the rest of the team followed the starting defence to centre field, 37 helmets were raised together in a gesture of solidarity and determination. Walking out with helmets up "made the hair on your neck stand up," says safety Dave Van Belleghem. "Get the fans even more riled up, so they can boo us even longer."

In his spotter's booth high above the field, defensive co-ordinator Dennis Meyer watched Harding point his finger at the A on his helmet, and just knew what was going to happen. "There was no doubt in my mind we were going to win the game. Hey, we're ready for this! When Rodney did that, it just sealed the deal."

* * *

Despite the monstrous wind chill, 51,985 hearty souls had packed into Winnipeg Stadium. More than a third of them squeezed together on temporary metal benches in the end zones.

The contrast between the enthusiastic sellout crowd and the previous year's Grey Cup was stark. Despite Ornest's belief that only the big cities could provide a revenue bonanza, the 1990 game in Vancouver had been a disaster, with thousands of empty seats. The league's eight teams came away with just $145,000 each from gate receipts. In 1991, teams received $375,000 each from the $3 million sent to the league.

Organizers in Winnipeg had succeeded in doing what Murphy and Houssin believed possible. They had made money "scalping" tickets, and used it to pay down the Blue Bombers' debt.

They had also done something else, which few were able to foresee at the time. The league inadvertently discovered the value of playing the game outdoors in cities where it meant the most, and where there was less competition for attention. It may have been freezing, but the enthusiasm of Winnipeggers for the Grey Cup was palpable. Everyone in town was caught up in football fever. "This is the soul of the CFL," Grey Cup committee chair Art Mauro said after the game. "It's not in Toronto or Vancouver. [In smaller cities] we feel strongly about this national event. It's not just a football game; it's part of the fabric of Canada."

A year later, the Grey Cup would return to SkyDome, with the Argonauts hoping for big profits. There was virtually no buzz in Toronto about the game, and ticket sales were so challenging that the Argos were only too happy to cede the rights to the 1993 game to Calgary. By 1995, the final had even been played in little Regina, and over the past 25 years it has gone to "small cities" 16 times, including three more games in Winnipeg. Far from ruining the Grey Cup, the small markets breathed new life into it and, surprisingly, earned more revenue.

Cal Murphy, who died in 2012, the year of the Grey Cup's centennial, would be proud.

The Pride and the Glory

O NE OF THE THINGS that made Chris Gaines' locker-room announcement that this was his last game so poignant is that teammates knew he wasn't going to get much of a chance to leave it all out on the field. The spiritual leader of the Argonauts defence would be playing a drastically reduced role, for the good of the team.

Under the direction of offensive co-ordinator John Hufnagel, the Calgary Stampeders had been successful with a scheme never used before: the six-pack. Calgary regularly took its running back and fullback off the field and replaced them with two receivers, in addition to the usual four. (The formation is now used regularly in the CFL, as is a "five-pack" variation in the 11-man football played south of the border.)

Standard CFL defences played with five defensive backs, so defending against six receivers meant having a linebacker cover one of them. That could create a mismatch since linebackers tended to be heavier and slower. To counter the six-pack, Argos defensive co-ordinator Dennis Meyer elected to have veteran defensive back Jim Rockford enter the game in passing situations. Going off the field would be Gaines.

"They were probably going to be in that offence a lot," says Gaines. "It's the biggest game of the year and you're not even going to be a starter. But it was brilliant, and the best thing to do for the team."

It was indeed best for the team. Calgary used the six-pack relentlessly. Quarterback Danny Barrett threw 56 passes, more than any Grey Cup quarterback before or since, and Rockford got inserted as the sixth DB for much of the game, with Gaines watching from the bench.

Barrett's first throw of the day was a disaster for the Stampeders.

On Calgary's initial possession, the quarterback looked to his right and lofted a pass towards receiver Pee-Wee Smith, the hero of a late-game comeback victory in the Western Final a week earlier. Barrett had thrown only five interceptions all season, but this pass sailed beyond Smith's reach and directly into the arms of Ed Berry.

Not exactly renowned among teammates for having great hands, the Toronto cornerback deftly snared the pass and raced untouched to the end zone for a 50-yard touchdown. As he hit the goal-line, Berry turned to celebrate. Teammates, including some who had run all the way from the Argo bench, piled on top, overjoyed to have taken the lead so early.

An interception returned for a touchdown, "pick-six," is one of the biggest momentum changers in football. Hugely inspiring to the team that scores, monumentally deflating to the team that's scored upon. In the opening minutes of a championship game, the impact is magnified. "It's like the first ten seconds of a hockey game and you score a goal," says Duguay. "The game just flippin' started, man!"

On one of the Argos' first plays from scrimmage, Calgary defensive tackle Stu Laird drilled Matt Dunigan into the rock-hard turf. Toronto fans, who had been surprised to see Dunigan on the field after the quarterback broke his collarbone the previous week, held their collective breath. Dunigan bounced right up.

"We're not getting him out of the game," Laird told teammates. "He's going to be playing the whole game.'"

It was the first of many hits Dunigan took as he was pounded repeatedly by a ferocious pass rush. His throwing arm hung limply at times, and he was examined on the sideline by club doctors after one particularly hellacious hit from Kent Warnock.

"He just crunched Dunigan," says Argo tackle Kelvin Pruenster. "Matt fell right on his shoulder, with Warnock on top of him. The cold just made that extra bad. It seemed like it would be way worse in that temperature."

Dunigan told Rita at one point that his arm "felt like a rag." Yet in keeping with his customary quarterback-who-thinks-he's-a-linebacker mentality, he barrelled straight into defenders whenever he carried the ball.

Dunigan's running was about the only offence the Argos could muster for much of the game. By halftime, they had accumulated just three first downs and a mere 50 net yards. Despite that, they led 11-10 at the break, thanks to Berry's touchdown, a single point on a kick, and a field goal by Lance Chomyc.

At times it seemed there were two games happening at once. Argos versus Stampeders, and both teams versus the cold. The sun shone brightly for most of the game (the last Grey Cup played in daylight hours), but the Argo sideline was on the shady west side of the stadium. Calgary coach Wally Buono "must have been a good Christian because he sat in the sun all day," says Rita. "I was in the shade freezing my butt off."

Large propane heaters were installed on the sidelines. Many players quickly deduced they were better off staying away from them. "As soon as you pulled away from it, it felt like your hands were frozen solid," says Berry.

Ball boys found a use for the heaters: to thaw bottles of water and Gatorade that otherwise froze solid almost instantly.

Equipment staff had about ten seconds to adjust shoulder pads before their fingers went numb. Helmets would freeze if removed, and become difficult to put back on.

Every time Dunigan took his helmet off on the sideline, the protective air bladder inside would burst. He wouldn't realize it and would return to the field without the added layer of air for protection. Finally, equipment manager Danny Webb instructed him to leave his helmet on at all times.

That wasn't the only problem with Dunigan's helmet. On one of the hits he took, his head hit the turf and the helmet cracked open. He would end the game wearing a spare helmet normally assigned to reserve running back Paul Palmer.

Players quickly discovered that playing on frozen artificial turf was like playing on concrete. "It felt like you fell from 20 feet when you hit the ground," says receiver David Williams.

They also found it difficult to understand coaches' instructions. "Their faces were frozen," says receiver Paul Masotti. "They couldn't move their mouths like they normally would."

Running was like trying to drive a car without oil lubricating the engine, says Rockford. "I mean, you couldn't move."

"You almost couldn't function," adds Pruenster "Neurologically, you weren't connected to your legs."

In addition to multiple layers of undergarments, some players slathered Vaseline petroleum jelly on their faces and arms to prevent their skin from cracking. Many had wrapped their ankles and wrists loosely, fearing they might cut off circulation if the tape was too tight.

The concern was well-founded. Cornerback Reggie Pleasant, who always tied his shoelaces tightly to prevent his feet from sliding around inside his cleats, would end up with severe frostbite. He was too numb

YEAR OF THE ROCKET

to notice during the game, but in the locker room afterwards, Pleasant's thawing feet "were purple and swollen. Excruciating pain. Believe it or not, there was talk of amputation—a toe or two." It took a couple of months for Pleasant to recover, and he had tingling sensations in his feet for a long time after that.

"You ask yourself, 'Was it worth it?' Honestly, I felt it would have been. But thank God they didn't have to amputate one or two toes."

On the CBC telecast, announcer Don Wittman, a Winnipegger himself, naturally mentioned the conditions. It was minus-17.5 Celsius (zero degrees Fahrenheit) at kickoff, with 13-kilometre-an-hour (nine-mile-an-hour) winds. On the scale used in 1991, that created a wind chill of 1,400 watts per square metre. In today's scale, that would be expressed as wind chill of about minus-25 C (minus-13 F).

Wittman updated viewers about the temperature throughout the game. Watching at home, countless Winnipeggers, sensitive about the habitability of their city, screamed at him to shut up. "The people in Winnipeg went nuts," says Brian Williams, who hosted CBC's pre-game coverage. "'How can you say that? You're one of us!'"

* * *

The effect of the nerve-numbing anesthetics Dunigan received before the game was unfortunately short-lived. He got shot up again at halftime. A few teammates recall seeing large needles and hearing howls of anguish from the quarterback as he was getting injected. "You could hear it, Matty screaming," says Webb. "You knew what he had signed up for, and we were going to war."

Dunigan knew Rita had made "a ballsy call" to start him at quarterback when the Argos had one of the league's best backups in Rickey Foggie. But

Rita's confidence extended only so far. In the third quarter, he threatened to yank Dunigan.

Rita generally allowed his quarterbacks to call their own plays, but from time to time he would insist on a particular call. Knowing Dunigan could be stubborn, Rita had given Foggie special instructions: "When I want a play and he doesn't want to call that play, I want you to warm up."

"You're not going to do that to him," Foggie said.

"Fuck yeah," replied Rita. "He wanted to play in this game, then he listens to what I have to say."

The head coach, who doubled as the team's offensive co-ordinator, had spotted a deficiency in Calgary's defence he wanted to exploit. He told Dunigan to call a deep pass that required the quarterback to fake a handoff and briefly turn his back to the defence. Dunigan, tired of getting slammed around by Calgary's pass rushers, said it was a "bullshit" idea.

"I don't want any contact," Dunigan told Rita. "I don't want to turn my back."

"Foggie!" Rita called out. "Get warmed up!"

"Oh, you're going to do me like this, eh?" Dunigan railed at his coach.

"I'll do whatever it takes," retorted Rita.

Dunigan says now that his reluctance to call the play was mainly because he had been struggling to read defensive coverages throughout the game, perhaps because of the painkillers he had received. "I was just not all there. It was like an out-of-body experience. It was like I was down here [but] watching it happen from above."

After Rita threatened to yank him, he acquiesced. "Yeah, I'll do it, Coach. Hell, you had the balls to put me out here, the least I could do is run the plays you want to call."

Dunigan called the play. He took the snap, turned his back to the defence and executed a fake handoff so effectively that the TV camera operator stayed on the decoy, Pinball Clemons.

Dunigan squared up, set his feet and, despite an arm that had looked to be practically falling off his body at times during the game, uncorked a beautiful deep spiral. "You think he can't throw it, and he's going to whistle one right by you," says Berry. "That's just how he plays."

Running into the clear up the middle, Darrell K. Smith adjusted to the ball's trajectory, looked it into his hands and stepped untouched into the Calgary end zone.

"I threw the ball as best I could and he was so wide open, it was a walk in," Dunigan says. "Adam knew it was going to work. He had set it up, and thank God my stubborn Irish temper didn't kick in."

The 48-yard touchdown pass ignited the small contingent of Argo fans in the crowd, and stunned everyone else.

"If there was any concern about Dunigan's ability to put some zip on the football, he certainly disproved [it] right there," said Wittman on CBC's broadcast. "He rifled that one down the seam."

"I don't know what they did at halftime," added colour commentator Joe Galat. "Maybe he got hypnotized. In this quarter he looks like he can zing that football."

As various angles of the TD were replayed, one showed a jubilant Dunigan thrusting both arms into the air. "Hey, he's lifting his right arm, too," Galat said. "That's supposed to be the bad arm."

Dunigan came back to the Argo sideline and went straight to Rita. "You are luckier than a dog with two dicks," he told the coach.

"I'm lucky I've got you," Rita replied.

* * *

Early in the fourth quarter, with the Argos up 19-14 after Smith's touchdown reception, Barrett was intercepted for a second time. Pleasant ran the interception back 28 yards to the Calgary 12, creating a glorious opportunity for Toronto to pad the lead. Dunigan, however, was forced to throw the ball away under pressure on first down, and a toss to Paul Masotti in the end zone was batted away by Calgary's Ken Watson. Chomyc, who had earlier missed two of three field-goal attempts, made one from 19 yards and the Argos led 22-14.

Toronto stopped Calgary on its next possession, got the ball back but was unable to pick up a first down. Ilesic managed only a 16-yard punt into the wind and Calgary started its next possession at the Argo 31. Barrett found David Sapunjis for 19 yards, then hit Allen Pitts with a pass near the goal-line. Pitts sidestepped a tackle attempt from Carl Brazley and scored a touchdown that cut the Argo lead to a single point, 22-21 with just under 11 minutes remaining.

Then came the play that will be remembered as long as they play football.

Rocket Ismail had not been having a great game. At one point, Dunigan ran up to him after a pass intended for Ismail had failed to connect. "Run the goddamn route or get off the field!" the quarterback yelled.

Just before halftime, Calgary's Jerry Kauric had launched a punt that Ismail fielded at his own five-yard line. He squeezed through a gap between tacklers, cut to the outside and began racing up the sideline. He easily dodged Kauric's attempted tackle, cut inside behind teammate Andrew Murray, and spun away from another tackler, only to fumble. Calgary's Paul Clatney pounced on the ball, ruining an inspiring 68-yard return.

On Calgary's next punt, Ismail fumbled again. The ball was recovered by an Argonaut, but the play was negated by an offside penalty that allowed the Stamps to retain possession.

The $4.5-million man had twice lost the football, and although neither fumble had cost the Argos any points, he was inconsolable at halftime.

"Hey, Rocket, you're fine," Gaines told him.

Gaines then turned his attention to teammates who manned the kick-return units. "All we've got to do, guys, is block for him. He's going to take one back. We're going to break one. You guys on the return team are doing your job; just keep doing what you're doing."

Other teammates echoed Gaines. "Let it go," they told Ismail. "It's no big deal. We've got the whole second half. Don't worry about it."

Murray, one of the blockers on kick and punt returns, put it to Rocket more forcefully: "What are you going to do about it? Complain and go in the tank? Shut up and let's go!"

But Ismail's second half wasn't going a lot better. After returning another Kauric punt, he stepped out of bounds at Toronto's 12-yard line. One of the three Stampeders who surrounded him was Dan Wicklum, whose late hit two months earlier had given the Rocket a concussion. This time, as the two men jawed at each other, Wicklum knocked his facebar into Ismail's. The Rocket responded by tossing the football at Wicklum, drawing a penalty for unsportsmanlike conduct.

Now, with just over ten minutes left in the game, things were looking grim for Ismail and the Argonauts. The clock was ticking down, and their margin had dwindled to a single, precarious point. Calgary had the momentum, completing pass after pass, moving the football up and down the field almost at will. The Argos' season and their owners' arguably insane decision to pay one player more than the rest of the team combined looked in jeopardy.

With the sun setting behind the west-side stands at Winnipeg Stadium, and the temperature dropping even lower, team owner Bruce McNall approached Ismail on the sideline. "Great game, man, whatever happens."

Ismail looked squarely at the man who signed his paycheques.

"I got this," he said matter-of-factly.

"You could see his excitement," says teammate Willie Gillus. "Him saying, 'It's my time now.'"

Rita called his kick-return team over for a conference before the kickoff after Pitts' touchdown. The group included three superb returners—Ismail, Clemons and Smith—as well as most of the Canadians who backed up on offence and defence. These guys considered themselves starters on special teams. "All of them were just nasty," says Gaines.

Rita felt certain Calgary would try to keep the ball out of Ismail's hands by kicking to Smith. He instructed the two to swap positions at the last second: "D.K., when the ball is kicked, rotate out. Rocket, you come over and field the ball. Pinball, you lurk out there and block somebody."

Ismail asked for confirmation: "I catch the ball?"

"Yeah," the coach replied. "I don't give a fuck where the ball is, you catch it, run up two, three steps, and head for the far end."

Smith objected: "I can do that!"

Murray, one of the blockers on the kick unit, told Smith: "Shut the fuck up and just listen to Coach."

As the players went onto the field, special-teams captain Paul Nastasiuk suggested a tweak to the blocking scheme. Assistant coach Mike Levenseller had called for the return to go up the middle of the field.

"Guys, he wants a middle return. Let's switch up and do a right," Nastasiuk said. "What do you say?"

Nastasiuk remembers that "everybody kind of made a collective decision" to have Ismail veer to his right.

As Rita had predicted, Calgary wanted to kick the ball away from the Rocket. The plan was to send it to Toronto's left, near the sideline, but the ball was hard and difficult to kick accurately in the cold weather. It bounced five or six times. Smith was in position to grab it, but instead yelled back at Ismail, "You! You! You!"

The ball popped into Ismail's arms halfway between the sideline and the hashmark. Calgary's coverage unit had too many men converging on the sideline to adjust to where it landed, says Andy McVey of the Stamps. "Everyone just got caught running deep right, and the ball didn't quite go there."

Ismail took a few quick steps forward, then cut to his right. Argonauts were furiously throwing blocks all around him, not all of them legal. "I held on that play," admits Bruce Elliott. "I grabbed the guy and Rocket ran by. I'm looking around for flags. There were no flags, so I'm OK."

On the TV broadcast, Wittman made one of his most memorable calls: "The Rocket looks for a hole. If he gets to the outside this time, he's gone!"

Clemons, who had wedged off one of the Calgary pursuers, heard what was going on more than he saw it. "The [crowd] noise is what told me he's moving. There were people between us, and I was trying to look over, but it was the noise that alerted me that something special was happening."

Further upfield, Dave Van Belleghem saw that if he managed to impede Calgary's Greg Peterson, Ismail likely would not be caught. "He was the last guy to seal off to get [Rocket] all the way to the outside. In the back of my mind was, 'Don't hold, don't clip.' I got him enough that there was no way he was going to make the tackle, and I let him go instantly."

On TV, Galat interrupted Wittman's play call with one word: "Goodbye!"

Calgary's McVey kept up his own futile pursuit. "I chased him down and was not far behind him . . . but he was gliding. I was pumping as hard as I could, and you could tell he probably had two more gears left in him if he needed to hit it."

Ismail stretched out his arms in triumph, looked over to the Argonauts bench and romped into the end zone. He had run 87 yards, the longest kickoff return in Grey Cup history.

"That [return] doesn't happen unless 11 other guys in front of him make the blocks," McVey notes. "They executed, he found a lane, and that was it."

The blockers did indeed execute superbly. But the play also wouldn't have happened without Ismail's speed, determination, and uncanny ability to make a big play when it mattered most. He had done it in titanic college matches for Notre Dame, he had done it with a punt-return TD to beat the Stamps late in the season (exacting revenge a month after he had been concussed by Wicklum), he had ended Winnipeg's playoff hopes a week earlier, and he had done it again in the Grey Cup.

In practice, Ismail ran all the way to the end zone every time he caught a pass or a kick, says teammate Jeff Braswell. "He wouldn't stop. He would keep going to the end zone." He was a firm believer that what you did in practice, you were going to do in a game.

Back at the Argo bench, Ismail went to Rita and acknowledged the late switch that had him, not Smith, field the kick. "Coach, that was an awesome play."

"Yeah," Rita replied, "you ran by four guys. I got you the ball, that's all."

* * *

The Argos were now up 29-21 with a little over ten minutes remaining, plenty of time for Calgary to make a comeback. But the Argos had a little more special-teams magic.

With the Argos kicking off into the wind after Ismail's touchdown, Rita and Levenseller sensed an opportunity. After Toronto's first touchdown of the game, kicker Hank Ilesic had deliberately punched the ensuing kickoff high into the air. Calgary's Pee-Wee Smith mishandled it, and Keith Castello of the Argos raced downfield and recovered. Toronto was unable to capitalize on the turnover for any more than a single point, but a seed had been planted.

Unlike almost every other kicker in pro football, Ilesic didn't kick soccer-style, from the side. Instead, he tied a shoelace between the toe of his kicking boot and his ankle, creating what amounted to a club, and approached the ball straight on. This old-school approach allowed him to "get underneath the ball lower than a soccer-style [kicker]," Ilesic says. "I can drive a ball straight up in the air. Almost like a scoop."

The frigid conditions this day made the football feel hard, "like kicking a brick," says Chomyc. A heavy ball doesn't travel as far as usual, and the strong wind made it even tougher to get distance. One of Kauric's punts for Calgary had gone just five yards before sailing out of bounds earlier in the game. But Ilesic, nicknamed Thunderfoot, had a strong leg, which meant Calgary had to respect his ability to drive the ball deep, even into the wind.

The Stampeders had a gap in their alignment: men deep, men up close, and a big open area in between. If the kick landed in the right spot, players up front would not want to turn around and go back for the ball; returners downfield would be too far back to come up in time.

"Can we do a sky-pooch kick?" Rita asked Levenseller.

The answer was yes.

"Who do we have in there to get the ball?" asked the coach.

The answer was Castello.

"Castello will get the ball," Rita said confidently.

As they returned to the field, Ilesic told Castello exactly where he was going to land the football. "I'm putting it up there," he said. "Go get it."

The high kick came down exactly where Ilesic intended. "The ball just died," says Levenseller. "It was like hitting it into a hurricane, and it dropped."

Returner Keyvan Jenkins frantically raced up from deep on the field in an effort to corral the ball. Instead, it bounced off his foot and into Castello's arms.

For perhaps the only time in football history, a single player had recovered two fumbles on deliberately pooched kickoffs in the same game.

Castello "is my player of the game, even today," says Rita. "He's my biggest hero."

"I don't know if I consider myself a hero," says Castello, "but looking back, it was two important possessions."

Castello's second fumble recovery of the game gave the Argos possession of the ball at Calgary's 36-yard-line. On second down, Dunigan took a deep drop, rolled to his left, planted his feet and somehow summoned the arm strength to hurl a pass 45 yards to the end zone. Five players were bunched tightly together: three Calgary defensive backs and Toronto receivers David Williams and Paul Masotti.

Williams was the intended receiver, but receivers are taught that if a ball is coming your way, you take it regardless of who it's aimed at. "You attack the ball," Rita says. "Masotti saw it first, and he got it."

"Everything was super quiet," Masotti says. "I didn't see or feel anybody around me. The ball was just slowly rotating, fluttering a bit and it just kind of fell into my hands. I just kind of stopped the ball, cradled it, and fell."

In his jubilation about scoring, Masotti raced to the bench to celebrate, forgetting that he was supposed to be the holder on the point-after attempt.

"He lost his mind and forgot the convert," says kicker Lance Chomyc. Andrew Murray dashed onto the field to fill his spot. "Thank God it went through," Murray says.

The Argos had scored two touchdowns in a span of 45 seconds. It was 36-21 with nine and a half minutes left. It was now up to the defence to close the game out.

Calgary started its next possession at its own 32-yard line. Barrett completed five passes and mixed in three running plays, setting up a first down at Toronto's two-yard line. Barrett tried a pass but had to throw the ball away under pressure from Harold Hallman.

On second down, Hufnagel sent his two backs onto the field, getting rid of the six-pack receiver set that had been working productively all day. That prompted the Argos to send in Gaines, who had watched much of the game from the sideline. It seemed all but certain that the Stampeders would attempt to run the ball in for a touchdown.

Instead, Barrett dropped back to pass again. Bursting with pent-up energy, Gaines roared in and sacked the quarterback for a 10-yard loss. Barrett's third-down pass bounced off his receiver's hands, turning the ball over to Toronto.

That would turn out to be Calgary's last best hope. One final shot at scoring resulted in Pleasant's second interception of the game, in the Toronto end zone.

With the clock running down, Matt Dunigan was finally able to do what he had dreamed of doing throughout his nine years in the CFL: take the snap and drop to one knee to down the ball as the Grey Cup-winning quarterback.

Time expired. The Argos were champs. The Hollywood season had its perfect ending.

* * *

The old saw that "offence sells tickets, defence wins games, and special teams win championships" may never have been truer than in the 79th Grey Cup. The Argo offence, despite all of its big-name stars, struggled mightily. Toronto managed just seven first downs, tying the record for fewest in a Grey Cup, and accumulated only 174 total yards (almost half of that on two plays, the Smith and Masotti touchdown receptions). The offence was opportunistic, however, scoring 11 points after Calgary turnovers.

Dunigan completed just 12 of 29 passes for 142 yards. His 44 yards on the ground led both teams, but he also fumbled three times, with Calgary recovering two of them. Somehow, he was able to throw long ten times, twice for touchdowns, and his repeated use of deep passes kept Calgary's defence guessing.

Despite surrendering 406 yards and 28 first downs, the Argo defence was superb. It made up some of the yards it gave up to Calgary with interception returns of 50 and 26 yards, as well as six quarterback sacks that cost Calgary 56 yards.

But it was Toronto's special teams that proved to be the difference in the game. The Argos scored 15 points directly as a result of the work of their kick-return and kick-coverage units: Ismail's touchdown return, plus Masotti's TD and a single point after Castello's two fumble recoveries.

The Argos accumulated 326 yards on 13 total returns (seven punts, six kickoffs), while limiting the Stampeders to a mere 113 yards on 15 total runbacks.

After the final gun sounded, spectators flooded onto the field. CFL commissioner Donald Crump hurriedly presented the Grey Cup trophy to the Argo co-captains, Dan Ferrone and Don Moen.

In a locker room jammed with family members, Hollywood interlopers, hangers-on and media, tears flowed freely. Dunigan sobbed as he hugged his mother. "I don't want to talk about my arm," he told her. "That might be my career right there."

Dunigan later told reporters, "Half these tears are joy, half these tears are pain. The shoulder feels like mush right now. I'm sure it's going to cost me, but it's well worth the price to know that for once in my life, I took the last snap in a Grey Cup victory."

Williams, one of Dunigan's favourite receivers dating back to their time in B.C., embraced his tearful teammate. "Matt went out there with half an arm and won the big game."

Carl Brazley sobbed openly in the locker room. So did John Candy. "I walk in with the Cup," says Moen. "John's standing right by my locker, crying like a baby. His tears, he was just so happy."

"I'm speechless," Candy told a camera crew. "I'm choked up. To be part of this team, and the emotion that's involved with it, I'll never forget it."

Wayne Gretzky, who had stayed warm with adult beverages, was loose and relaxed as he took in the scene with his wife, Janet. Equipment assistant Jason Colero, gathering gear in the midst of the bedlam, approached them. "Sorry, guys, I have to hang up a shirt," he said.

"Go over there and celebrate with everybody," Gretzky replied. "You're going to have plenty of time to hang your stuff up. This doesn't come very often. Go have some fun."

The Great One, a student of sports history, had noted to team executive Brian Cooper that if the Argos were to win, he would join Lionel Conacher in having his name on both the Grey Cup and the Stanley Cup. Conacher won the Grey Cup with the Argonauts in 1921, and the Stanley Cup with Chicago and the Montreal Maroons a decade later. Gretzky, who won four

Stanley Cups with the Edmonton Oilers, was named Canada's athlete of the century at the end of 1999. Conacher had been named athlete of the half-century in 1950.[22]

For some members of the team, winning represented a financial windfall. Each Argonaut received $16,200 from the league, pocket change to Ismail, but roughly half the entire season's pay for young Canadians like J. P. Izquierdo.

"Drinking out of the Grey Cup, and you get your bonus!" thought Izquierdo. "It wasn't much of a deal for Rocket, but it was a big deal for me."

The Rocket, whose deal with the Argonauts included endorsing Ford products, won a GMC Suburban as the game's most valuable player. He handed the keys to his mother.

Once the locker room cleared out, the entire Argonauts organization, family members, the Los Angeles contingent and many of the Argo fans who had made the trek to Winnipeg gathered for a raucous celebration at the team's hotel. Chomyc shared the joy of winning with his wife, his infant daughter and celebrities like Janet Gretzky and Martin Short. Candy picked up seven-week-old Andrea Chomyc: "Your daddy kicks the ball so far, and have you seen my movie *Planes, Trains and Automobiles?*"

As the owners and executives gave blissful, drunken speeches, says Jeff Boyd, "everybody seized the moment to say: no matter what happens, there'll never be a year like this. Not just the game itself; there'll never be a year like this."

---

22 Carl Voss (Grey Cup with Queen's University in 1924, Stanley Cup with Chicago in 1938) is the only athlete other than Conacher to win both trophies. Norm Kwong won the Grey Cup as a player with Calgary and Edmonton, and the Stanley Cup as an executive with the Calgary Flames. Harold Ballard won both as an owner of the Toronto Maple Leafs and Hamilton Tiger-Cats. Oddly, Gretzky's prediction that his name would be on both Cups did not come true until 2007, when the CFL replaced the silver plate listing members of the 1991 Argonauts. The original plate had McNall's name engraved, but omitted Gretzky's and Candy's names.

The Throw

FOR NEARLY THREE DECADES it has been a mystery, a bit of Canadian folklore that everyone who saw it remembers vividly. And yet nobody who saw it seems to know the full story.

Who threw the beer can at Rocket Ismail?

With just over ten minutes to go in the 79th Grey Cup, Ismail scooped up Mark McLoughlin's bouncing kickoff and cut to his right behind a wall of blockers. By the time he crossed the Calgary 10-yard line, there were no Stampeders within 20 yards of him. Ismail spread his arms in triumph and looked to his left.

At that instant, something landed on the field to his right, almost hitting his feet. In those days of fuzzy, low-definition television, it looked at first like a snowball, and was identified as such by CBC play-by-play announcer Don Wittman.

On closer inspection, however, it was no snowball. It was a beer can, spinning its contents out into instantly frozen foam on the rock-hard artificial turf. It had been thrown from the stands. But by whom? Why? And what type of beer?

Although the beer can appears from time to time on TV features about crazy moments in sports, nothing much has been written about it since it was thrown. But there had to be a story behind it.

Surely someone in Winnipeg would know something. As Gary Lawless, then a Winnipeg-based reporter, said in a 2015 feature for TSN, "no one really knows who threw it. But everyone knows someone who knows someone who knows the guy."

Based on a seating map of the now-demolished Winnipeg Stadium, it was evident the throw had likely come from Section S, the northernmost section on the building's east side. Section S was known as the student section, notorious for heavy drinking and partying.

Denizens of Section S in the 1980s and 1990s liked to throw peanuts at other fans (later switching to marshmallows at the behest of security). If someone left a game before it was over, dozens of fans in the section would start jangling their keys and chanting, "Beat the traffic!" Winnipeg's famous "beer snake," hundreds of emptied Solo cups stacked together and winding their way through the stands, was by several accounts inaugurated in Section S.[23]

In a Zapruderesque twist, a close look at Grey Cup video replays reveals a second can flying onto the field seconds later from the corner of the end zone, likely Section P or O. Watching replays shown to him by CBC in 2006, Ismail noticed the second shot: "Oh, that was a beer can, too. It just didn't have the same oomph."

After this book's quest to find the thrower was revealed to Winnipeggers by Doug Speirs, award-winning humour columnist and feature writer for the *Winnipeg Free Press*, several individuals came forward claiming to have information.

---

23 The tradition lives on in Winnipeg's new IG Field. Other cities and leagues sometimes claim to have invented the beer snake, but Winnipeggers know better.

Trevor Finch did not attend the 1991 Grey Cup, but was later told by fans whose season tickets predated his own that the thrower sat in Section S. "One person says it was this guy Dwayne; someone else says no, it was another guy. It's amazing how everyone remembers that, and it's also amazing that no one has sat around and trumpeted, 'Yeah, I was the one.'"

Claudette Thibert had become a Section S season-ticket holder in 1990. Guys named Glenn and Dave sat near her, and although she didn't know them well, or even know their last names, she knew Dave as "Gotchman," a guy who attended games in his underwear. She was certain the can had been thrown by his buddy, Glenn.

"He threw his can of beer. We saw it fall and we went, 'Oh, what are you doing?' Some guy said, 'You're wasting your beer.' And that's pretty much the story. No security came. He just threw it, and everybody was laughing."

Patrick Dirks bought season tickets in the late 1980s, when the Bombers offered a deal for students: 50 bucks for the full season, in Section S. Like Thibert, he remembers "the underwear man," who sat one row lower and a few seats to his left. The can was thrown from the area where the underwear man sat, he says, comparing his recollections to a famous *Seinfeld* episode in which baseball star Keith Hernandez was accused of spitting on characters Kramer and Newman:

The trajectory of the beer—this sounds like the magic-loogie episode— just from where it landed, we could tell it had been thrown from our area.

You quickly look over and what I remember is the usual crowd: underwear man and his buddy. Everyone going, what the heck happened?

And there was only one person who wasn't doing that. It had to have been him. From the trajectory of the beer, it would have been within a

ten-foot-square area, and he was the only one who was sort of looking guilty.
He was just sort of sitting there, with his head down.

The break in the case came when it emerged that there really was an underwear man named Dave, and he was ready to talk. "I know everyone says they know the guy that threw the beer," Dave Heywood wrote to Speirs. "But this is legit. He is my best friend; I have known him for 50 years. I was standing right beside him when he threw his half-frozen OV [Old Vienna] tall boy from our seats in Section S Row 7 at the old stadium."

Heywood says the underwear tradition was started by his older brother and some buddies, who started kitting up for games in "gotch." As many as 20 or 30 guys would show up to their Section S seats in underwear. Snapshots found on the Internet confirm clusters of young fellows wearing briefs or Y-fronts instead of pants. "You're 18, 19, 20, you're drinking, that's what you do: you put your underwear on and go to the Bomber game."

The original gotchmen are now in their sixties and no longer dress up, but Heywood still does. "I'm the last. They call me the lone gotchman."

He matter-of-factly describes sitting seven rows above field level, near the north end goal-line. The can, he says, was thrown by a guy he has known since they were in kindergarten.

Throwing it was "not something we planned to do. Spur of the moment. When it splatted, it looked like a snowball" because the beer was half-frozen.

Security guards tried to identify the thrower, unsuccessfully. All the fans looked the same in their heavy parkas—except Gotchman, of course. "I don't wear parkas to the games, ever."

The thrower hasn't talked much about the incident since it happened. "For a while he didn't want to because he didn't want to get into trouble," says Heywood. "He didn't want to say anything. 'Don't tell anybody.' But the inner circle knew."

Over the phone, the thrower is initially reluctant to be interviewed because of "the reality of the megaphone we've given through social media to put a shame on people."[24]

Eventually he agrees to speak on condition of anonymity, although he can be described as 55 at the time of the interview, living a quiet life tending to gardens on Canada's west coast. His name is neither Dwayne nor Glenn; for the purpose of recounting his tale, he'll be known as Oswald.

He confirms most of what Heywood had said. Like his buddy, Oswald was kitted up in gotch at the 1991 Grey Cup. Underwear was a handy way to smuggle in beer. "I'd stuff a couple of cans in my bra." (Although beer was available at concession stands during the game, sneaking beer into the stadiums was a gotchmen tradition).

Some have speculated, based on the silvery appearance of the can in the grainy TV footage, that the beer was a Coors Light. Heywood insists it was Old Vienna, and Oswald confirms it. Asked if OV was his beer of choice in 1991, the thrower responds immediately: "Beer was my beer of choice back then."

Oswald grew up in Winnipeg but had moved to Calgary and was cheering for the Stampeders that day. He was unhappy that the Argos, by signing Ismail to his record-breaking contract, were flouting the league's salary-cap rules.

---

24 A 2015 incident involving another tossed beer can lends credence to the thrower's reluctance to be identified. At a Toronto Blue Jays playoff game at the Rogers Centre (the renamed SkyDome), a fan threw a full can towards a Baltimore Orioles outfielder. Unlike the 1991 Grey Cup, this immediately ballooned into a big deal. The culprit was identified though social media, charged with mischief (and later convicted), and lost both his job and his career in journalism.

He never planned to hurl the beer. It was a split-second decision based on a flood of thoughts and emotions.

"He was running down the field and was obviously gonna score. Things can flash through your mind in a millisecond." Things like, "They've bought the Cup. They've changed the CFL."

Like, "There he goes. That kind of sucks."

Like, "I've got a three-quarters can of OV in my hand that I can't drink because it's mostly frozen."

In an instant Oswald stood, took aim, and fired, narrowly missing his target.

"It landed almost between his legs, kind of went through his legs. Whatever liquid was in there blew up."

Although about a hundred people in Oswald's immediate circle have known he threw the can, few people at the game could have identified him as the culprit because few actually saw him throw it. "They were watching the play; they weren't watching Bozo in the stands throwing a can."

But a security guard, long accustomed to the antics of the gotchmen, knew.

"Hey, take it easy, man," he said.

"Oh yeah, won't do that again this game," Oswald replied.

After the final gun, the victorious Ismail laughed it off. When he played for Notre Dame at the University of Tennessee, he told reporters, "they'd throw Jack Daniel's bottles at us."

"I'm just glad that guy didn't have a good aim, man," Ismail said years later. "He could have knocked that ball out of my hand. I'm showboating on the 10-yard line. What the heck was I thinking?"

Asked if he has any regrets, Oswald says, "Oh, sure. Of course. You go, holy shit." If he had actually hit Ismail, "that could've been problematic."

If he were to meet the Rocket now, "I'd probably say, 'Hey man, no harm meant.'"

Oswald saw Ismail break-dancing on a morning TV show years later. "He was absolutely horrible." One of the show's hosts apparently felt the same way, saying, "Where's the guy with the beer can when you need him?"

Stomped

MERE WEEKS AFTER HE showed unparalleled leadership in piloting the Argos to the Grey Cup championship, Matt Dunigan's two-year contract expired. The CFL's best-paid and most frequently injured quarterback, the face of the league before Rocket Ismail arrived, was up for grabs to the highest bidder.

Dunigan had moved up a class with his remarkable performance in the Grey Cup, from "star" to "legend." There was no question of his talent and leadership ability, but general managers around the league had serious misgivings about his health. The succession of injuries had fans calling him the "glass quarterback," or Matt Down-Again.

The Argonauts brass certainly appreciated what Dunigan had done to win them a Grey Cup. But backup Rickey Foggie was responsible, in whole or in part, for ten of the team's 15 wins in 1991, and even some Argos executives believed the team would have performed just as well, perhaps even better, if he had played in the championship.

As he plotted out his 1992 roster, general manager Mike McCarthy kept hearing the same comments about Dunigan from head office. "He's always hurt, Mike. Why not let Rickey play?"

"Everybody was very loyal to Matt and they recognized not only what he had sacrificed for that [Grey Cup] game, but that he was an Argonaut," says Suzan Waks, the team's primary financial executive. "On the other hand, you have to look at the finances and say, how much can I afford to pay a guy who at this stage of his career appears to be on the downside? He's more injury-prone and he's missing more games."

The bosses in Los Angeles wanted McCarthy to make Dunigan an offer with an unusual contingency arrangement. His base salary would still be among the highest in the league, but to really cash in, he would need to play most of the team's games. "It's sort of like, we recognize how great you are . . . and for the games you can play, we'll pay you," Waks says. "A way to try and keep him without taking too much risk."

McCarthy resisted. "You don't get it," he told Waks. "He's the leader. He has the swagger. He's the guy, even on the sideline. Why Foggie did so well was Matt standing there with him."

But head office was insistent, and McCarthy eventually followed orders. "He's only played 16 [regular-season] games in two years," he told Dunigan's agent, Ron Perrick. "And some of those 16 games, he didn't play the whole game."

Not surprisingly, Dunigan wanted no part of a contingency arrangement. Injuries are part of football, especially for a quarterback who played with a ferocious, "I'll hit you first" mentality.

"This is a collision sport, and people are going to get hurt," Dunigan says. "Why would I sign something like that? You've got to be out of your frickin' mind."

He felt confident in his position. At the huge party the team threw to celebrate winning the Grey Cup in Winnipeg, owners Bruce McNall, Wayne Gretzky, and John Candy had all been effusive in their praise. "Most incredible performance, gutsy performance, that they'd ever seen in a championship, in any sport," is what Dunigan remembers them telling him. That was then, however. "Two or three months later, this is how they're treating [me]? It didn't seem to mesh."

Still, he seemed to have few alternatives. Most teams already had veteran quarterbacks.

Lying in a tanning bed in preparation for a week-long Florida bachelor party for teammate Andrew Murray in early 1992, Dunigan received a call from an unlikely source: Cal Murphy.

"What do you think about becoming a Winnipeg Blue Bomber?"

"Hell, yeah, I'd be interested," Dunigan replied.

Players changing teams through free agency was not commonplace in 1992. A gentleman's agreement to leave other teams' free agents alone, intended to prevent salary escalation, had been in place for years. But the Ottawa Rough Riders had chosen to ignore it and go on a free-agent spending spree in 1990, signing six players from other organizations. Murphy, the crusty general manager of the Bombers, had been one of the league's most outspoken opponents of signing other teams' free agents. Yet here he was, wooing a free agent.[25]

The seeds for this had been planted the previous season. During a game against Toronto in 1991, Murphy pointed down to the field from the private box he shared with a few confidants, including the team's lawyer, Bob Sokalski. "We're going to get that guy," he said. He was pointing at Dunigan.

The Blue Bombers had a consistently superb defence that had helped them win two of the past four Grey Cups. Their offence could usually run the football effectively. But their quarterbacking had been pedestrian at best since Tom Clements retired after the 1987 season.

---

25 Murphy later justified going after Dunigan, telling the *Winnipeg Free Press*: "All I said was I wouldn't be the first to start signing other teams' free agents. I never said I'd be the last."

"Operation That Guy" was launched, a plan so secret that even the partners in Sokalski's law firm were kept in the dark. "I opened a file named *Winnipeg Football Club re: Quarterback to be named later*," Sokalski says. "I was at a firm with 60-odd lawyers. Fifty-nine of them traipsed through my office saying, 'Who is it?' I can't tell you. 'But we're your partners.' I can't tell you."

Getting Dunigan would not be easy for the community-owned Bombers. The profit the team had made as host of the 1991 Grey Cup (about $1.1 million), was only enough to cut the team's long-term debt in half. Signing a quarterback to the half-million dollars Dunigan was demanding would require a collective effort.

Murphy and Sokalski approached Winnipeg Enterprises Corp., which ran Winnipeg Stadium. It agreed to provide about $100,000 towards a contract for Dunigan.

Murphy also asked veteran players on the Bombers to accept pay cuts so money could be funnelled to the quarterback.

"They told us they were going after him, but they had to have the money," says offensive tackle Chris Walby, who agreed to a ten-per-cent pay reduction. "Cal's big selling point was we'll go to the Cup every year and we'll get playoff bonuses."

Cornerback Rod Hill remembers his own conversation with Murphy.

"We've got a chance to sign Matt Dunigan. I'm going to need some extra money for him," said Murphy.

"OK, how much do you want to give him? A thousand dollars?"

"No, Rod. A thousand dollars is not enough."

"Three thousand?"

"No, Rod. That's not enough."

The two eventually "settled on a number," Hill says. "I gave him that number and it worked out well. It was worth it." The Bombers would go to the Grey Cup in 1992 and 1993.

The deal the Bombers offered was, unlike most CFL contracts, guaranteed. Dunigan would be paid regardless of whether he got injured. The team got Lloyd's of London to underwrite an insurance policy on the contract.

The Winnipeg deal paid Dunigan $500,000 per season. The Argos, news reports at the time indicated, had offered a base salary of $250,000, plus games-played bonuses that could earn him as much as $270,000 more. The CFL's second-highest-paid player in 1992, after Ismail, was Doug Flutie, who also took advantage of free agency to sign with the Calgary Stampeders for a million dollars per season.

Months after Dunigan signed in Winnipeg, McNall continued to defend the decision to offer a contract contingent on games played. "I like Matt, I really do," the majority owner told a reporter. "But I just couldn't justify guaranteeing a guy money when I knew he wouldn't be around for all of our games." Dunigan dressed for every Blue Bombers game in 1992, but did miss some playing time due to injuries.

Toronto's decision to let Dunigan leave was blasted by Steve Simmons in the *Toronto Sun*. The team, he wrote, "lost their leader. They lost their guts. They lost their soul."

* * *

Losing Dunigan was the first sign for Argo players that things were not going to be as joyful as they had been in 1991. The next sign came when training camp opened. McCarthy delivered unwelcome news: "There's going to be pay cuts. If you don't like it, you're going to get cut. Anyone who doesn't go along with it is going to be gone."

It was "a pretty sobering way to start the season," says offensive tackle Kelvin Pruenster. "You don't go into the first day of practice with your head right after that."

With Dunigan gone, the Argos handed the QB reins to Foggie. Also a pending free agent heading into 1992, he had re-signed with Toronto, a contract that gave him a nice pay increase, but nothing like what Dunigan received from Winnipeg.

What should have been a straightforward transition from Dunigan to Foggie was mucked up by another attempt at a Hollywood-style splash. Unlike the signing of Rocket Ismail, this one was ill-conceived at best.

Since the McNall group had arrived a year earlier, its owners had been pushing for the league to expand into the United States. One of the cities considered a hot prospect for a franchise was Portland, Oregon. Paul Allen, who made a fortune co-founding Microsoft with Bill Gates, was said to be interested in adding a CFL team to his sports stable, which already included the NBA's Portland Trail Blazers.

To push the expansion idea forward, McNall and Larry Ryckman, who purchased the Calgary Stampeders late in the 1991 season, agreed to stage an exhibition game between the two clubs in Portland. The game would feature the league's two "marquee players," Ismail and Flutie, both of whom had high profiles in the United States as former college football stars.

On June 25, 1992, the CFL played its first contest in the United States in 34 years. It was not a particularly memorable game, with a crowd of 15,362 watching the Stamps trounce the Argos 20-1.[26]

---

26 There had been three previous Canadian pro football games played on U.S. soil: two exhibition matches and one regular-season game. The Hamilton Tigers defeated the Ottawa Rough Riders 11-6 in an exhibition game on December 11, 1909, in Van Cortland Park, New York City. The Hamilton Tiger-Cats edged the Argonauts 14-8 on August 25, 1952, in an exhibition contest at

The game result was completely overshadowed by a stunt pulled by McNall.

With Foggie working to establish himself as a No. 1 quarterback for the first time in his five years as a pro, the publicity-hungry Argo owner paraded his next potential marquee signing around the field at Portland's 70-year-old Civic Stadium: Mark Rypien.

Born in Calgary but raised in Spokane, Washington, Rypien had quarterbacked the NFL team in Washington, D.C. to victory in Super Bowl XXVI five months earlier. Now a free agent, he was looking for a new contract, and eager to float the possibility of signing with Toronto. It might give him a bit of leverage in negotiations with Washington.

McNall told reporters he might ask the seven other CFL teams to share the cost of signing Rypien (an idea those teams scoffed at). Behind the scenes, the Argos spent weeks exploring whether they could find a way to add Rypien. Brian Cooper, the team's executive vice-president and chief operating officer, sent a memo to McCarthy (copied to McNall and Waks) on July 9: "I have started my search for additional funds outside of a straight salary for the possible securing of Mark Rypien for the team. To date, I have had a negative response from most parties I have spoken to, including Molson, Coca-Cola, and the Bitove organization."[27]

McNall piled another indignity on Foggie early in the season. While the new No. 1 quarterback was smoothly directing the Argos to a 61-20 annihilation of the B.C. Lions at SkyDome, Rypien was up in the owner's box, then down on the sideline right behind the Argo bench, his face up

War Memorial Stadium in Buffalo, New York. And the Tiger-Cats defeated the Rough Riders 24-18 on September 14, 1958, at Municipal Stadium in Philadelphia, a regular-season game.

27 The Bitove group owned concession rights at SkyDome, and would later bring the NBA Raptors to Toronto.

on the JumboTron for 36,000 fans to see. He told reporters he might soon be signing with the Argos. Although he was too polite to say it, he was talking about taking Foggie's job.

"It just makes [Foggie] tougher," head coach Adam Rita told reporters afterwards. "It'll put another coat of armour on him."

Foggie had little to say about Rypien. "I don't worry about what's happening in the front office. [Rita is] the guy I've got to please."

The dalliance with Rypien continued for a few more weeks until he finally re-signed with Washington. But even before that seemingly inevitable occurrence, it was evident that McNall no longer had any faith in the quarterback he had weeks earlier urged McCarthy to move on to. In one of his weekly memos to the majority owner, McCarthy wrote: "I know how you feel about Foggie, but when the ball is dropped or the receivers don't go where they are supposed to go and the ball is intercepted and a TD is scored, it is not the QB's fault."

Foggie's jovial personality may not have endeared him to the brass. He never stopped smiling, regardless of whether he had just made a spectacular play or a horrendous one. "Sometimes he'd throw an interception and be smiling. People would get mad," says receiver David Williams. "That's how he is. He's always smiling, whether he's good or bad. You would never know if Rickey played great or bad."

He also tried to keep teammates happy. Foggie realized in the fourth quarter of a game that he hadn't thrown a pass all day to Darrell K. Smith, whose streak of consecutive games with a reception had reached 96. "D.K., to keep the streak alive, I'm just going to throw you the ball," Foggie said in the huddle.

The pass was thrown. Smith batted it down.

"What the hell was that?" the quarterback asked after the game.

"If I'm not good enough for you to throw me the ball for three and a half quarters, I'm not going to take some kind of pity shit from you," the intensely competitive Smith replied icily.[28]

In ascending from "the best backup quarterback in the history of the Canadian Football League," as labelled by Dunigan, to the role of starter, Foggie fell victim to an old phenomenon, says teammate J.P. Izquierdo: "The thing you love about your girlfriend is the thing you hate about her as a wife. The things that people want you for become the things that people don't want you for later. They loved him [in 1991] because he was loose and didn't give a guy shit too often. The next year, 'You're too friendly and too loose.'"

McCarthy's memo to McNall defending Foggie also highlighted other problems that had begun to plague the Argonauts. A stunning collapse in Week 1 against the Ottawa Rough Riders was an ugly harbinger of a year in which it seemed that whatever could go wrong, would go wrong.

There was dissension in the ranks. As McCarthy put it in his fax message to McNall: "We have a few jerks who we came down on hard. We cut Dave Bovell, who was a problem. And D.K. Smith has started his B.S. again. The next time he does this, he is gone! . . . He is always shooting his mouth off in the huddle, and was one of the receivers . . . who dropped nine balls in the fourth quarter."

There had been no dissension, no bad-asses, no jerks, in 1991. This was due in large part to two leaders, Matt Dunigan and Chris Gaines. "Matt is the first player I've ever seen lead the team when he's hurt," says Pinball Clemons. "[Normally] when guys get hurt, they check out, people just don't hear their voice. But Matt was still the leader of our team even while being hurt."

---

28 Smith's mark of 96 consecutive games catching a pass remains the team record.

"Matt leaving kind of messed up some of our chemistry," says Foggie. "Even though he was hurt, guys still loved him. His personality was a huge part of our football team. I was happy I was the starter, but something just wasn't right with that team after Matt left. It was bad mojo that year."

On the day of the Grey Cup parade in 1991, Gaines had been pulled into a pub by owner John Candy and offered a job as strength and conditioning coach, which he gratefully accepted. But as a member of the coaching staff, he could not maintain his role as the team's spiritual leader. And in 1992 the team was bereft of spiritual leadership.

"The whole atmosphere is different," says Williams. "Gaines is gone, Matt's gone, and that's huge. Everything felt different."

Added punter Hank Ilesic: "If you want to take the legs out of a football organization, take out the guy who pulls the trigger and the guy who's the heart of the defence. You can't replace that."

Health was also a factor. Darrell K. Smith, an iron man who had missed just two games over the previous five seasons, had to sit out five games with an assortment of injuries. The painful turf-toe injury Clemons had suffered late in 1991 lingered throughout the entire season. Clemons says he played the season "running on one foot."

With the team also plagued by undisciplined penalties, dropped passes, missed blocks and imprecise pass routes, the normally laid-back Rita quickly became fed up. He gave Smith a tongue-lashing so severe the star receiver came away from the conversation believing he was being released by the team. And it was the coach's decision to unload Bovell, whose arrival late in 1991 from Winnipeg had provided the final piece of a superb defensive secondary.

In a game against Hamilton, the free-spirited, outspoken Bovell had taken three penalties, including one for unnecessary roughness (for a head butt) and one for illegal substitution after he sauntered onto the field before a Toronto punt. "I can't take it anymore," Rita told the *Toronto Star*. "I really, really wanted him in there, but he proved me wrong. I thought he could change, I thought he could fit in. I was wrong."

"I was an idiot, and Adam was an idiot," says Bovell, reflecting on his brief tenure as an Argo. "It was a marriage of convenience that had a shelf life."

With the season not yet two months old, the Argos had lost four of six games, and rumours spread that the coach of the defending champions might be fired. Rita himself invited such speculation when he told reporters he was not going to bench Foggie. "They're going to have to fire me to make a quarterback change. The easiest thing for them to do is change coaches, and then they can change the quarterback."

When Foggie went out briefly with an injured ankle, the Argos turned initially to John Congemi and Mike Kerrigan at quarterback. They lost Congemi's first start in Edmonton, then won the next game at home against Ottawa, with Kerrigan coming off the bench to engineer two fourth-quarter touchdown drives.

Kerrigan started the next game in Hamilton, when the Argos turned the ball over eight times: five lost fumbles and three interceptions thrown by Kerrigan before he gave way to Foggie. Ismail, returning to the Argo lineup after missing the previous three games with an injury, fumbled five times, although he managed to recover all but one. The Ticats won 27-24.

* * *

The Argonauts' season was already a wreck when the Calgary Stampeders rolled into town for a rematch of the previous year's Grey Cup championship game. Just halfway through the schedule, Toronto had already lost six games, more than in all of 1991, with just three wins. The

Stampeders, with new quarterback Flutie tearing up the league, had six wins and were on a mission to make up for 1991's heartbreak by getting back to the Grey Cup. And what better way to make a statement than by kicking the defending champions' ass?

On a sweltering September afternoon in SkyDome, Calgary laid an ugly pounding on the Argos. As the score become lopsided, boos cascaded down from the 29,044 spectators baking under the open roof.

Tension built on the field throughout the game. Despite being beaten almost from the opening kickoff, members of the Argos taunted the Stampeders. "Hey, how do you like my Grey Cup ring?"

Out of action because of an injury, Smith was on the Argo sideline "jawing the Stamps constantly throughout the game," says Jason Colero, an Argo equipment assistant.

Ismail, like pretty much ever other Argo, had a bad game. He'd been targeted several times but managed just two receptions while being manhandled by defenders. In the third quarter, he veered into the end zone and attempted to catch what might have been a touchdown pass, but a Stampeder blatantly interfered with him. No penalty was called. Ismail exploded at the officials, and was still seething moments later as he stood in the Toronto end awaiting a punt.

What happened next became one of the most-replayed sequences in Canadian football history.

Tony Martino's punt bounced in front of the Rocket and rolled harmlessly out of bounds to end the play. With CBC's camera focused on Ismail trotting off the field, viewers at home heard announcer Don Wittman's voice suddenly rise in intensity: "There's pushing and shoving at the Argo bench!"

Toronto's Dave Van Belleghem was grappling with Calgary's Andy McVey, both men falling to the ground. Suddenly the Rocket appeared in the frame. He took a flying leap and came down feet first on McVey's head. He then kicked towards the Calgary player.

The in-stadium producer, showing an ironic sense of humour, started playing the *Hockey Night in Canada* theme song over the PA system.

When things calmed down, CBC queued up replays to show how the whole scene had unfolded.

Van Belleghem, peeling back towards Ismail on the Argos' punt-return unit, threw a blind-side block on Calgary's Paul Clatney near the Toronto sideline. Absorbing the blow, Clatney thrust his arms forward and slammed into the nattily dressed Smith, who was propelled backwards about 20 feet, landing on his backside.

Argo receiver David Williams retaliated by pushing Clatney. Head coach Adam Rita angrily approached Clatney and gave him a shove. The Stampeders' McVey came over to grab Williams. Both men fall to the ground, knocking over a trash can. Van Belleghem jumped on McVey.

Then Rocket jumped in and stomped on McVey's helmet. Bill Harcourt, a side judge on the officiating crew, grabbed Ismail by the collar as he jumped, pulling him backwards and possibly preventing a more direct and heavier blow to McVey's head.

Watching and describing a replay, CBC's usually unflappable Wittman was incredulous. "It looked as if he was trying to jump on top of Andy McVey! Watch the Rocket come in. . . . It almost seemed as if he was trying to jump on the head of Andy McVey and trying to kick him."

After the scuffle ended, referee Bud Steen announced the penalties: rough-play disqualifications against Ismail, Williams, and McVey. As he headed to the locker room after being kicked out of the game, the Rocket leaned into Steen and gave the ref an earful, earning a further penalty for objectionable conduct.

The highest-paid player in football had been kicked out of the game for stomping on an opponent whose pay for the entire season was roughly equal to what Rocket made for a single quarter of one game.

Although replays showed Clatney being hit by Van Belleghem just before he rammed into Smith, some Argo players believed at the time, and still believe, that Smith had been deliberately knocked over.

"I blocked [Clatney] to the point where it was almost out of bounds," says Van Belleghem. "And then, instead of stopping, he accelerated right into D.K. Smith."

Clatney, who grew up in Toronto cheering for the Argonauts, insists the Van Belleghem block that ignited the brawl was "a big-time late hit. He clips me directly from behind. All of a sudden, I'm flying toward Darrell K. Smith.

"I feel bad now hitting Darrell K. I probably could have gone the other way, could have avoided him more than I did. But hit me into your guy? It's your fault. If you want to hit me into your bench, a late hit from behind, then you can hit me into your guy. It was just a sea of blue around me and before long, guys came to my rescue."

One of those guys was McVey, who attended North Toronto Collegiate and the University of Toronto before being drafted by the Stampeders. With family members and friends in the crowd, he had scored a touchdown earlier in the game.

"When one of your players goes into a bench and there's pushing and shoving and things start happening, you obviously go in there with them as well," says McVey. "You don't really process or think it through. It was just pushing and shoving, and all of a sudden the whole pile goes down and it was a bit of a brawl."

McVey couldn't believe what he saw on a TV replay in Calgary's locker room after the game. "You really don't realize what's going on because you're at the bottom of a pile. You really can't do much, so you clench up and wait and see what happens.

"I do remember something banging on my head. It wasn't until I saw the replay and realized what Rocket had done: he was trying to come down on my head with both feet. The ref [Harcourt], from what I could see in the highlights, kind of gave him a shove and knocked him off a little bit, so he didn't really get a clean whack on my head."

Carl Brazley, Ismail's roommate on road trips, remembers seeing the Rocket's reaction and thinking, he should get out of there.

"Everybody was just going crazy and berserk," Brazley says. "He was in the middle of the fight. I was more scared about him getting hurt . . . because you know there's guys saying, 'Hey, I'm going to run and take a shot at him.'"

In the Argo locker room afterwards, Ismail was distraught. Tears streamed down his face as his roommate Brazley tried to console him.

"I screwed up," the Rocket forlornly told his friend. "I messed up. I can't believe it."

Brazley got a brainwave. "Dude, just tell everybody else. Who better than to come from you? Let's go to Speakers' Corner and just tell them the same thing you're telling me."

There was no Twitter in 1992. No Instagram. No Facebook. No TikTok. No way to get your message out directly, in your own unfiltered words, short of buying an ad in a newspaper or on radio or TV. But in Toronto, there was another way, and it was just a ten-minute walk from SkyDome.

Speakers' Corner was an early, innovative form of social media, launched by Citytv, a low-budget, hyper-local television station. It was a simple booth set up outside the station on Queen Street West. Anyone could pop a dollar coin into a slot, look into a camera lens, and record a video. The most interesting videos were broadcast on a program called *Speakers' Corner*.

On the evening of September 13, 1992, a young man in a grey hoodie and white ballcap took a deep breath. Staring into the tiny camera lens embedded in the wall before him, he began speaking in a calm, controlled voice, occasionally pausing and looking upward, as if searching his brain for the correct words.

> *Hi, my name is Rocket Ismail and I'm here at Speakers' Corner for the first time ever in my life. The reason I'm here is because . . . we had a game today against [pause] the Calgary Stampeders. And, during the course of the game, emotions ran high and wild and whatever-whatever, and a fight broke out on the sidelines.*
>
> *And during the time of the fight, I [pause] got involved and [pause] did some pretty bad things. I'm just saying that the reason I did those things was stupid. And for any of those young people out there, little guys who always come up to me and say they want to be like the Rocket, I'm just here telling you that that is not the way to go about being like me. That was [pause], this is a situation that I got caught up in that I had no business being caught up in.*
>
> *And I just want to apologize to the player from Calgary because I'm not generally that person to go off their heads and resort to physical violence.*
>
> *Until next time, peace and love, again I apologize. Thanks a lot.*

As he signed off, Ismail flashed two fingers in the traditional peace sign and opened his mouth into a gentle—if somewhat enigmatic—smile. Watching it today, it's fair to say he seems somewhat relieved at the end of his 70-second spiel.

Ismail had gone to Speakers' Corner without consulting anyone from the Argonauts, other than Brazley. The video had not yet been shown on TV when McCarthy suggested to Ismail the next day that he might want to make a public statement about the incident. "I've already done that," he told the GM. "I did it last night."

Unfortunately for the Rocket, the apology (of sorts) was not the end of the story. The incident was shown repeatedly on sportscasts across North America. While many blows had been struck during the brawl, coverage naturally focused on the stomp.

"I had calls from my friends all over America," Ismail told the *New York Times* in 1993. "They called me Bruce Lee, Chuck Norris, Kung Fu."

Stampeder players ripped the Rocket and his teammates. "They were just looking for any excuse to get in a fight because they were getting their butts whipped," Clatney told reporters. "Most championship teams, when they get down, play tougher. These guys just gave up and figured they'd make a circus out of it."

McNall told a reporter that Ismail's actions "showed his devotion by coming to the aid of his teammates." That notion is supported even now by some of those who played with the Rocket. "It was his passion to win and to protect his players and be a part of the team, because he was like that," says fellow receiver Paul Masotti. "He was being protective of somebody he felt was hit without equipment on, and protecting his teammate."

Brazley says his roommate bore the brunt of criticism only because of his massive contract. "They don't show the folks swinging and hitting. They just showed him kicking some guy. He did what I hope anybody would do when you understand being in this mentality—it's like going to war. You're all on the same team and when it breaks out, everybody's there. Hopefully you keep your head, but when it goes nuclear, hey, it is what it is."

Forced to talk to reporters a day after making himself scarce following the game, Ismail sounded contrite as he contemplated the punishment that awaited him. "Whatever happens, it won't be anything I don't deserve. It came from frustration, man. Everything just got to a boiling point."

A suspension seemed inevitable, if not blindingly obvious, but the next Argo game was in Vancouver against the B.C. Lions. That caused a problem for the league, which was desperately seeking a buyer for the club after owner Murray Pezim went bankrupt. Would Larry Smith, in the job of CFL commissioner for barely eight months, really remove one of the league's star attractions from a game in a market that needed help with ticket sales?

Under the CFL's collective agreement with the players' association, the largest fine Smith could levy was half of one game cheque. Ismail's official league contract paid him about $110,000, so his maximum fine would be about $3,000. Chump change.

Describing Ismail as "an irate child," the commissioner announced the Argo star could either be fined $1,000 and suspended for a game, or avoid the suspension and fine by making a voluntary $10,000 donation to the Special Olympics. Ismail opted to make the donation.

Asked by TSN's Rod Smith whether he felt $10,000 was an excessive amount to fork over, the Rocket reverted to his usual childlike demeanour. "I find anything over five dollars to be an excessive amount of money!" he said, before seeming to calm down. "But hey, it's like the situation warranted it. It's not excessive when you take into account what happened."

Smith's decision was not received well in Calgary. *Herald* columnist Allan Maki wrote that the Rocket, "who probably leaves $10,000 bills in his pants pockets when he sends out his laundry," had considered both options Smith gave him "and decided to go the tax-credit route."

* * *

Desperate to improve the team's fortunes, McCarthy reverted to an oft-used, generally ill-advised practice from the past known as the Argo Airlift. He brought in a new quarterback, an eight-year NFL backup named Blair Kiel, whom McCarthy claimed was similar to Matt Dunigan, but "bigger than Mathew and his arm is a lot stronger than Mathew's. . . . We shouldn't underestimate how good Blair is."

Eleven years earlier, McCarthy's predecessor as Argo GM, Ralph Sazio, had made similarly grandiose predictions about a Buffalo Bills castoff named Dan Manucci, recruited in mid-season to take the quarterback job away from Condredge Holloway. Manucci had six of his 68 passes intercepted, and was soon looking for a new job. Kiel would surpass that burst of mediocrity.

Inserted into the lost-cause game against Calgary that featured Ismail's stomp on McVey, Kiel immediately threw an interception that was returned for a nail-in-the-coffin touchdown. Before the next game in Vancouver against the B.C. Lions, McCarthy laid things out for Rita.

"You're starting Blair Kiel," he told the coach. "And you've got to win the next two games."

"OK, no problem, Mike," Rita replied in his usual low-key manner.

Kiel had an idea what he'd gotten himself into: "Coach," he told Rita before the game, "you know you're going to get fired for playing me."

"Don't worry about me getting fired," Rita replied. "[If it happens] they've still got to pay me."

"Poor Blair," Rita says now. "He was there a week and had never been in an offence like mine. He hadn't played for ten years. He was a backup quarterback."

Kiel managed just three completions in 13 attempts before pulling himself out of the game. "Coach," he said, "this is ridiculous. Put Foggie in."

Foggie didn't play much better than Kiel. But thanks to two defensive touchdowns, the Argos kept the score close before suffering their eighth loss against three wins. The *Star* and the *Sun* both reported that the defeat had probably cost Rita his job.

There was no "probably" about it.

McCarthy broke the news on September 21, Rita's 45th birthday. The reigning CFL coach of the year was finished, replaced by defensive co-ordinator Dennis Meyer.

The decision to fire Rita had been made in Los Angeles, the GM says.

"Enough!" McCarthy remembers hearing from Waks. "Our attendance is going down!"

"Why don't you fire him, Su?" McCarthy asked.

"You're the GM," she replied.

McCarthy told reporters that firing Rita was "the hardest thing for me to do in my life. I love this man."

Rita, known to some of his players as the Happy Hawaiian, was, as usual, smiling and jovial when he met with the media. "Who's responsible?" he asked, before pointing to himself. "I'm not bitter. I thought I was given every opportunity to turn this team around, and I wasn't able to do it, so they had to do what they had to do."

After the informal news conference, some reporters took the ex-coach to a bar. Rita celebrated his birthday and his sudden departure from the pressure cooker by drinking more than his usual one beer. "It was probably the only time I had ever seen him hammered. He couldn't even get the key in the lock of the door," says Jocelyne Meinert, who married Rita a couple of months later.

The Argos won three of their first four games under Meyer, but lost the last three games of the 1992 season to end the year with a miserable record of six wins against 12 defeats. The dreaded championship hangover.

"Championship fat," says safety Don Wilson. "You think you're focused, you think you're determined, you think you're on point, but you really aren't. You're still kind of living off last year's championship."

"We went into that season as individuals, not as a collective," adds Chris Schultz. "We fractured as a team. . . . We acted like a bunch of spoiled brats."

Nowhere to Hide

I T WAS GREY CUP WEEK in 1992, and ticket sales for the game
at Toronto's SkyDome were not going well. With the Toronto
Argonauts not in the big game, and a team from the distant prairies,
the Winnipeg Blue Bombers, representing the East Division, the only real
fan interest in southern Ontario was among the small band of diehard
CFL fanatics who went to every Grey Cup regardless of who was playing.
There were plenty of tickets left to be sold, and time was running short.

When they purchased the Argonauts in early 1991, Bruce McNall and
his partners had negotiated the rights to the championship game in back-
to-back years, 1992 and 1993. They assumed the events would generate
big profits and earn back some of their investment in the team. What
they hadn't banked on was the defending champion Argos falling out of
playoff contention by Labour Day in 1992, en route to a last-place finish
with just six wins in 18 turbulent games.

To help spur last-minute sales, Brian Cooper, the Argos' executive
vice-president, who had primary responsibility for the Grey Cup game
and festival, arranged to have his two most high-profile players make the

rounds of morning radio. Pinball Clemons and Rocket Ismail would go on air, talk up the big game and try to build some hype for an event that was sorely lacking in excitement.

One of their stops was CJCL, which had rebranded itself as the Fan 1430 and launched Canada's first all-sports radio format just two months earlier. Clemons and Ismail were booked for an appearance on the mid-morning show hosted by Toronto sportswriters Steve Simmons of the *Sun* and Mary Ormsby of the *Star* (although Ormsby was not on the air that day).

Clemons arrived and was his usual effusive, friendly self. Ismail was another story. He was apparently surprised to encounter Simmons who, in addition to hard-hitting columns, had co-written a story two months earlier that said Argo management was eager to get out of its contractual obligation to Ismail, and teammates felt the Rocket was "playing out the string."

"We're about to go on air," Simmons says. "Rocket sees it's me, looks at me and [utters] the last words he ever spoke to me: 'Fuck off.'"

Although they might not have heard such harsh language from the Rocket, it was a sentiment senior Argo executives had become accustomed to over the past year.

Reluctant to speak to journalists almost from the moment he arrived in Toronto, Ismail became even less co-operative during his second year with the club. The massive amount of money he was being paid was not because of his football talent, but to put the Argonauts and indeed the entire CFL into the collective consciousness.

The Argos needed Ismail to sell tickets and sponsorships as the face of Canadian football. They even harboured aspirations that he might attract sponsors and a significant TV rights package in the United States.

To most Americans, Canadian football was at best a peculiar diversion one might catch a glimpse of from time to time on obscure cable channels, played on a weirdly huge field, with a slightly fatter, striped football and a couple of extra players. Signing a guy who had twice been on the cover of *Sports Illustrated* and who was expected to be the first pick in the NFL draft was supposed to change that. If Rocket couldn't be "the Wayne Gretzky of Canadian football," executives with the club hoped he at least might become Toronto's version of Earvin "Magic" Johnson, star of the Los Angeles Lakers basketball team.

"We were hoping to do with Rocket what [Lakers owner] Jerry Buss had done with Magic Johnson," says Suzan Waks, a senior executive with the Argo ownership group. "He was very well spoken, educated, likeable, very personable, and very childlike. Magic Johnson [came to transcend his sport] because of his personality. Everybody talked about his smile or how excited he got. Rocket's childish, boyish kind of thing would have sold, like Magic's did. Rocket had the potential. . . . I think he could have transcended Canada."

The Argos did manage to land a handful of high-profile sponsorship deals that offset part of the personal-services contract that paid Ismail $4.5 million US per year. A TV commercial for Pepsi had him popping open a bottle of the soft drink, taking a swig, and pronouncing it "Rocket fuel." For Reebok, he narrated a 30-second spot depicting him dancing, strutting, working out, and breaking into the clear for a touchdown. Ismail also pitched for automaker Ford, shooting an ad at Toronto's Varsity Stadium in which he raced against a Ford Escort.[29]

But none of that commercial activity made a dent in the ten-times-larger

---

29 Despite his endorsement deal with Reebok, Ismail wore Nike cleats, with the logo covered up.

U.S. market. As well-known and popular as the Rocket had been at Notre Dame, he might as well have moved to Estonia when he jetted north to Canada.

This came as no surprise to Joe Theismann, whose own path to pro football was oddly similar to Ismail's. Both had starred at Notre Dame. Both finished second in voting for the Heisman trophy as the top U.S. college football player. Both initially spurned the NFL to sign with the Argos and become the CFL's highest-paid player, although at $50,000 a year in 1971, Theismann was paid barely one per cent of what the Rocket earned 30 years later.

Like Ismail, Theismann had finished his college football career as one of the biggest names in the sport. Yet when he returned home after the CFL season, "everybody wanted to know where I'd been." When Theismann was an Argonaut, the league had deployed him as an emissary of sorts to U.S. broadcasters. Even with that help, all it could muster was a tiny network of small, independent American stations to broadcast a few games, often aired days or even weeks after they had been played.

While Theismann has always had good things to say about his three years in Canada with the Argos, he harboured doubts about the organization's ability to leverage the Rocket into big U.S. revenue. "I think they were trying to take it to the next level, but I didn't know if the next level would be willing to accept it. How big was it going to be in the United States?"

After the Argonauts won the 1991 Grey Cup in storybook fashion, the organization was stunned to be faced with a decline in fan interest. The novelty of celebrity owners and the highest-paid player in football had worn off, ticket prices had been increased, and enthusiasm among Toronto sports fans was heavily weighted towards baseball's Blue Jays, who seemed to be on the cusp of a championship after nearly a decade of contending. (The Jays did win the World Series in 1992, and again in 1993.)[30]

In an effort to stoke interest in the Argos, team executives in Los Angeles pushed to have the Rocket featured more on offence. While it might have been possible to make greater use of Ismail in the passing game—targeting him, say, eight to ten times a game—head coach Adam Rita knew he could not build an entire offence around a single receiver. "I can't have too much focus on Rocket," he said privately. "I've got 12 guys on the field and they've all got to participate. If it's all about Rocket, it's not a balanced team."

Still, Rita gamely tried to extract maximum value from the team's marquee player. At times it seemed as if Foggie and the other Argo quarterbacks had eyes only for Ismail, yet he never managed more than nine offensive touches in a game all season.

Meanwhile, the coach also tried to insulate Ismail from all the demands on his time for off-field work promoting the team. Shortly after the 1991 season ended, Rita and several Argo executives had been invited to attend a training session in Los Angeles led by Andrea Kirby, a renowned media coach. "Rocket was a hot topic of conversation during those discussions," says communications executive David Watkins. Rita insisted Ismail was doing everything required of him. It was, says Watkins, "a difficult conversation."

When Watkins had to advise Rita about Ismail's off-field commitments in 1992, the coach often replied, "Rocket's not gonna be up for that."

There were a lot of things Rocket did not seem up for in 1992. He appeared less engaged in general. At practices, he would sometimes be

---

30 Interest in the Argos waning after the team wins the championship seems to have become a peculiar, perpetual phenomenon. It happened in 1984 after the team ended a 31-year Grey Cup drought, and has been repeated after most of the team's championships since then.

spotted talking on a cell phone (a device few people had in those days) when he was supposed to be on the field. He regularly fell asleep in meetings.

Before a trip to Winnipeg, he checked in for the team's flight, but failed to board. The plane backed away from the gate, then the captain's voice came over the intercom. "Folks, we have to go back to the terminal to pick up a passenger."

The plane returned to the gate. The door opened and on came Ismail, complaining about being besieged for his autograph. "Shut up and get in your seat," more than one teammate said.

Ismail did so, pulled his hoodie over his head and promptly fell asleep.

Watching the scene unfold, head trainer Kevin Duguay turned to his seatmate, assistant coach Jim Hilles. "If that was you or me," Duguay said, "the plane ain't going back to the terminal. You catch the next plane, you're going to get fined."

That apparent double standard had started to grate on teammates.

"Last year he never took advantage of his position," offensive guard Dan Ferrone said. "This year, I do think he's taking advantage of his position by missing practices. [In 1991] he still would sleep, but at least he was in the room."

Rita could not abide Rocket blowing off team activities. Reports indicated Ismail was fined repeatedly for missing meetings or medical treatments. (He suffered several injuries in 1992, including two diagnosed concussions, giving him at least four of those in two seasons in Toronto.)

On the field, Ismail wasn't the same player as in the championship season. "Right from the start," said Ferrone, "I noticed guys were tackling him with arms. You couldn't do that last year because if you used an arm, he'd rip it off as he went by. His feet kept kicking and he was gone. That's not really prevalent this year."

In 1991, opponents tried to avoid kicking to him. In 1992, Ferrone said, "they're kicking to Rocket now because they know that cowboy's just running around." Early in a game in Hamilton, after Ismail fumbled the football, Jason Riley of the Tiger-Cats crossed paths with Ferrone on the field. "Man," Riley said, "he's a liability, an expensive liability."

Publicly, McCarthy defended Ismail, telling the *Toronto Star* somewhat hyperbolically: "The Rocket-bashing is unbelievable. . . . The kid has done more for this league than any other individual in the history of this league."

In the locker room, players weren't buying it. "If I was an owner and I'd done this investment on a guy like him, I would be really disappointed," Ferrone said. "He's not getting paid this money for his football. He's paid because he's the Rocket. Some people have the personality to do this job and others don't. Rocket does not have the personality to do this job. Those who thought he could, made a mistake."

That was the bitter conclusion the team's owners also had privately reached, especially after Ismail began skipping out on appearances arranged by the organization. In one infamous incident, he avoided a commitment by calling in sick, only to be spotted hours later at a concert.

"He wasn't really performing the personal services that we'd hoped he'd perform off the field," says majority owner Bruce McNall. "I talked to him myself. 'You've really got to help us here a little bit.' He was always very nice, and he'd say, 'Yeah, yeah, absolutely.' But it never really happened."

Part of the problem, says Waks, was that Ismail was paid the bulk of his personal-services contract before the season started. "Everyone had skin in the game except him, because he got his money up front.

"At least in year one he showed up, even if it was for a short period of time," adds Waks. "In year two he'd say, 'Yeah, I'll be there,' and then not show up. He was put on notice many times that he wasn't living up to his side of the bargain. He was just not in."

Faced with a contract that would run two more years and pay another $9 million, the organization began searching for a way out of the obligation. In December 1992, Watkins and marketing executive Bret Gallagher were asked to document every promotional appearance that had been booked for Ismail that year. Watkins put his observations into a memo with some devastating details:

> *Sprinted past a photographer who was set up at the practice to shoot a cover for Toronto Life magazine . . .*

> *Failed to show at a scheduled interview with a Wilkes-Barre [Pennsylvania] TV crew . . .*

> *Failed to attend a scheduled appointment with Jeff Ross of TSN that caused Mr. Ross to complain in writing to Bruce McNall . . .*

Rocket had blown off TSN at least twice before that. In a mid-season segment about problems that beset the Argonauts after winning the Grey Cup, reporter Rod Smith described Ismail's "apparent aversion to the media. Twice we brought our cameras to Argonaut practice to interview the Rocket for this story. Both times, he refused to talk to us."

Rumours about Ismail going to the NFL had circulated almost from the moment he signed with the Argos. Although he had been touted as a possible No. 1 overall draft pick, after signing with Toronto he slid to the fourth round, where he was selected by the Los Angeles Raiders.

Perhaps unknown to Ismail, McNall had contemplated his departure even before he signed with the Argonauts. The majority owner made what he called "a secret arrangement" with one of his counterparts in the L.A. sports scene, Raiders owner Al Davis.

"What if I sign him and take away the NFL thing, and you draft him like in the third, fourth or fifth round?" McNall suggested. "I keep him for two years and make sure he moves on to you."

Publicly, Argo management's position on the rumours was always the same: we signed him for four years, but we won't stand in his way if he ever wants to try the NFL. McNall says now it had become clear during the 1992 season that Ismail "really wanted to be in the NFL. He started to make that more clear, both in the on-field performance and not being around too much, ducking everything even more than he had before."

Ismail insisted he was going nowhere, telling CBC viewers at halftime of the game in which he later stomped on Andy McVey's head, "Basically, I just want to play out the next two years, and not even worry about that option."

By the end of the 1992 season, the Argos were so desperate to engineer Ismail's departure that Waks and her colleagues devised a hardball strategy: threaten to sue him for breach of contract, while promising not to do so if he voluntarily opted out of the remainder of his contract.

"He was on notice that this was a problem," says Waks. "We started to let him know that if he wanted to explore options elsewhere, we wouldn't be going after him for breach of contract. It was like, you don't have to finish out your contract if you don't want to be here and you don't want to do the marketing."

"We had a pretty good case if we wanted to just shut the thing down," says McNall. "I don't think anybody wanted to fight. I don't think Rocket wanted the bad publicity of that. I think we would have won that if we had pursued it."

There was just one problem, however, with the notion of Rocket happily decamping for the NFL. There was no chance the Raiders would offer him a contract even close to what the McNall group was paying him. He would have to take a gigantic pay cut to move to Los Angeles.

That he was now trapped in Toronto seems to have encouraged Ismail to take a provocative public stand on the question of his leaving the Argos. Taking an apparent poke at the rotund McNall, he said, "It ain't over until the extremely fat person sings or the extremely fat person cuts you." (Ismail's agent, Gus Heningburg, would later tell *Sports Illustrated* that "among his peers, the term 'fat' refers to rich.")

Ismail finally showed up for an interview at TSN to help stir up interest in the 1992 Grey Cup. Interviewer Michael Landsberg opened the segment by saying, "It's ironic that the Rocket is hyping a game that he's not playing in, because he seldom did it for games that he was playing in this season."

Ismail denied the suggestion he had not helped promote the Argos as required by his contract. Wearing a white hoodie emblazoned with the slogan "Racism is an illness," he noted that the previous week, while in a New York hotel room, he had seen himself in a highlight reel on a U.S. sports channel. He then elaborated in a way that was not helped by his rather childlike speaking style.

"The question was, is Ismail gonna stay, whatever. I'm just saying that before that happened, no one knew about Toronto or the CFL. . . . If Mr. McNall and the people who bought the Argonauts hadn't gone out and done what they did, it probably wouldn't be like it is right now. So I don't feel that I'm not doing what I should be doing, as far as promoting the CFL and the Argonauts."

Landsberg closed the clip by saying, "Even though he is evasive, there's something likeable about him. Even though he's not a hundred per cent answering your question, there is something there, a boyishness about him that I quite like."

While Landsberg was willing to cut Ismail some slack, Doug Smith, who covered the CFL for *The Canadian Press,* says the bottom line is that Rocket "never took responsibility for his greatness. He wouldn't do it. With the right personality, he could have owned the city. But he never had that. He never had that desire."

As the 1992 season ended, and fans and media began looking to the future, stories on the possibility of Ismail jumping to the Raiders were published regularly, as were items about the Argos' disenchantment with him. A lengthy piece in *Sports Illustrated* outlined both the organization's enmity and the player's insistence that he had fulfilled his obligations. It also underlined the absurd disparity between Ismail's salary and that of the average CFL player: "I mean, here I am," Ismail was quoted, "endorsed by Ford, getting a new Explorer every five minutes, and there's a teammate chugging out of the parking lot in a 1972 Toyota."

With Ismail back at Notre Dame continuing his studies in the spring of 1993, the *Toronto Star* sent reporter Paul Hunter to South Bend in hopes of landing an interview. Two years earlier, *Star* reporter Rick Matsumoto had cornered the Rocket in his dorm room, sticking his foot inside to force Ismail to make a comment. Hunter wasn't as lucky.

The reporter tracked down Ismail at a gym, but the Rocket saw him and slipped out a back exit. Hunter ran out in pursuit, although his 40-yard dash time had never been in Ismail's league. "Is this ever stupid," Hunter said to himself. "I don't think I'm going to catch him."

By mid-summer, Ismail had signed with the Raiders, negotiating a contract that paid him about one-third of what he would have received in Toronto.

When the *Star's* Rick Matsumoto caught up to him in October of 1993,

Ismail was relaxed enough to drive the reporter around L.A. He clearly was relishing being just another player, a backup receiver at that point.

"It's so awesome to not have to go out and be the guy everyone's looking at to make things happen," he said, "to not have to worry about just being *the* man all the time. It's so much better to know that I'm not the one everyone's attacking after the game. I always felt pressured to the point that, man oh man, if I don't do something, no one is.

"The only thing that made me mad was that they made it seem like I never tried to do anything or went to interviews or never spoke to anybody. That was ludicrous, man. I was waking up at 5 o'clock in the morning doing media blitz things. We must have talked to every radio and television station in the country. For them to say I wasn't doing my job . . ."

Carl Brazley, who as Ismail's road-game roommate was the Argo who got to know Rocket best, says the club miscast his friend by surmising he would embrace the spotlight.

"Their thinking was, what kid wouldn't want all this money, be at all these parties, be out in the limelight and meeting all the people? And they're absolutely, 100 per cent, 180 degrees the wrong direction with him.

"He's the guy who wanted to stay in, sleep, watch TV, hang out with the boys. He didn't want any of the limelight. He was not a limelight guy. Can you imagine every week somebody putting you in the worst scenario possible for you, and then saying, now perform? Rocket is one of the nicest, most lovable people you could ever meet. But he's not fake. He's not a performer where you can just ask him to be someone he's not."

Despite his eagerness to discard Ismail after two years, McNall insists he and the Rocket parted on good terms, although he hasn't spoken to him for years. "I think he realizes that in his whole football career, that was the biggest thing he ever had. He played [in the NFL] for ten years. He was a very good player, but not the superstar that he was in the CFL.

Nobody came to see him, where they did in the CFL. I think he would say that for that moment in time for him, it was probably the most exciting time he's ever had."

Ismail did acknowledge, years later, that he had not been prepared for the role that was thrust upon him by signing such a massive contract. On a TSN radio program in Toronto, he was asked about a line in Elton John's *Rocket Man*, which had been played at the news conference where his signing was announced: "I'm not the man they think I am at all."

"I was faking like a man," the Rocket replied, "but I was desperately looking for a blueprint on what it took to actually be a man. I don't think I actually felt like a grown, mature man capable of handling whatever came my way probably until I was about 35."

Fun While It Lasted

EVERYTHING THE MCNALL GROUP did in 1991 seemed bigger than anything ever done in the Canadian Football League. So it was only fitting that the Argos' post-game celebration a few hours after winning the Grey Cup was the biggest of all time.

In the same Sheraton hotel ballroom where, 24 hours earlier, Matt Dunigan had secretly tested his ability to throw the football with a broken collarbone, about 350 individuals gathered on the evening of Sunday, November 24, to toast the Grey Cup champions. The crowd included players, coaches, and staff of the Argonauts. Also, family members, the Hollywood entourage, and more than a few hangers-on.

Amidst the revelry, with Champagne and beer being drunk out of the Grey Cup, the seeds of despair, which would become the prevailing emotion of 1992 and 1993, were sown. The three owners of the Argos all made celebratory speeches. But it was a remark by Bruce McNall that inadvertently signalled the magic was coming to an end.

The gregarious majority owner took to the podium to marvel over what a great day it had been and how gratified he was to win a championship in his first year in the CFL. "If you're in this room, you're going to Disney World with us. We're going to take everybody." The ballroom erupted in euphoria.[31]

"We were high-fiving. Bruce is taking us to Disney World!" says David Watkins, the team's director of public relations. "Everyone's yelling, 'You're the best, Bruce! Yeah!'"

But there would be no trip to Disney World. It was one thing to make a big promise when the drinks were flowing and the mood was high. It was another to deliver on it when the financial bottom was about to fall out of the organization.

From the day the Argonauts were bought by McNall, Wayne Gretzky, and John Candy, money had flowed freely. They had signed Raghib "Rocket" Ismail to the richest contract in the history of football. They had staged the grand opening-night spectacle featuring Dan Aykroyd and a Blues Brothers band flown in from Europe. The private jets, the Roots jackets, the cappuccino maker. On it went.

When the new owners arrived, "they couldn't spend too much money," says journalist Doug Smith. "You wondered whether it was sustainable. You started thinking, how can this go on for a year, let alone forever? When would the other shoe drop?"

It started dropping even before the first season ended. Although Hollywood celebs (mostly B-listers, truth be told) and musical acts like the Barenaked Ladies still showed up on the JumboTron at home games, there were no more big post-game concerts.

---

31 McNall's announcement came four years after the most valuable player in the 1987 Super Bowl, Phil Simms, agreed to yell, "I'm going to Disney World" in a TV commercial. The Disney corporation then hired other athletes, including Magic Johnson of the Los Angeles Lakers, to make similar advertising pitches after winning championships. For a time in the late 1980s and into the next decade, "I'm going to Disney World" (or alternatively Disneyland) was a "thing."

A major reason was that revenue was not meeting expectations. The McNall group had figured that by injecting a dash of celebrity into the product—whether that was Ismail, a celebrity solely because of his stunningly high salary, or genuine celebs like Candy and Gretzky—the team would fill SkyDome and rake in money. But the home opener's crowd of 41,000, although roughly twice what the Argos had typically drawn in 1990, was still 13,000 below a sellout. And crowds for subsequent home games were in the 30,000s, far below expectations (although the team did manage a near-sellout for the Eastern Final).

Suzan Waks, the McNall organization's senior financial executive, knew early on that the gravy train couldn't continue indefinitely. Before the end of 1991, she acknowledges, "we were saying, 'I'm not sure we can make this work financially.' We were in the red, and you figure it's probably never getting better than this."

That revenue shortfall was just one of many problems for McNall. Unbeknownst to virtually everyone in the Argonauts organization other than McNall and Waks, the whole McNall empire had been built on fraud. A financial house of cards he had constructed over a five-year period was starting to collapse. The earliest evidence of that, although it wasn't fully apparent for a few years, came in Toronto, with the Argonauts.

* * *

Bruce McNall's story was the stuff of legend. He had acquired some business acumen early: as a five-year-old playing Monopoly at home, he always tried to buy the high-priced properties "and he always seemed to get them," his mom once said.

As a teenager, he had been astonished to discover he could buy ancient Roman coins for just a buck or two. He got hooked on coin collecting, kept trading his way into richer deals (some of which required smuggling coins illegally across borders, sometimes in his pants pockets) and eventually became wealthy enough to buy private jets, fancy cars, and multiple luxury homes. He became a major mover in sports and entertainment circles as owner of the NHL's Los Angeles Kings and a successful film producer. "I came in with nothing, I'm going out with nothing, and I'm going to have a good time in between," he said at the height of his rise to prominence.

McNall Sports & Entertainment conned banks out of massive loans, often backed by assets that didn't exist. It fooled rich individuals and corporations into funding investment opportunities based on false premises. Starry-eyed investors and lenders bought the hype, didn't ask many questions, and signed hefty cheques. Each new project, whether it was a film production or a sports team, was relied on to finance previous projects.

In one classic example of McNall's scheming, he purported to have gigantic assets in the bull market of sports collectibles. He and Gretzky had very publicly spent nearly a half-million dollars on a rare 1909 baseball card featuring a legendary player named Honus Wagner. So when McNall showed off stacks of essentially worthless cards, gullible lenders eagerly bought the fiction that they were worth a fortune. He also passed off collectibles borrowed from their actual owners, like Babe Ruth's New York Yankees contract, as his own.

One of McNall's ex-wives, Jane Cody, once found her own signature forged on a document that put her home up as collateral for a loan. McNall told her it had been done by "some underling," without his knowledge. "He's very smart, very talented—and very crooked," Cody once told a journalist.

Perhaps the first sign of trouble for McNall came just a few months into his ownership of the Argos. A piece in *Forbes* magazine exposed some stories he had told (such as attending Oxford University and doing deals with billionaires J. Paul Getty and Howard Hughes) as pure fiction. In a retrospectively telling anecdote, McNall was described by a rival coin dealer as "the Donald Trump of the coin world—a master promoter."

In 1993, Scott Carmichael, a Los Angeles Kings communication executive, called his Argo counterpart David Watkins to say a journalist would be meeting with McNall when the owner visited the team's offices at Exhibition Stadium. The journalist turned out to be Bryan Burrough, renowned for breaking big stories about corporate wrongdoing. He published an article in March 1994 in *Vanity Fair* entitled "Raider of the Lost Art." It revealed that McNall had stolen and smuggled ancient artifacts—not just coins, but also larger antiquities—out of countries around the Mediterranean, and found wealthy buyers eager to turn a blind eye to the items' provenance.

McNall cheerfully admitted it was all true.

"Bruce loved to talk," understates Carmichael. "The exposé perhaps wouldn't have been as impactful had Bruce not been Bruce."

The Vanity Fair story focused mostly on shady dealings in antiquities, and didn't delve deeply into the ugly financial realities of McNall's sports and entertainment businesses. But a whistle had been blown on his dishonest practices.

McNall was later described by *Fortune* magazine as a "preternatural schmoozer who seemingly could get anyone to lend him money . . . with a Ponzi-esque balance sheet."

A *GQ* profile said McNall "had a ten-year party with other people's money [and] created a culture of fraud."

When it was all tallied in 1996, the McNall companies had ripped off lenders and investors, including the Bank of America and Credit Lyonnaise, for almost a quarter-billion dollars. Both McNall and Waks went to penitentiary for the schemes.

* * *

After McNall obtained Wayne Gretzky for his Los Angeles Kings in 1988, the NHL essentially "handed him the keys to the league," says Stephen Brunt, lead sports columnist for the *Globe and Mail* in those days. "He was a brilliant, charming, charismatic conman. He was this kind of nerdy, roly-poly guy . . . which made him endearing. Kind of giggly, kind of goofy. Which is why he was such an effective conman."

McNall had a way of persuading people to see things his way. "If he pointed to a window and said he could fly, you'd have to believe him," says Gord Miller, a TSN announcer who covered the Argonauts closely in 1991.

One person over whom McNall held considerable sway was Gretzky. McNall was not only the Great One's boss; he was also his partner in ventures like racehorses that had made money for the pair.

One day in late 1990 or early 1991, Gretzky had called Brian Cooper, a marketing executive in Toronto who had established a business relationship and friendship with the hockey star after he increased the scope of Gretzky's charity tennis tournament. McNall was thinking of buying the Argonauts and bringing the Great One along as a partner. "What do you think of this?" Gretzky asked.

"I don't think it's going to fly," Cooper replied. "You're going to have to put too much money in. It's going to take years to build."

It seemed obvious to Cooper that the Argos were a poor investment. "[None of] my colleagues were buying tickets to Argo games. Like, no one. The NFL had a strong following up here. The Argos, because of the way Harry [Ornest] ran them into the ground . . . their relevance in the marketplace was at its lowest point."

Gretzky shrugged off Cooper's pessimistic analysis, and went along with McNall's plan to purchase the club. Cooper was then hired to run the team day to day, in an unconventional organizational structure. Cooper has described himself as a former Argo president, but in 1991 and 1992 his official title was executive vice-president and chief operating officer. The team had no president (although a few sports executives were approached about the possibility, including Richard Peddie, who at the time ran SkyDome, the Argos' home stadium).

Vying with Cooper for control of the Argonauts was Waks. By coincidence, the two had gone to high school together in New York City. Waks's official title with the Argos was alternate governor, but "the whole Argonauts venture became more Su's thing than anybody's," says McNall. "It was Su's team, that was the bottom line. From a business standpoint and an emotional standpoint, that was her baby."[32]

As one of the first female executives in football, Waks regularly endured sexist, dismissive remarks and whispers. Standing barely five feet tall, with big, imposing hair and a wide, endearing smile, she was often described as "a pit bull in a dress."

Sometimes that characterization had a slight variation: "pit bull in heels." Which would inevitably revive the story about her supposed demand to have a pair of shoes flown to Toronto from L.A. for her use. Waks simply rolls her eyes when that tale—possibly apocryphal, or at least incomplete—is mentioned. McNall doubts it ever happened. "She probably had them put some shoes on a plane that was coming anyways. I don't think I would have been very happy if she used the private jet for a hundred thousand [dollars] to take some shoes."

---

32 Waks delivered an actual baby early in her time with the Argonauts. Peddie recalls Waks as "a little dynamo" who insisted on continuing negotiations over the team's stadium lease almost until the moment she gave birth.

While the Argos were Waks's baby, Cooper was the senior on-site executive, and it was up to him to make things work financially. Any hopes he had of turning a profit had been dashed the moment Rocket Ismail signed his contract. Asked how much money the team lost in 1991 and '92, Cooper says between $7 million and $8 million. Ismail was paid $9 million US for those two seasons.

"I can juggle books with the best of them," Cooper says, but after Ismail was paid up front, "I had no money left to operate for the rest of the season. Even though we increased the gate receipts tremendously, probably by over 150 per cent, we weren't going to make up the four-million US hole we started in."

During meetings to plan for the 1992 season, Cooper was stunned to hear Waks say Argo fans "deserved" a ticket-price increase after the Grey Cup season. "You guys are making a big mistake," he snapped. "This is not the time to do this. Our foundation is not solid. This can turn on us real quick."

In addition to raising ticket prices, the Argos slashed spending to try to cover the revenue gap. That's why there would be no trips to Disney World, or trips to Hawaii, or big cash bonuses, as were also rumoured when the Argos won in 1991. In the end, the organization gave a small payout, reportedly in the range of $1,000 to $1,500, to players and other staff members. And some player salaries were cut at the start of the 1992 season.

Another broken promise involved the team's championship rings, which had been touted as unlike any ever seen before. The rings received by the players had the Argos' A logo in white embedded on a blue background, with team slogan "The Pride, The Glory" etched around it. On one side of the ring band was the player's name and uniform number, a rendering of the Argo helmet and "fifteen-five" (a reference to the team's won-lost record in 1991). The other side had the score of the Grey Cup game and a depiction of the trophy.

As attractive as the ring would be to anyone who has never earned one, it was far less glitzy than players had expected. "Those rings were just a big letdown," says linebacker Chris Gaines. "I mean, it was big and it was nice, but . . . they were talking about all these diamonds. The players were like, what is going on?"

David Bovell, a late addition to the Argos after being released by the Winnipeg Blue Bombers, was the only individual to earn a Grey Cup ring in both 1990 and 1991. The Blue Bombers' ring from 1990 had an almost identical design, with Winnipeg's W logo set into a blue background. "If [manufacturer] Jostens had an entry-level championship ring, that's what this would have been," Bovell says.

Based on weight of gold, the Argo ring was as big as any issued to that date, says Pruenster, who also has a smaller Grey Cup ring from the team's 1983 championship. He had seen prototypes because of his close relationship with co-owner John Candy. "But it had one diamond in it. Those diamond chips don't cost anything. I always wondered why they didn't just spend a few hundred bucks to . . . bling it out with not-valuable diamonds."

Led by receiver Darrell K. Smith, notorious for his love of bling, several Argo players had extra diamonds added to their rings, at their own expense.

To be fair, a number of players were happy with the ring. "I've got the same one John Candy had," says defensive end Mike Campbell. "That's good enough for me."

Even if McNall had been everything he said he was, the Argos faced an uphill battle to financial solvency in Toronto. Attendance at SkyDome dropped almost 20 per cent in 1992 as Torontonians turned their attentions elsewhere after the magical championship run. "The people of Toronto," says McNall, "were like, hey, we won, goodbye, see you later, we'll do something else.

"We just couldn't replicate the excitement of that first year. There was nothing we could do to top that. It's like making a sequel to a giant film; the odds are not great to do that easily. That's what it felt like—the sequel just wasn't there."

The first year "was the honeymoon," says Greg Campbell, the Argos' CFO. "It was a battle to try to maintain that excitement level. I don't want to say that the fans felt entitled, but I think we needed to dazzle them almost as much in the second and third year as we did in the first year."

Except there was no money available to do so, no matter how aggressively the organization chased new revenues and how tightly it controlled spending.

Blaine Schmidt, who sold cell phones while working as an offensive lineman and long snapper, was close friends with sales staff at CHUM, which had broadcast the team's games on radio in 1991. He was appalled to discover that Argo management jacked up sponsorship rates for CHUM and other partners. "They were the head sponsors throughout the lean years and now you're [gouging them] just because you won one Grey Cup? That's not right." (CFRB took over radio broadcasts in 1992.)

Executives in Toronto learned the hard way that Los Angeles was taking its time paying bills. The Argos' chief operating officer was enjoying a relaxing dinner with his wife at a restaurant one night when a fellow approached their table. "You're Brian Cooper," he said. "You stiffed me." The man ran a printing company that had done some work for the Argonauts and didn't get paid for nine months. Cooper was mortified. In a matter of months, the Toronto Argonauts had mutated from the talk of the town into a bad receivable for a bunch of small-business owners.

At head office, McNall, Waks, and a few others were desperately trying to stay current on loans and keep McNall Sports & Entertainment afloat. They instructed Cooper to try to wheedle new credit, McNall's standard approach. The three banks he approached weren't as credulous as their American counterparts; they needed to see tangible evidence of real assets. All Cooper could offer was a thin prospectus for one of McNall's investments. It "wasn't actual documentation. It was just the prospectus, but it had Merrill Lynch [a globally known investment banking firm] at the top. [McNall] assumed Canadian banks, like Americans, were going to fall for that. I struck out very quickly."

Meanwhile, Cooper was making regular cash calls to L.A., and not getting any answers. "Brian Cooper would tell me that he himself was having to phone them to get [financial] transfers," says John Tory, who was the CFL's legal counsel at the time. "They would quibble and equivocate."

"Looking back," says Cooper, "they had no money and they had bigger conversations than how the Argos are doing. Like where the hell are we going to get this money before somebody finds out?"

While their own finances and McNall's crumbling empire were one set of problems for the Argos, the state of the CFL was another. Cooper's pre-purchase analysis advising his friend Gretzky not to buy into the club had focused primarily on the Toronto market. It came as an unpleasant shock to the McNall group that the league as a whole, both financially and from a governance perspective, was a mess.

A couple of franchises were teetering on the edge of bankruptcy, and the Ottawa Rough Riders needed to have their bills paid by the other clubs for several months until their buyer was found. This sunk the Argos' chances of getting the other franchises to help pay Ismail's salary, which was perhaps a pipe dream to begin with.

"When we came in to find out that some of the teams were in really bad shape, the likelihood that we were going to get anything more than what we generated [from ticket sales] dissipated," says Waks. "The league didn't have as much leeway to give us what we wanted in order to cover the cost of Rocket, which everyone was benefitting from."

The prevailing attitude from other clubs, she says, was, "It's not my responsibility to help you with your contract with Rocket. I didn't tell you to sign him. I'm happy to take whatever comes into my stadium, but I'm not giving you anything."

One of the biggest fights was over TV rights. The league sold rights nationally to CBC, which would then resell some games to TSN. The McNall group demanded the right to sell Argo home games to local broadcasters. Waks says this had been promised by commissioner Donald Crump, whom she describes as "a nice guy [who] didn't have a really great handle on the big picture." Cooper says Crump was "in way over his head."

Tory confirms the McNall group had been granted permission to sell some games to local broadcasters, but those would be games that were not included in CBC's national package. "The league couldn't have survived without the national TV contract, which included a number of Argo home games—usually more than you might expect, because the Toronto market is the biggest." In 1991, only one Argonauts game was not televised nationally by either CBC or TSN. The following year, 20 league games were not televised; none involved the Argos.

Argo executives also clashed with their fellow clubs over gate equalization. Dating to the early 1970s, the Argonauts (who led the league in home attendance in that era) shared ticket revenue with visiting teams, an arrangement that supported clubs in smaller markets. This was still in effect in 1991, even though the Argos were paying $100,000 per game to rent SkyDome. Toronto was still expected to pay $300,000 into the gate-equalization fund; the Hamilton Tiger-Cats, who paid virtually no rent at Ivor Wynne Stadium, expected to receive a total of $400,000 from the fund. The McNall group demanded this subsidy be scrapped.

McNall went public with his displeasure just before the 1992 season began. "I feel a little hurt, a little peeved," he said. "I thought we had done some things to create excitement and bring some credibility and financial stability to the league. Now that that's been done, they've forgotten about the things they promised us before we bought the team. The attitude seems to be, 'They've got deep pockets, don't worry.'"

Tory made countless pilgrimages to McNall's corporate headquarters in California. "Look," Argo executives would tell him, "we're not going to invest all this money and build up this franchise just to totally benefit all the other teams." While sympathetic to the McNall group's desire for a favourable return on investment, Tory would remind them the league as a whole was in a precarious state: "If you don't have anybody to play against, I guess it won't be a very valuable franchise to own."

Battles were protracted and, at times, rancorous. Old-school executives from community-owned clubs, like Winnipeg's Cal Murphy, and private owners like Hamilton's David Braley accused the Argos of trying to run the entire league. Nor were the other teams happy dealing with an upstart like Cooper, who, although he had lived in Canada for decades, retained a heavy accent from the New York borough of Queens.

"They're muttering, 'The Yankee fuck' under their breaths," he says. "I had some classic battles with them. Some of the shit that was coming out of the mouths of the other governors, I was like, 'Help me. We're all going to go down if we listen to this shit.'"

Argonauts executives behaved arrogantly, says Phil Kershaw, who became chair of the CFL board in 1991. "They were not afraid to throw

YEAR OF THE ROCKET

their weight around. Anytime you . . . start a conversation with, 'Do you know who I am?' it's not going to . . . build a relationship."

Toronto's attitude was "we're the saviours of this league, so . . . rules don't apply to us," Tory says. "They were 'first among equals,' therefore they should get different treatment on everything. We were 'so lucky to have them here.'

"It became evident as we went through all these disputes: this wasn't an attempt to resolve a long-term issue, but rather it was a short-term attempt to try and improve cash flow. It wasn't just points of principle. There really was an inability, or unwillingness, or a combination, to write these huge cheques that were needed."

Adds Kershaw: "We were all under the [impression] that these guys . . . had more money than God, almost. After the first year, it became apparent that the emperor had no clothes."

Larry Smith saw that first-hand. Soon after being hired as CFL commissioner in early 1992, he flew to Los Angeles to meet with McNall at his offices in Century City. "He had a large staff of people; I think he had three or four floors in the building. About six months later, I went down and he had half the number of staff. About a year and a half later, there were about two people left."[33]

Another contentious issue that flared up in 1992 not only drove a wedge between the Argonauts and the other seven franchises, but also put John Candy in an untenable position.

Candy's passion for promoting the Argos and the league had been relentless and incredibly effective throughout 1991. Everywhere he visited,

33 When McNall was interviewed for this book in 2018, the discussion took place in a tiny office in a nondescript building in downtown Santa Monica. McNall's "desk" was essentially a slab of wood resting on two sets of desk drawers.

more tickets were sold for the Argos' visit than for the average of all other games in that city. Some of this was because of the circus atmosphere surrounding Toronto and Rocket, but a lot of it was due to Candy making the rounds of local radio and TV stations hawking tickets.

As overjoyed as fans were to see him in every stadium, the tour took a toll on the actor, who had to put his career on hold. In August 1991, Candy had told the *Edmonton Journal*: "We didn't realize the problems we were facing coming in, the amount of travel it would involve for myself. . . . It's a lot more than I thought."

In 1992, Candy resumed his acting career. He still attended many Argo home games, but did not go on the road with the club. The Argonauts, meanwhile, presented the league with a bill for $400,000 to cover expenses Candy had incurred flying by private jet to each city the previous year.

"We can't do that," Kershaw huffily told Argo executives. If the Argonauts had approached other teams in advance offering to have Candy visit in exchange for expense reimbursement, the response would have been, "There's absolutely no way we're doing that."

Waks says Candy had asked Argo management to reimburse his 1991 expenses. Kershaw says the actor did not seem to know the Argos were going to seek recompense from the league. "I think he was embarrassed. It probably revealed to him that the people he thought were his partners in the Argos weren't who they said they were. The fact they didn't want to pay the travel expenses . . . I just think they didn't have it."

Candy making the rounds of the league in 1991 was "a huge plus," acknowledges Tory. "But we didn't have the money to pay his expenses for economy airfare, let alone a private jet."

In the end, Tory worked out a compromise. Each team would cough up about $18,000 in 1992 and '93, meaning the Argos would be repaid

$250,000 in total—below the requested $400,000, but still a tough pill for the other franchises to swallow.

All of the pressures bearing down on the Argos had a predictable impact on people in the team's front office. Waks had flown to Toronto regularly in 1991, but was becoming too enmeshed in McNall's tangled financial affairs to visit as often the following year. The relationship between business operations in Toronto and head office in L.A. became dysfunctional, a situation compounded when a new executive entered the mix.

Cooper and general manager Mike McCarthy received a letter from Waks and McNall in August 1992 advising that "Tony Tavares has been given the assignment of being the sole Owners' Representative to the Toronto Argonauts Football Club for the balance of the season."

A consultant with a reputation as an up-and-coming sports executive, Tavares had been given "full executive powers and authority to oversee routine club operations. Please accept his directives and advice as if it were coming directly from us."

No public announcement was made about Tavares' appointment to the oddly titled position of "owners' representative." But word of his involvement leaked to the *Globe and Mail*, which said he had concluded that the organization was riven with internal conflicts. "There are damned few people in that Toronto organization who get along with each other," Tavares was quoted as saying.

There were indeed tensions in Toronto. Cooper and McCarthy clashed at times. For the most part, Cooper stayed out of matters related to football, and kept McCarthy out of matters related to business. But Cooper could not resist needling the GM. One day, before Matt Dunigan signed with Winnipeg, Cooper spotted something in the daily digest of newspaper clippings circulated around the office. A story had quoted Waks, rather than McCarthy, speaking about negotiations with the quarterback. Cooper, knowing McCarthy would see the report, scribbled a note in the margins asking whether Waks was now "your assistant GM?"[34]

A larger source of conflict, however, was not within the Toronto operation, but between Cooper and Waks, the former schoolmates who now seemed at odds with one another. The mere fact the Tavares report was leaked to the media gave credence to its thesis of internecine warfare. In a follow-up *Globe* story, Cooper took what appears to have been a thinly-veiled shot at either Waks or Rosanne Rocchi, an aggressive Toronto lawyer who did a lot of work for McNall. "Who's your source?" Cooper was reported to have asked reporter Marty York. "I'll tell you this: whoever she is obviously has it in for me."

It was an altogether unpleasant time for Cooper, who had another huge challenge in the fall of 1992. As part of their agreement to buy the Argonauts a year earlier, the McNall group had been granted the right to stage the Grey Cup in SkyDome in 1992 and 1993. McNall and his partners believed they could profit from hosting one of Canada's biggest sports events. They hadn't anticipated that the Argonauts would tank in 1992, and that the Toronto Blue Jays would be filling SkyDome with 50,000 spectators, night after night, while contending for a championship of their own. Canadian football was swamped by baseball fever.

Cooper tried desperately to drum up interest in the Grey Cup game, sweeping away some of its tired traditions, such as the Grey Cup parade and the anachronistic Miss Grey Cup pageant. He introduced a "fan bowl" featuring interactive exhibits, and made Gretzky and Candy

---

34 McCarthy could get under Cooper's skin, too. During a meeting one day, Coper recalls, "I had a big potted plant, and he goes over and spits in the planter. He had tobacco in his mouth. I told him, 'Don't ever fucking do that again.'"

available for autograph sessions. He hired Celine Dion, then on the verge of international superstardom, to sing at the gala Grey Cup dinner. None of it moved the needle.

There was virtually no buzz in Toronto about the 1992 final. With two western-based teams (Calgary and East Division representative Winnipeg) advancing the week before, any hopes of a big last-minute rush for tickets was dashed. Attendance was announced at fewer than 46,000; some of those were freebies handed out in a bid to make SkyDome look almost full.

"It was a tough, tough sell," says Cooper. "We put on what I thought was a great Grey Cup, it was just that nobody came."[35]

With nothing but bad news coming out of Argos offices, Wayne Gretzky began to express disenchantment with his investment in the club. In a candid interview on TSN, he more or less waved a white flag.

"The problem with the CFL is it's been struggling for 15 years. This is not an overnight problem," he said, echoing his friend and adviser Cooper's warnings from 1991. "You've got teams such as Toronto, who in this city are viewed as not a professional team. . . . The people in Toronto, people in Hamilton, are saying, 'We don't want to watch it right now, we're not interested in it.' My feeling is, hey, if the people in Toronto don't want CFL, that's fine. . . . If people aren't going to support it, we've got to think of the alternatives."

Asked if the Argo owners might pull the plug, the Great One offered at best a half-hearted commitment: "I don't think we'll pull the plug, but I think we've come to the point where now we're saying, 'OK, we can't take any more losses. Now we've got to think of the alternatives.' John

---

35 Not willing to play host again in 1993, the Argos sold the rights to the next Grey Cup to the Calgary Stampeders.

[Candy] and I being from around this area, we've got too much respect for the people of Canada to quote 'pull the plug.' But . . . common sense tells you that if us three are having trouble making this work, it's going to be very difficult for anyone else to come in and make it work."

A year later, Gretzky was less equivocal. Enough was enough. "The fact is, people in Toronto don't want the CFL," he told the *Toronto Star* in November 1993. "I've told McNall, I think it's time [to sell]. . . . As far as I'm concerned, time's up."

Unhappy Ending

By the spring of 1993, the Argonauts were bleeding cash, and there was no prospect of improvement. Even with Rocket Ismail about to be released from his contract, which would save the club nine million dollars over the next two years, things looked bleak. It was increasingly common for the team's suppliers to wait months to be paid. And word began to spread that the problems were shared with others in Bruce McNall's crumbling empire.

The L.A. Kings were advancing towards the 1993 Stanley Cup final when Danny Webb, the Argos' equipment manager, got a phone call from his counterpart with the hockey club. "We just had a stick order rejected," the Kings' equipment guy said. "I'm just wondering if things are OK up there."

Things weren't OK up there. Brian Cooper was offering to pay vendors and suppliers with game tickets, "anything but cash." He flew to L.A. to show his bosses the team's ledgers and plead for help. "I can't say it any clearer," he told them. "I need some money."

When he agreed to buy a 20-per-cent stake in the club, John Candy had ensured that his investment would be capped at $1 million. While majority owner Bruce McNall has since tried to claim this was his idea, it was actually Candy's wife, Rose, who had insisted.

"You put a cap on this or we're not doing it," she had told her husband in 1991. "This is going to be fun, but you cap it."

"Our mom was always supportive of our dad," daughter Jennifer says, "but she was also the [one with] common sense. Our dad probably would have shelled out everything he owned to put into that team."

The other 20-per-cent partner, Wayne Gretzky, had no such limitation on his contribution. Gretzky had to dip into his own pocketbook at times to float money to the football club. He was not happy about it, and perhaps forgetting that Cooper had warned him against the investment, complained to him: "This is costing me."

McNall had already given Cooper two instructions: find a buyer for the Argos, and don't tell John. McNall didn't explain the reasoning behind the second point, but Cooper surmised that the majority owner was afraid of Candy finding out how desperate things were in the crumbling empire.

Cooper quickly got into serious discussions with John Labatt Ltd., a brewery that already owned the Blue Jays and owned TSN, at the time Canada's only cable sports network.

The proposed deal made sense for Labatt: if no one else bought the Argos (and no other buyers had emerged from Cooper's search), the CFL might become a western-based league, and TSN's telecasts would be far less attractive to sponsors. The brewery was also part of the consortium that owned SkyDome, and having the Argonauts in the building for ten games a year was better than the alternative.

From the CFL's perspective, "all we wanted was some kind of stable ownership for Toronto," says John Tory, the league's legal counsel. "Somebody who could write the cheques and not fight with us." He was thrilled to have Labatt, a rich company in the sports television business, at the table.

Before a deal could be consummated with Labatt, Cooper's employment was terminated.

So was Cooper's friendship with John Candy, who had suddenly stopped talking to him. The actor had somehow found out the team was up for sale, and he needed somebody to blame, Cooper says. "He wasn't going to blame Bruce or Wayne. He felt I had betrayed him, and maybe he felt that way because I hadn't told him. But my boss was Bruce, and Wayne was my closer friend. It wasn't for me to tell John if they didn't want me to tell him." Candy and Cooper never spoke again.

McNall appointed Scott Carmichael, the senior communications executive for the Kings, as temporary head of the Argonauts. In the summer of 1993, Carmichael and Candy met regularly at the actor's favourite steak house in Toronto, Barberian's. Sipping his rum and Diet Coke, Candy would fret that his public image was suffering because things had gone so sour with the Argonauts, on and off the field. "What do you think people think of me?" he'd ask Carmichael. "I'm concerned about my reputation."

Although Candy was shooting movies again, he continued to attend home games, hosting family and friends in his skybox. He still had the same passion for the team that he'd had as a kid.

The dawning realization that his team was in deep trouble and that McNall had financial difficulties seemed to sap Candy's enthusiasm. Whereas two years earlier, he had eagerly sat through ten-hour league meetings, paying attention and contributing input throughout, now his weary reply to problems presented to him was "do what you want."

After Cooper was fired, Candy got actively involved again. He reached out to Ron Barbaro about becoming president of the Argonauts. Barbaro, who had just retired after a successful career as an insurance executive, had made a name for himself in Toronto as the man who "saved" the city's Santa Claus parade when it lost its traditional sponsor, the Eaton's department-store chain. And back in the 1960s, he had founded the Argo Playback Club, which attracted hundreds of fans to gatherings in which Barbaro would interview coaches and players.

Barbaro mulled over the idea for a few weeks, during which the Argos kept losing; they would finish the 1993 season with three wins in 18 games. SkyDome crowds often barely topped 20,000.

Intrigued by the challenge, Barbaro accepted Candy's offer and became the new Argo president. Almost immediately, he dismissed GM Mike McCarthy and head coach Dennis Meyer, bringing back Bob O'Billovich to take over both roles.

Barbaro also flew to L.A. to meet with his new boss. "I don't have any money," McNall told him. Lovely, thought Barbaro.

He came back to Toronto and told Candy, "We've got to sell this team."

"We've got to keep it going," insisted Candy, still emotionally invested.

It's unclear whether Candy did anything other than ponder the situation over the ensuing months. Meanwhile, things only got worse at McNall Sports & Entertainment. It was on the verge of collapse with debt in the range of $200 million, much of it backed by phony collateral. McNall was desperate to sell assets. Finally, in February 1994, he was ready to close a deal for the Argos.

That's when a call was made to Candy, who was in Mexico shooting a movie called *Wagon's East*. Standing on a dusty desert plain, wearing a scruffy beard and a big cowboy hat, Candy took the call on a large satellite phone. It was his business manager, Gary Kress.

It was a call Candy had been expecting. And dreading.

Kress informed him that the Argos were going to be sold. Candy was about to lose his direct connection to the team that had brought him to tears of joy in the locker room after the 1991 Grey Cup.

"I wouldn't go so far as to say the colour went out of his face, but it was close," says Candy's assistant Bob Crane Jr., who stood nearby as Candy talked to Kress. "This was a cold, corporate, 'we're dumping this.' He deserved better than that."

Candy briefly toyed with the idea of putting together an ownership group of his own. "I still believe in the Argos," he told another assistant, Bret Gallagher. Candy called a journalist he had befriended to say he was trying to muster a group to buy the club. He promised to call back as soon as he found out whether his efforts were successful.

But he apparently couldn't find a partner with deep enough pockets, and couldn't afford to take the lead himself. "However successful he was," says Tory, "he wasn't rich enough to lose four to five million bucks a year."

A week or two after he learned the team was being sold, any hope Candy had of continuing with the Argonauts in any capacity was moot.

On the morning of March 4, 1994, one of his aides went to the actor's trailer on the set of *Wagon's East*. When Candy didn't answer the door, the aide broke in. John Candy was on his bed, dead of an apparent heart attack at the age of 43.

The Money Trail

TWO MONTHS AFTER John Candy died, his beloved Toronto Argonauts were sold on May 5, 1994. TSN, a subsidiary of the Labatt brewing company, said it was paying $6.5 million for the club.

The reality was much different. As when Harry Ornest had bought the club in November 1988, and when Candy teamed up with Bruce McNall and Wayne Gretzky to buy it from Ornest in February 1991, the story the public was told about how much money changed hands was little more than plausible fiction.

Getting a firm grip on financial realities in the CFL has always been a mug's game. League and team executives, and journalists, have historically thrown figures around with abandon. Whether it's revenues, expenses, profits, or attendance, reality is usually bent into saleable storylines. But it's safe to say that none of the three buyers paid, and none of the three sellers received, the amounts reported at the time.

"Harry Ornest was the only owner in Toronto Argonauts history who made money selling the team" is a statement that has been written so often over the years, it has entered into the realm of conventional wisdom. But is it true?

After buying the Argonauts from the Carling O'Keefe brewery in 1988, Ornest told reporters, "The total price is a little more than five million." Some journalists were skeptical, especially given Ornest's reputation for driving a hard bargain. "He bought the Argos for an actual outlay of about $1 million," Wayne Parrish insisted in the *Toronto Sun*.

When Ornest was looking for a buyer in early 1991, the *Globe and Mail* reported that his $5-million deal to buy the team from Carling O'Keefe had included a payment to him of between $3 million and $4 million for marketing rights to the Argos. This fits with an estimate provided all these years later by Ornest's son Mike, who believes the club cost his father $1 million, not $5 million.

When the club was sold to McNall, Gretzky and Candy, the announced price was again $5 million. In theory, Ornest made a profit as high as $4 million on his short-term investment. But that does not appear to be the case, either.

What journalists weren't told when Ornest sold the club was that he had agreed to accept notes—promises of future payment—to cover a substantial portion of the sale price. "He got two million down and the balance was going to be paid over the course of whatever period of time," says Mike Ornest.

Much, if not all, of that two million appears to have come from Candy and Gretzky. Each had been announced as owning 20 per cent of the club, with McNall owning the other 60 per cent. So, $1 million each from the two minority partners in a deal said to be worth $5 million.

McNall, who later went to prison for bank fraud, wire fraud and conspiracy, is said by associates to have a great memory for details of financial transactions. But asked how much money Ornest received up front, he offers only a vague recollection. "I don't remember the exact initial payment, but it was probably half [of the sale price] or something like that.

"Whatever it was, I remember there were several contingencies. It was so much money down; maybe it was a couple of million dollars down, or half, or something in that ballpark. And then he'd be paid as economic things occurred, and I don't think anything occurred."

There's clear evidence that at least a million dollars of Ornest's take was to be deferred to a later date. In December 1993, Ornest wrote a letter to McNall "to clarify our agreement regarding the stock and monies that are due and owing . . . in connection with the $1-million promissory note executed May 31, 1991." (The sale of the team had been announced in February, but details were not finalized until May.)

The letter documented a series of agreements Ornest and McNall had subsequently reached that increased the overall value of what Ornest was owed to more than a million dollars. Among them, McNall was to transfer shares of the Hollywood Park racetrack to Ornest in lieu of some of the money owed. "Unfortunately, to date you've neither delivered the stock to me nor paid me the money you owe me."

By Ornest's calculation, the total he was owed as of December 2, 1993, was $1,195,000: $518,368 in cash plus 105,724 shares of Hollywood Park, which Ornest valued at $676,632.

Ornest died in 1998 before McNall's debt could be settled, but the Ornest subsidiary that had owned the Argos pursued the matter.

After he got out of prison in 2001, McNall settled with creditors in bankruptcy proceedings. By then the Ornest company (OFE & Partners) had submitted a claim for $2,071,750. The final payment issued to that company with respect to the bankrupt estate of Bruce Patrick McNall was for $202,938. Or, as the cheque noted, 9.8 per cent of the claimed amount, less than ten cents on the dollar.

Intriguingly, the claim for two million is substantially less than what Ornest at some point apparently believed he was owed. This came to light in a disdainful note, found in a file saved by his daughter Laura, that Ornest wrote sometime after he had sold the Argos. On a photocopy of a page from the team's 1989 media guide that included a biographical sketch of Ornest, the former owner had typed this addendum: "Sold to McNall/Gretzky/John Candy—May 31/91. McNall took ONLY one year to ruin club financially after I left him and Candy [Gretzky was passive partner, essentially] a top-notch, profitable club. McNall stiffed me for 'only' $3.5 mil."

In a fond remembrance of Ornest published in March 2020, Steve Simmons of the *Toronto Sun* wrote: "He told me he never was paid the money McNall owed him. What he told me earlier and forgot: he never did pay for the Argos in the first place."

That's the mug's game of CFL finances.

* * *

Candy's investment in the Argonauts had been capped at a million dollars. Most of the executives interviewed for this book maintain the actor was not asked to pony up more, even when team management made cash calls to ownership in 1992 and '93. But Gretzky's investment was not capped, and he apparently anted up more than his $1 million.

A *Globe and Mail* report in August of 1992 said Gretzky's "personal losses on the Argos" would amount to $1.36 million by the end of that season, part of an overall loss projected at $6.8 million over the first two years of the McNall group's ownership. "Bruce owns 60 per cent of the club," the Great One said then, "but I pay my own way on every business venture with him. So I'm losing money on the Argos just like he is, and it's not a pleasant feeling."

Gretzky insists now he ultimately didn't lose money on his investment. "John and I didn't lose a penny. [McNall] said, 'I promise you guys you won't lose one penny.' That was the one thing about Bruce McNall. He didn't want our money. . . . If there was an upside, we would have benefitted, because that's how Bruce is. If there's a downside, then we were fine."

Suzan Waks, an executive who had detailed knowledge of McNall's tangled financial affairs, says if his partners lost money on a particular venture, he would try to make up for it through other deals. Gretzky was McNall's partner not just in the Argonauts but also in racehorses, sports memorabilia, coins, and other things. "This was the thing with Bruce. You buy a horse with him that didn't do well, and he'd be, 'OK, I'll just trade you into another one.' To him that was a big thing, that his partners should do well. They had very intertwined businesses. Wayne did fine. He lost here and he made it up there."

McNall says it was Gretzky's decision to not have his investment capped. "I could always pay him more money [to play hockey] so he's OK. When money was needed [to run the Argonauts], I basically put it up. I covered most of it, but Wayne was technically on the hook for it a little bit."

When the losses kept piling up in 1993, McNall says, "I couldn't go to him and ask for additional funds. Because he was Wayne Gretzky, for God's sake. Doing everything he's done for me, I couldn't ask him."

The $6.5 million Labatt/TSN allegedly paid to the McNall group for the Argonauts mostly involved settling with creditors who hadn't been paid by the team for goods or services. The new owner shelled out far less than the reported price.

"That number, like many numbers in those days, was concocted," says John Tory, the CFL's legal counsel at the time. "It was nowhere near that amount of money. That number of $6.5 million was meant, from the McNall perspective, to make it look like they sold it for [more than] they paid, and from the league's perspective, that the franchise still had a value."

Before he stepped down as team president after eight months in the job, Ron Barbaro worked to make sure creditors were compensated. "I paid all the little suppliers, all the small businesses, with the proceeds," he says.

Bob Nicholson, who replaced Barbaro as team president, adds: "It was really us picking up all the pieces. There were obviously bills, people we agreed to make whole. We bought those liabilities so we could continue to operate. Guys we'd have to work with in the future—you don't want to see them get stiffed and look at you the same way they might look at the previous owners."

There wasn't enough money coming from Labatt/TSN to pay one creditor, though. "The guy we owed two million to was really pissed off," Barbaro says. "Harry Ornest. He was owed and he wanted his money, but I used up all the money before I got to his name."

As for how the sellers made out in the deal, McNall says his group received "some cash, but it wasn't huge. Maybe a million bucks or something like that."

Nicholson, however, is adamant: the McNall group received nothing. "No money transferred. The owners didn't see a dime."

Epilogue

A FEW MONTHS INTO RESEARCHING this book, I drove to Erie, Pennsylvania, to interview Roy Mlakar, one of the executives who helped make 1991 the most magical, mesmerizing year in a century and a half of Argo football.

"What's the purpose of your visit?" asked the U.S. border patrol agent at the Peace Bridge.

"I'm writing a book about the 1991 Toronto Argonauts," I replied.

He broke into a wide grin. "Did you know John Candy?"

Sadly, I did not, although, like most who have seen his work in film and on television, I felt as if I did.

And, like every fan of Canadian football in the early 1990s, I came to understand how much John loved the Argos—and especially how much he loved being swept up in the circus of 1991.

Even living in far-away Edmonton, I managed to experience John Candy that year.

I took my son, David, to the Argos' opening game in Ottawa. Rocket Ismail stood on the sideline in street clothes, his launch delayed by a week, but it was Candy who stole the show. When he came up into the stands that night, fans at Lansdowne Park went bonkers over "Uncle Buck."

David and I were joined by my daughter, Rachel, the following week at SkyDome to see the Rocket make his debut in Toronto's home opener. The building was electric when Candy walked the sideline beforehand, and when he joined the reformed Blues Brothers Band for a halftime performance.

The Argos' visit to Edmonton a month later provided another opportunity to catch the show. The day before the game, I packed eight-year-old David and six-year-old Rachel into our minivan and drove to the field outside Commonwealth Stadium where the Argos were holding their "walk-through" routine. We watched agog as they spent more time break-dancing than practising.

Candy made the rounds that day. He offered warm, often hilarious, greetings to those on hand. He signed autographs and posed for pictures.

The next morning, adorning Cam Cole's column on the front of the *Edmonton Journal* sports section was a large colour photo of Candy alongside David. Rachel was, sad to say, cropped out of the image—ironic, in retrospect, since she ended up a bigger Argo and CFL fan than her older brother.

Since choosing the Argos as my team in the late 1960s, I had experienced all the pain and pleasure that comes with being a serious sports fan. I had endured many of the worst seasons in what eventually became 31 years of misery for the football club in Canada's largest city. I had suffered through failed big-name imports like Forrest Gregg, Anthony Davis and Terry Metcalf; through the sad second act of the legendary Leo Cahill; through the brief era of the tragically flawed Willie Wood. I had been at Bob O'Billovich's first game as head coach in 1982, and the game that triggered his dismissal in 1989.

Along with disappointment and in some cases humiliation, I had been fortunate enough to experience triumph and joy. I was at waterlogged Exhibition Stadium, thankfully in the covered north grandstand, when the surprisingly entertaining 1982 Argonauts improbably played in the Grey Cup just a year after the worst season in team history. They lost, but it was exhilarating, nonetheless. I was in Vancouver's B.C. Place Stadium a year later when the championship drought finally ended in a heart-stopping one-point victory.

My vocation as a journalist occasionally intersected with my avocation as an Argo fan. The first CFL game I ever covered was the Argos' 1986 home opener, after which I had my first encounter with Carl Brazley. Aghast over an official's ruling that had gone against the team, Brazley (my favourite player during his years with the Argos) told me afterwards that even his "good friend Steve Wonder"—the legendary musician, who happens to be visually impaired—would have known it was a terrible call.

But none of that could, or ever will, top 1991, when John Candy, Wayne Gretzky, and Bruce McNall ignited the most electrifying year in the history of a team that had been around since Canada was six years old.

A year when the funniest Canadian, the greatest hockey player, and a slick sports magnate with an apparent Midas touch brought Hollywood to Toronto.

When a kid so fast he was nicknamed Rocket became the highest-paid player in history, and rose to the occasion when it mattered most.

When a linebacker with the heart of a quarterback barked out inspirational raps, and a quarterback with the heart of a linebacker endured agonizing injections to lead his team to the ultimate victory.

And so much more . . .

The coldest Grey Cup ever played. The frozen beer can that almost beaned the Rocket as he was about to cross the goal-line.

It was a year that has never been topped for excitement and enthusiasm and craziness.

A year that came to a sad, sudden end.

After the three amigos took control of the ancient Argonauts franchise, after all the breathtaking highs of 1991, came two years of failure and strife.

The Rocket's ill-advised stomp on the head of Andy McVey was as far from the pride and glory of 1991 as anyone could possibly imagine.

The Argonauts' Hollywood era was a classic "how the mighty fall" tale. "They had the win," says broadcaster Matthew Cauz, who watched it unfold from the perspective of a fan in his late teens. "Then they got the stomp. John Candy's dead, Bruce McNall's in jail, and Wayne Gretzky's in St. Louis. It was like all these mini deals with the devil for this one moment."

"Just a special, divine era in Canadian football," says journalist Dave Naylor. "And ultimately unsustainable."

Soon after the 1991 Grey Cup, it became clear how much winning it had cost. "It was like New Year's Day," says broadcaster Gord Miller. "The party's over, and now you're sweeping up. You had that high, and no matter what you did, it was going to be a low the next year. It was an impossible act to follow. But for that one summer, they were the happening thing in Toronto. They made it matter, for a short time."

A short time. Indeed, the magic dissipated almost instantly. The triumph and joy of 1991 were followed by a well-deserved last-place finish, then by 15 defeats in 18 games, half of them played in a SkyDome that was barely one-third full. By 1994, only ten players who showed up for the start of training camp had a Grey Cup ring from 1991.

John Candy was gone by then. He died far too young, just days after coming to the bitter realization he had to walk away from the team he had adored since childhood.

Not long after selling the Argos out from under Candy, Bruce McNall acknowledged his multiple, massive frauds and began serving six years behind bars, including hard time in a couple of America's nastiest penitentiaries.

Just as he had duped credulous investors and lenders, McNall gamed the prison system. The six months he spent in "the hole"—solitary confinement—for refusing to rat out dirty guards was an act of self-preservation: he had negotiated special treatment from those crooked minders in exchange for hockey memorabilia brought in by his loyal friends Wayne Gretzky and Luc Robitaille. McNall even faked an alcohol addiction to wheedle his way into a cushier prison.

The guy one skeptical CFL governor had suggested should be properly vetted before being allowed to buy the Argos had turned out to be much, much less than he was cracked up to be.

"Icarus flying too close to the sun," says Phil Kershaw, one of the governors who shouted down that skeptic, lest the apparent golden goose fly the coop. "He had all of this ambition and wanted to be this highly influential power broker, but there was a moral, ethical lapse in his thinking. And somewhere in there, a lot of people ended up getting screwed."

Gretzky, whose desire to own a piece of the action waned almost as soon as the championship put him in the record books for winning both the Grey Cup and the Stanley Cup, spent the next decade playing out the string. Still a superb hockey player in St. Louis and New York, but never producing memories that came close to matching his glory years in Edmonton and Los Angeles.

The Rocket, stubbornly unwilling to live up to the promotional obligations that accompanied his outlandish pay packet, settled for the consolation prize of a much less generous, but still lucrative, NFL contract. He spent nine seasons down south, a far longer career than most players, but never developed into the superstar his raw talent had suggested.

Ismail has laughed over the years about the beer can hurled at him, and mildly lamented his stomp on McVey. Lessons learned from teammates Carl Brazley and Pinball Clemons seem to have taken root: in contrast to his diffidence in Toronto, he's now an inspiring motivational speaker, relaxed and comfortable in front of an audience. Yet many requests to interview him for this book, conveyed over more than a year, went unanswered until he finally, characteristically, said No. "He hopes the team will share their wonderful and meaningful stories with you," an intermediary told me. "However, he has declined to be interviewed."

Matt Dunigan, who jeopardized his health and career to courageously play in the Grey Cup despite a broken collarbone, recuperated well enough to play four more mostly successful seasons after leaving the Argonauts. However, a career filled with violent collisions—and countless concussions—left him suffering continuing health challenges that can be traced back to the "linebacker-playing-quarterback" mentality that so endeared him to fans, teammates and coaches.

Chris Schultz protected Dunigan's blind side as left tackle, and later sat to his left on TSN's CFL panel. Like Dunigan, he put his health at risk for the Argos. A blow to his head from an opponent's knee during the 1991 Grey Cup knocked Schultz unconscious and gave him a concussion. He went back into that game, because that's what players did back then. Schultz died suddenly in 2021, just a month after the 30th anniversary of the McNall group's purchase of the Argonauts.

Also gone is Darrell K. Smith, who fell quickly from record-setting brilliance and primal screams to rock bottom. Traded to Edmonton in 1993 with seven teammates, he made virtually no contribution to the Eskimos' Grey Cup win that year. D.K. played just four more CFL games before his career ended.

His addiction to crack cocaine became public knowledge when a police officer was accused of stealing Smith's 1991 blinged-up Grey Cup ring, which had been seized from a drug dealer. The officer had hoped to quietly return the bauble to Smith.

In late 2016, Sherman Smith was stunned to see how much weight his visiting brother had lost. Sherman sent Darrell to a doctor, who diagnosed cancer. Despite the removal of a kidney and his spleen, the cancer spread quickly. D.K. died five months after the initial diagnosis.

Near the end of his life, he overcame his demons and re-embraced his Christian faith. "Darrell had that rough spell of drugs . . . but he finished up strong," says Sherman. "He had accepted responsibility for some of the things that didn't go well for him. To listen to him take responsibility for where he was and where he wasn't, the mistakes he had made, it was just like God had spoken to his heart."

For some members of the team, things worked out better. Gaines, whose inspirational raps set the tone in 1991, still has the swollen, painful ankles that forced his retirement. But his glower is as menacing as it was three decades ago, and he can still bust an original rhyme on a moment's notice. When the 1991 Argos held their 20-year reunion, Gaines gave a New Jack-style pep talk to the 2011 edition of the team, then led ex-teammates in a halftime celebration so long and boisterous that the referee threatened to penalize Toronto for delay of game.

Pinball Clemons was a lone bright light on bad Argo teams from 1993 to '95. His career was reinvigorated in 1996 when Don Matthews returned for a second stint as head coach. The Don cannily converted

Clemons to slotback; the Pinball racked up enormous yardage (and back-to-back championships) in the high-octane passing attack orchestrated by quarterback Doug Flutie.

He also channeled the New Jack spirit of Gaines. The 1996-97 Argos powered up for games through Pinball's effusive call-and-response: "Who's in the house? Daddy's in the house! What time is it? It's time to get busy!"

Clemons is now revered as the greatest Argonaut of all time, a three-time champ on the field who also won Grey Cups as a coach and team executive. He gained more yards than anyone in the history of Canadian football. His uniform number, 31, is one of just four permanently retired by the Argonauts.

Things worked out OK, too, for Adam Rita, after an ugly departure. A couple of months after he was fired in 1992, statements attributed to him in a newspaper story—remarks that don't sound remotely like anything the Happy Hawaiian would ever say—prompted the club to stop paying the balance of his contract. Rita claimed misquote, but concluded it wasn't worth fighting over.

He came back to the Argonauts as an assistant under Don Matthews in 1996, winning another Cup, and also won a ring as general manager in 2004. Since leaving the CFL in 2010, Rita has shared his offensive wizardry and relaxed coaching style with aspiring football players all over Europe.

After replacing Dunigan as the starting quarterback in 1992, Rickey Foggie had difficulty shaking his reputation as someone better suited to be a backup. He won another Grey Cup with Edmonton in 1993 (as Damon Allen's backup), then played eight seasons in the Arena Football League, including a 2002 stint with the short-lived Toronto Phantoms.

Nearly half of the men named in 2007 to the Argos' all-time roster played for the team in 1991: Brazley, Clemons, Lance Chomyc, Dan

Ferrone, Rodney Harding, Hank Ilesic, Paul Masotti, Don Moen, Reggie Pleasant, Schultz and Don Wilson.

Clemons, Dunigan, Ferrone, Harding, Ilesic, Wilson, James Parker and David Williams are all in the Canadian Football Hall of Fame; cases can be made for three or four others from 1991.

A case can also be made for John Candy as the greatest owner any team ever had. He is unquestionably the most beloved owner in Argonauts history.

For everyone associated with the team during Candy's three years as co-owner, the shock and grief caused by his sudden death in 1994 have been supplanted by fond memories of the man who loved the Argos as deeply as any hard-core fan.

Suzan Waks, McNall's financial lieutenant who followed her boss to prison for enabling the frauds the organization perpetrated, still treasures a large crystal vase, etched with the Argos logo, that Candy gave her. Waks uses it, appropriately enough, as a candy dish.

"John was completely passionate about the Argos," says Brian Cooper, the executive Candy stopped speaking to after finding out the team was for sale. His office wall still bears a poster of Candy, triumphantly holding a helmet aloft at the 1991 Eastern Final. "It was nothing to do with money. It all had to do with him growing up as an Argo fan, what it meant to him and the city."

The legacy of the Hollywood years is not McNall's financial failings, Gretzky insists, but Candy's impact on Canadian football. "Bruce and I were there in spirit. John was there, heart and soul. Had it not been for John being involved, I don't know if the Toronto Argonauts would be there today."

Despite spending far too much money on the Rocket, and failing to pay the team's bills by the end, McNall says owning the Argonauts was one of the greatest experiences of his life, in large part because of Candy. "The idea of not only taking a team but an entire league, a whole country for that matter, and lifting it all up to the world—I thought that was really cool. We won a championship, and John made it so much fun."

That fun, that heart and soul, that passion. Those ineffable qualities that John Candy brought to the Argos and his hometown for three years were recognized at last in 2007.

Years after romping around their dad's skybox as kids, Jennifer and Christopher Candy were on hand with their mother, Rose, when a wrong was finally made right.

The original plate attached to the Grey Cup listing members of the 1991 champs had included only one owner's name: Bruce McNall's. Inexplicably and inexcusably, John Candy's and Wayne Gretzky's names had been left off.

Thirteen years after Candy died, the league belatedly rectified this omission by engraving his name on the Grey Cup, along with Gretzky's.

"Finally, the recognition he deserves," said his friend Dan Aykroyd.

Acknowledgments

WITH SO MANY INTRIGUING STORYLINES, plot twists and characters, this was bound to be a big project. It turned out even bigger than I had imagined, and I could not have finished it without help from hundreds of supportive individuals over the past four years.

I am indebted to executives, managers, coaches, players, family members, support staff, journalists and others connected with the early-1990s Argonauts. Many of those who graciously shared memories and perspectives are quoted in the book; those whose comments I have not quoted also helped me discover and understand what happened back then.

I was, sadly, unable to speak to a few important figures. John Candy died far too young, of course. Harry Ornest died almost two decades before I began the project. Don Matthews and Darrell K. Smith both died when I was still in the early stages of research. Others whose deaths precluded them being interviewed include Harold Hallman, James "Quick" Parker, Doran Major, Keith Kelly, and R.D. Lancaster. I was fortunate enough to interview Chris Schultz, an astute observer as well as one of the Argos' all-time best players, before he died in early 2021. His insights helped shape my understanding of the subject matter.

Particularly generous and helpful were Dan Aykroyd, Carl Brazley, Lori Bursey, Jason Colero, Matt Dunigan, Michael P. McCarthy, Laura Ornest, Kelvin Pruenster, Adam Rita, David Watkins, and Danny Webb. Especially deserving of thanks is Crista Bazos. Although she played an important role in the Argo football operation in the early 1990s, Crista declined to be interviewed, insisting (inaccurately, I'm certain) that she had not contributed enough back then to be worth speaking to. She did, however, make an invaluable contribution to this book.

Mike Hogan has been a fabulous friend and supporter. Thanks as well to Bill Manning, Mike Clemons, Chris Shewfelt and Dave Haggith of the Argonauts, and Jonathan Rubinoff of the CFL.

The following helped in many different ways: Ryan Ballantine, Donnovan Bennett, Dean Berkers, Susan Gee Berry, Saundra Boyd, John Bradley, Raymond Brassard, Steve Cameron, Jamie Campbell, Christopher Candy, Matthew Cauz, John Cerney, Lucinda Chodan, Paul Clatney, Cam Cole, Gary Collins, Michael Cooke, Wendy Cox, Gordon Craig, Bob Crane Jr., Roger Currie, Steve Daniel, Neil Davidson, Susan Davy, Nick DeNobile, Kevin Duguay, Jamie Dykstra, Nehal El-Hadi, Dave Elston, Leo Ezerins, Dan Ferrone, Trevor Finch, Sean Fitz-Gerald, Doug Flutie, Frances Foster Brooks, Chris Gaines, Margo Goodhand, Clyde and Matthew Hencher, Dave Heywood, Paul Hunter, Rob Hynes, Bob Irving, Chris Karwandy, Lee Knight, Stu Laird, Don Landry, Astrid Lange, Pierre LeBrun, Gord Lewis, Janice Linton, Daniel Lombardi, Gail Longworth, Jill Loosley, Reg Low, Steve Lyons, Allan Maki, Matt Maychak, Robyn McCabe, Hartley Millson, Steve Milton, Sarah O'Donnell, Mary Ormsby, Joe Pascucci, Susan Patricola, Cary Paul, Bill Pierce, Dr. David

Posen, Katelyn, Amanda and Carmelle Price, Dan Ralph, Roy Rosmus, Graeme Roy, Joe Ruscitti, Paul Samyn, Ian Sanderson, David Sapunjis, Kyle Scott, Terry Scott, Katherine Sedgwick, Steve Simon, Daryl Slade, Doug Smith, Robert Sokalski, John Sokolowski, Doug Speirs, Glenn Stevenson, Ed Tait, Ariel Teplitsky, Maureen Trovo, Will Tudoroff, Walter Tychnowitz, Alison Uncles, Beth Waldman, Scott White, Paul "Willy" Williamson, and Gabriel Witkowski.

I am deeply grateful to the fine folks at Sutherland House, especially publisher and editor Kenneth Whyte, for taking on and believing in this book.

A special thanks to my two closest partners in the project. Don Gibb superbly guided me through the long and often tortured process of writing and self-editing; one of these years he will be inducted into the coaching Hall of Fame. Sharon Hockin patiently, efficiently and cheerfully transcribed the interviews, giving me hundreds of thousands of words to sift through in search of gold nuggets.

Most importantly, I am full of love and gratitude for Lauraine Woods, who through four long years of this project (not to mention 40-plus years of collecting—she might call it hoarding—Argo memorabilia) offered unending support and reassurance. I simply could not have done it without her.